T0353479

Architecture and Security Issues in Fog Computing Applications

Sam Goundar
The University of the South Pacific, Fiji

S. Bharath Bhushan
Sree Vidyanikethan Engineering College, Tirupati, India

Praveen Kumar Rayani
National Institute of Technology Durgapur, India

A volume in the Advances
in Computer and Electrical
Engineering (ACEE) Book Series

Published in the United States of America by
IGI Global
Engineering Science Reference (an imprint of IGI Global)
701 E. Chocolate Avenue
Hershey PA, USA 17033
Tel: 717-533-8845
Fax: 717-533-8661
E-mail: cust@igi-global.com
Web site: http://www.igi-global.com

Library of Congress Cataloging-in-Publication Data

Names: Goundar, Sam, 1967- editor. | Bhushan, S. Bharath, 1990- editor. |
  Rayani, Praveen Kumar, 1989- editor.
Title: Architecture and security issues in fog computing applications / Sam
  Goundar, S. Bharath Bhushan, and Praveen Kumar Rayani, editors.
Description: Hershey PA : Engineering Science Reference, [2020] | Includes
  bibliographical references. | Summary: "This book examines security and
  privacy issues in intelligent fog applications"-- Provided by publisher.

Identifiers: LCCN 2019018305 | ISBN 9781799801955 (paperback) | ISBN
  9781799801948 (hardcover) | ISBN 9781799801962 (ebook)
Subjects: LCSH: Cloud computing. | Cloud computing--Security measures. |
  Internet of things.
Classification: LCC QA76.585 .A73 2020 | DDC 004.67/82--dc23
LC record available at https://lccn.loc.gov/2019018305

This book is published in the IGI Global book series Advances in Computer and Electrical
Engineering (ACEE) (ISSN: 2327-039X; eISSN: 2327-0403)

British Cataloguing in Publication Data
A Cataloguing in Publication record for this book is available from the British Library.

For electronic access to this publication, please contact: eresources@igi-global.com.

Advances in Computer and Electrical Engineering (ACEE) Book Series

ISSN:2327-039X
EISSN:2327-0403

Editor-in-Chief: Srikanta, Patnaik, SOA University, India

MISSION

The fields of computer engineering and electrical engineering encompass a broad range of interdisciplinary topics allowing for expansive research developments across multiple fields. Research in these areas continues to develop and become increasingly important as computer and electrical systems have become an integral part of everyday life.

The **Advances in Computer and Electrical Engineering (ACEE) Book Series** aims to publish research on diverse topics pertaining to computer engineering and electrical engineering. **ACEE** encourages scholarly discourse on the latest applications, tools, and methodologies being implemented in the field for the design and development of computer and electrical systems.

COVERAGE

- Programming
- Power Electronics
- VLSI Design
- Electrical Power Conversion
- VLSI Fabrication
- Computer Hardware
- Circuit Analysis
- Microprocessor Design
- Sensor Technologies
- Computer Science

IGI Global is currently accepting manuscripts for publication within this series. To submit a proposal for a volume in this series, please contact our Acquisition Editors at Acquisitions@igi-global.com or visit: http://www.igi-global.com/publish/.

Titles in this Series

For a list of additional titles in this series, please visit:
https://www.igi-global.com/book-series/advances-computer-electrical-engineering/73675

Novel Practices and Trends in Grid and Cloud Computing
Pethuru Raj (Reliance Jio Infocomm Ltd. (RJIL), India) and S. Koteeswaran (Vel Tech, India)
Engineering Science Reference • copyright 2019 • 374pp • H/C (ISBN: 9781522590231)
• US $255.00 (our price)

Blockchain Technology for Global Social Change
Jane Thomason (University College London, UK) Sonja Bernhardt (ThoughtWare, Australia)
Tia Kansara (Replenish Earth Ltd, UK) and Nichola Cooper (Blockchain Quantum Impact, Australia)
Engineering Science Reference • copyright 2019 • 243pp • H/C (ISBN: 9781522595786)
• US $195.00 (our price)

Contemporary Developments in High-Frequency Photonic Devices
Siddhartha Bhattacharyya (RCC Institute of Information Technology, India) Pampa Debnath (RCC Institute of Information Technology, India) Arpan Deyasi (RCC Institute of Information Technology, India) and Nilanjan Dey (Techno India College of Technology, India)
Engineering Science Reference • copyright 2019 • 369pp • H/C (ISBN: 9781522585312)
• US $225.00 (our price)

Applying Integration Techniques and Methods in Distributed Systems and Technologies
Gabor Kecskemeti (Liverpool John Moores University, UK)
Engineering Science Reference • copyright 2019 • 351pp • H/C (ISBN: 9781522582953)
• US $245.00 (our price)

Handbook of Research on Cloud Computing and Big Data Applications in IoT
B. B. Gupta (National Institute of Technology Kurukshetra, India) and Dharma P. Agrawal (University of Cincinnati, USA)
Engineering Science Reference • copyright 2019 • 609pp • H/C (ISBN: 9781522584070)
• US $295.00 (our price)

For an entire list of titles in this series, please visit:
https://www.igi-global.com/book-series/advances-computer-electrical-engineering/73675

701 East Chocolate Avenue, Hershey, PA 17033, USA
Tel: 717-533-8845 x100 • Fax: 717-533-8661
E-Mail: cust@igi-global.com • www.igi-global.com

Table of Contents

Detailed Table of Contents

Chapter 1

Gowri A. S., Pondicherry University, India

Shanthi Bala P., Pondicherry University, India

Internet of things (IoT) prevails in almost all the equipment of our daily lives including healthcare units, industrial productions, vehicle, banking or insurance. The unconnected dumb objects have started communicating with each other, thus generating a voluminous amount of data at a greater velocity that are handled by cloud. The requirements of IoT applications like heterogeneity, mobility support, and low latency form a big challenge to the cloud ecosystem. Hence, a decentralized and low latency-oriented computing paradigm like fog computing along with cloud provide better solution. The service quality of any computing model depends on resource management. The resources need to be agile by nature, which clearly demarks virtual container as the best choice. This chapter presents the federation of Fog-Cloud and the way it relates to the IoT requirements. Further, the chapter deals with autonomic resource management with reinforcement learning (RL), which will forward the fog computing paradigm to the future generation expectations.

Chapter 2

Shanthi Thangam Manukumar, Anna University, India

Vijayalakshmi Muthuswamy, Amity University, India

With the development of edge devices and mobile devices, the authenticated fast access for the networks is necessary and important. To make the edge and mobile devices smart, fast, and for the better quality of service (QoS), fog computing is an efficient way. Fog computing is providing the way for resource provisioning, service providers, high response time, and the best solution for mobile network traffic. In this chapter, the proposed method is for handling the fog resource management using efficient offloading mechanism. Offloading is done based on machine learning prediction technology and also by using the KNN algorithm to identify the nearest fog nodes to offload. The proposed method minimizes the energy consumption, latency and improves the QoS for edge devices, IoT devices, and mobile devices.

Chapter 3

D. N. Kartheek, Sree Vidyanikethan Engineering College, India
Bharath Bhushan, Sree Vidyanikethan Engineering College, India

The inherent features of internet of things (IoT) devices, like limited computational power and storage, lead to a novel platform to efficiently process data. Fog computing came into picture to bridge the gap between IoT devices and data centres. The main purpose of fog computing is to speed up the computing processing. Cloud computing is not feasible for many IoT applications; therefore, fog computing is a perfect alternative. Fog computing is suitable for many IoT services as it has many extensive benefits such as reduced latency, decreased bandwidth, and enhanced security. However, the characteristics of fog raise new security and privacy issues. The existing security and privacy measures of cloud computing cannot be directly applied to fog computing. This chapter gives an overview of current security and privacy concerns, especially for the fog computing. This survey mainly focuses on ongoing research, security challenges, and trends in security and privacy issues for fog computing.

Chapter 4

Aravind Karrothu, Vellore Institute of Technology, India
Jasmine Norman, Vellore Institute of Technology, India

Fog networking supports the internet of things (IoT) concept, in which most of the devices used by humans on a daily basis will be connected to each other. Security issues in fog architecture are still a major research area as the number of security threats increases every day. Identity-based encryption (IBE) has a wide range of new cryptographic schemes and protocols that are particularly found to be suitable for lightweight architecture such as IoT and wireless sensor networks. This chapter focuses on these schemes and protocols in the background of wireless sensor networks. Also, this chapter analyses identity-based encryption schemes and the various attacks they are prone to.

Chapter 5

Vaishali Ravindra Thakare, Vellore Institute of Technology, India
K. John Singh, Vellore Institute of Technology, India

Cloud computing is a new environment in computer-oriented services. The high costs of network platforms, development in client requirements, data volumes and weight on response time pushed companies to migrate to cloud computing, providing on-demand web facilitated IT services. Cloud storage empowers users to remotely store their information and delight in the on-demand high quality cloud applications without the affliction of local hardware management and programming administration. In order to solve the problem of data security in cloud computing system, by introducing fully homomorphism encryption algorithm in the cloud computing data security, another sort of information security solution to the insecurity of the cloud computing is proposed, and the scenarios of this application is hereafter constructed. This new security arrangement is completely fit for the processing and retrieval of the encrypted data, successfully prompting the wide relevant prospect, the security of data transmission, and the stockpiling of the cloud computing.

Chapter 6

Peyakunta Bhargavi, Sri Padmavati Mahila Visvavidyalayam, India
Singaraju Jyothi, Sri Padmavati Mahila Visvavidyalayam, India

The moment we live in today demands the convergence of the cloud computing, fog computing, machine learning, and IoT to explore new technological solutions. Fog computing is an emerging architecture intended for alleviating the network burdens at the cloud and the core network by moving resource-intensive functionalities such as computation, communication, storage, and analytics closer to the end users. Machine learning is a subfield of computer science and is a type of artificial intelligence (AI) that provides machines with the ability to learn without explicit programming. IoT has the ability to make decisions and take actions autonomously based on algorithmic sensing to acquire sensor data. These embedded capabilities will range across the entire spectrum of algorithmic approaches that is associated with machine learning. Here the authors explore how machine learning methods have been used to deploy the object detection, text detection in an image, and incorporated for better fulfillment of requirements in fog computing.

Chapter 7

Xalphonse Inbaraj, PACE Institute of Technology and Sciences, India

With the explosion of information, devices, and interactions, cloud design on its own cannot handle the flow of data. While the cloud provides us access to compute, storage, and even connectivity that we can access easily and cost-effectively, these centralized resources can create delays and performance issues for devices and information that are far from a centralized public cloud or information center source. Internet of things-connected devices are a transparent use for edge computing architecture. In this chapter, the author discusses the main differences between edge, fog, and cloud computing; pros and cons; and various applications, namely, smart cars and traffic control in transportation scenario, visual and surveillance security, connected vehicle, and smart ID card.

    Korupalli V. Rajesh Kumar, Vellore Institute of Technology, India
    K. Dinesh Kumar, Vellore Institute of Technology, India
    Ravi Kumar Poluru, Vellore Institute of Technology, India
    Syed Muzamil Basha, Vellore Institute of Technology, India
    M Praveen Kumar Reddy, Vellore Institute of Technology, India

Self-driving vehicles such as autonomous cars are manufactured mostly with smart sensors and IoT devices with artificial intelligence (AI) techniques. In most of the cases, smart sensors are networked with IoT devices to transmit the data in real-time. IoT devices transmit the sensor data to the processing unit to do necessary actions based on sensor output data. The processing unit executes the tasks based on pre-defined instructions given to the processor with embedded and AI coding techniques. Continuous streaming of sensors raw data to the processing unit and for cloud storage are creating a huge load on cloud devices or on servers. In order to reduce the amount of stream data load on the cloud, fog computing, or fogging technology, helps a lot. Fogging is nothing but the pre-processing of the data before deploying it into the cloud. In fog environment, data optimization and analytical techniques take place as a part of data processing in a data hub on IoT devices or in a gateway.

    Ravi Kumar Poluru, Vellore Institute of Technology, India
    M. Praveen Kumar Reddy, Vellore Institute of Technology, India
    Rajesh Kaluri, Vellore Institute of Technology, India
    Kuruva Lakshmanna, Vellore Institute of Technology, India
    G. Thippa Reddy, Vellore Institute of Technology, India

This robotic vehicle is a farming machine of significant power and incredible soil clearing limit. This multipurpose system gives a propel technique to sow, furrow, water, and cut the harvests with the least labor and work. The machine will develop the ranch by considering specific line and a section settled at a fixed distance depending on the crop. Moreover, the vehicle can be controlled through voice commands connected via Bluetooth medium using an Android smartphone. The entire procedure computation, handling, checking is planned with engines and sensor interfaced with the microcontroller. The major modules of the vehicle are cultivating, sowing seeds, watering, harvesting the crop. The vehicle will cover the field with the help of the motors fixed which is being controlled with the help of the voice commands given by the user. The main motto of this project is to make the vehicle available and should be operated by everyone even without any technical knowledge.

Cloud computing is an emerging field. With its three key features and its natural favorable circumstances, it has had a few difficulties in the recent years. The gap between the cloud and the end devices must be reduced in latency specific applications (i.e., disaster management). Right now, fog computing is an advanced mechanism to reduce the latency and congestion in IoT networks. It emphasizes processing the data as close as possible to the edge of the networks, instead of sending/receiving the data from the data centre by using large quantity of fog nodes. The virtualization of these fog nodes (i.e., nodes are invisible to the users) in numerous locations across the data centres enabled the fog computing to become more popular. The end users need to purchase the computing resources from the cloud authorities to process their excessive workload. Since computing resources are heterogeneous and resource are constrained and dynamic in nature, allocating these resources to the users becomes an open research issue and must be addressed as the first priority.

Preface

Fog computing is an emerging area of research that expands mobile cloud computing services to satisfy customer's requirements between the devices and cloud. Current cloud computing architecture has been reported as unsuitable for the Internet of Things (IoT) where sensors and actuators are embedded in physical objects that are linked to the Internet through wired and wireless networks. Billions of devices now being connected (IoT) produce terabytes of data daily that need a better infrastructure for dissemination, data mining and analytics (Big Data). Fog Computing works in conjunction with cloud computing to tackle these challenges and optimizes the efficient use of all resources.

Currently, most enterprise data are pushed up to the cloud, stored and analyzed, after which a decision is made and action taken, but this isn't efficient. Fog Computing allows computing, decision-making and action-taking to happen via Internet of Things (IoT) devices and only pushes relevant data to the cloud. Organisations have begun to look for solutions that would help reduce their infrastructures costs and improve profitability. Fog Computing is becoming a foundation for benefits well beyond IT cost savings. Yet, many business leaders are concerned about Fog Computing architecture, security, privacy, availability, and data protection.

Fog computing is playing a vital role in the communication between lightweight devices and cloud computing. However, there are very few books which have specifically focused on the architecture of intelligent fog applications enabled with machine learning. This book summarises the type of issues and challenges architecture of intelligent fog applications are facing. Besides, this book also focuses on the security and privacy issues in intelligent fog applications. This will help industry practitioners manage their works in smart way. This will lead to better utilization of bandwidth and latency for data transmission when associated with centralized cloud solutions. Additionally, the book summarises the recent research developments in the area of intelligent fog applications enabled with machine learning.

The fog extends the cloud to be closer to the things that produce and act on Internet of Things data. These devices, called fog nodes, can be deployed anywhere with a network connection: on a factory floor, on top of a power pole, alongside a railway track, in a vehicle, or on an oil rig. Any device with computing, storage, and network connectivity can be a fog node. Examples include industrial controllers, switches, routers, embedded servers, and video surveillance cameras. It is estimated that the amount of data analysed on devices that are physically close to the Internet of Things (IoT) is approaching 60 percent. There is good reason: analysing IoT data close to where it is collected minimizes latency. It offloads gigabytes of network traffic from the core network, and it keeps sensitive data inside the network. Analysing IoT data close to where it is collected minimizes latency. It offloads gigabytes of network traffic from the core network. And it keeps sensitive data inside the network. (Cisco, 2015).

FOG COMPUTING APPLICATIONS

Fog computing applications are as diverse as the Internet of Things itself. What they have in common is monitoring or analysing real-time data from network-connected things and then initiating an action. The action can involve Machine-to-Machine (M2M) communications or Human-Machine Interaction (HMI). Examples include locking a door, changing equipment settings, applying the brakes on a train, zooming a video camera, opening a valve in response to a pressure reading, creating a bar chart, or sending an alert to a technician to make a preventive repair. The possibilities are unlimited. Production fog applications are rapidly proliferating in manufacturing, oil and gas, utilities, transportation, mining, and the public sector.

Generally speaking the fog computing suits applications with low latency requirements, therefore fog computing has the potential to be used in any application that is latency sensitive, such as health care, urgent services and cyber-physical systems. Researchers (Hu, et al., 2017) list some of the applications of fog computing as: 1). Health care; 2). Augmented reality; 3). Brain machine interface; 4). Gaming; 5). Smart environments; 6). Vehicular fog computing; 7). Fog in Internet of Things (IoT); 8). Fog in Cloud of Things; 9). Smart energy grids; and 10). Urgent computing. Another application of fog computing is in web optimization. Since all web requests that the user makes first goes through the edge (or fog) servers, which subsequently obtain them from the core network where the web servers reside and potentially modify and locally cache these files. Fog devices have the potential to be used as local caching points.

To demonstrate the applications of fog computing, (Stojmenovic & Wen, 2015), used six motivating scenarios to elaborate on the advantages of fog computing. The scenarios were:

1. **Smart Grid**: Energy load balancing applications may run on network edge devices, such as smart meters and micro-grids. Based on energy demand, availability and the lowest price, these devices automatically switch to alternative energies like solar and wind.

2. **Smart Traffic Lights and Connected Vehicles**: Video camera that senses an ambulance flashing lights can automatically change streetlights to open lanes for the vehicle to pass through traffic. Smart street lights interact locally with sensors and detect presence of pedestrian and bikers, and measure the distance and speed of approaching vehicles.

3. **Wireless Sensor and Actuator Networks**: Traditional wireless sensor networks fall short in applications that go beyond sensing and tracking, but require actuators to exert physical actions like opening, closing or even carrying sensors.

4. **Decentralized Smart Building Control:** The applications of this scenario are facilitated by wireless sensors deployed to measure temperature, humidity, or levels of various gases in the building atmosphere. In this case, information can be exchanged among all sensors in a floor, and their readings can be combined to form reliable measurements.

5. **IoT and Cyber-Physical Systems (CPSs):** Fog computing-based systems are becoming an important class of IoT and CPSs. Based on the traditional information carriers including Internet and telecommunication network, IoT is a network that can interconnect ordinary physical objects with identified addresses.

6. **Software Defined Networks (SDN):** Fog computing framework can be applied to implement the SDN concept for vehicular networks. SDN is an emergent computing and networking paradigm, and became one of the most popular topics in IT industry. It separates control and data communication layers.

FOG COMPUTING ARCHITECTURE

A number of Fog Computing Architectures have been proposed by a number of researchers. For example, Datta, Bonnet, and Haerri (2015) in their paper "Fog Computing Architecture to Enable Consumer Centric Internet of Things Services" discusses the architecture for connected vehicles with Road Side Units (RSUs) and Machine to Machine (M2M) gateways including the Fog Computing Platform. Machine to Machine (M2M) data processing with semantics, discovery and management of connected vehicles are consumer centric Internet of Things (IoT) services enabled by the distinct characteristics of Fog Computing. Their architecture comprises of: (i) virtual sensing zones with vehicular sensors acting as source of Machine to Machine

(M2M) data, (ii) Access Points Road Side Units (RSU) and Machine to Machine (M2M) gateways (DataTweet Box) and (iii) cloud system (DataTweet Cloud). The vehicular sensors report Machine to Machine (M2M) data in a uniform format as described in Sensor Markup Language. These data are communicated primarily to the Road Side Units (RSU) or Machine to Machine (M2M) gateway which include the Fog Computing platform. The Machine to Machine (M2M) data are sent over one-hop or multi-hop communication.

Fog computing is a new computational paradigm, which extends the traditional cloud computing and services to the edge of network. It provides the computation, communication, controlling, storage and services capabilities at the edge of network. The decentralized platform is different from other conventional computational model in architecture. A hierarchical structure of fog computing is proposed by (Hu, et al., 2017). They claim that the reference model of fog computing architecture is a significant research topic. In recent years, a number of architectures have been proposed for fog computing. They are mostly derived from the fundamental three-layer structure. Fog computing extends cloud service to the network edge by introducing fog layer between end devices and cloud. The hierarchical architecture is composed of the following three layers:

1. **Terminal Layer:** This is the layer closest to the end user and physical environment. It consists of various IoT devices, for example, sensors, mobile phones, smart vehicles, smart cards, readers, and so on. These devices are widely geographically distributed in general.
2. **Fog Layer:** This layer is located on the edge of the network. Fog computing layer is composed of a large number of fog nodes, which generally including routers, gateways, switchers, access points, base stations, specific fog servers, etc. These fog nodes are widely distributed between the end devices and cloud, for example, cafes, shopping centres, bus terminals, streets, parks, etc. They can be static at a fixed location, or mobile on a moving carrier. The end devices can conveniently connect with fog nodes to obtain services.
3. **Cloud Layer:** The cloud computing layer consists of multiple high-performance servers and storage devices, and provides various application services, such as smart home, smart transportation, smart factory, etc. It has powerful computing and storage capabilities to support for extensive computation analysis and permanently storage of an enormous amount of data.

FOG COMPUTING SECURITY

Given the widespread use of fog computing applications and computing with devices at the edge, Fog Computing Security becomes a critical issue that needs serious attention. There are several challenges that must be overcome in order to create an ecosystem where all actors (end users, service providers, infrastructure providers) benefit from the services provided by fog computing. Not surprisingly, one of the greatest challenges is security. According to (Roman, Lopez & Mambo, 2018), there are several reasons for this. First, at the core of most edge paradigms, there are several enabling technologies such as wireless networks, distributed and peer-to-peer systems, and virtualization platforms. It is then necessary not only to protect all these building blocks, but also to orchestrate the diverse security mechanisms.

This is by itself a complex issue, as we need to create a unified and transversal view of all the security mechanisms that allows their integration and interoperability. Second, the whole is greater than the sum of its parts: by assuring the security of all the enabling technologies, we do not assure the security of the whole system. Once cloud computing-like capabilities are brought to the edge of the network, novel situations arise (e.g. collaboration between heterogeneous edge data centres, migrating services at a local and global scale) whose security has not been widely studied. (Roman, Lopez & Mambo, 2018)

There are security solutions for Cloud computing. However, they may not suit for Fog computing because Fog devices work at the edge of networks. The working surroundings of Fog devices will face with many threats which do not exist in well managed Cloud. According to (Stojmenovic & Wen, 2015), the main security issues are authentication at different levels of gateways as well as (in case of smart grids) at the smart meters installed in the consumer's home. Each smart meter and smart appliance has an IP address. A malicious user can either tamper with its own smart meter, report false readings, or spoof IP addresses. Man-in-the-middle attack has potential to become a typical attack in Fog computing. In this attack, gateways serving as Fog devices may be compromised or replaced by fake ones. They gave the examples of KFC or Star Bar customers connecting to malicious access points which provide deceptive SSID as public legitimate ones. Private communication of victims will be hijacked once the attackers take the control of gateways (Stojmenovic & Wen, 2015). With research and development, many security issues have now been mitigated and neutralised.

ARCHITECTURE AND SECURITY ISSUES IN FOG COMPUTING APPLICATIONS

The internet is progressively adapted with smart cities, smart homes, smart industries, and transportation systems for simplifying the end user's desires through intelligent applications of lightweight devices. Lightweight devices might be Internet of Things (IoT), Smartphones, Wearable devices, Internet of Medical Things (IoMT) and so on. These lightweight devices are enabled with several sensors to acquire data from user. For processing acquired large amount of raw data, light weight devices needs highly configured hardware. To reach this constraint, light weight devices are connected to fog computing which reduces bandwidth and latency for data transmission when associated with centralized cloud solutions.

For handling large amount of raw data, machine learning algorithms are incorporated in fog nodes. The machine learning algorithms might be supervised learning algorithms or unsupervised learning algorithms. This book addresses all innovative aspects of communication between lightweight devices and fog computing (intelligent traffic, intelligent buildings, intelligent environments, intelligent businesses, intelligent medical applications, intelligent smartphones, intelligent wearable devices, intelligent cyber-physical systems, security and privacy applications, and precise solutions for security vulnerabilities) with a sole goal of simplifying individual desires.

This book addresses the architecture of intelligent fog applications enabled with machine learning in various domains. Lightweight devices capture real-time data from a human being and forward it to fog nodes for data processing which reduces bandwidth and latency for data transmission when associated with centralized cloud solutions. The received data from lightweight devices may be labelled or unlabelled corpus. This effort helps to make use of fog node for learning about useful patterns in making better predictions of mobile/IoT/IoMT cloud computing applications.

This book is positioned to be at the intersection of machine learning, lightweight devices and fog computing with outstanding and innovative work on-going at academic, and research laboratories. This book presents current progresses in machine learning for lightweight devices and fog computing and can be used by students having Network Security, Fog computing, Internet of Things, Wireless Networks as the mainstream of course. Graduate students, academics, researchers and practitioners in the industry will also find this book quite useful.

The primary objective of this book is to be a primary source for students, academics, researchers and practitioners to reference the evolving theory and practice related to fog computing, fog computing applications, fog computing architecture and fog computing security. It aims to provide a comprehensive coverage and understanding in the management, organisation, technological, and business use.

The secondary objective of this book is a thorough examination of fog computing applications, architecture and security with respect to issues of management, architecture, deployment, application, governance, trust, privacy, security, interoperability and access. The book intends to provide opportunities for investigation, discussion, dissemination and exchange of ideas in relation to fog computing applications, architecture and security internationally across the widest spectrum of scholarly and practitioner opinions to promote theoretical, empirical and comparative research on problems confronting all the stakeholders.

ORGANISATION OF THE BOOK

The chapters in the book are organised as follows:

Chapter 1: Fog Resource Allocation Through Machine Learning Algorithm

Internet of things (IoT) prevails in almost all the equipment of our daily life like health care unit, industrial productions, vehicle or banking insurance. The unconnected dumb objects have started communicating with each other thus generating voluminous amount of data at a greater velocity that are handled by cloud. The requirements of IoT applications like heterogeneity, mobility support, and low latency form a big challenge to the cloud ecosystem. Hence a decentralized and low latency oriented computing paradigm like fog computing along with cloud provide the better solution. The service quality of any computing model depends more on resource management. The resources need to be agile by nature which clearly demarks virtual container as the best choice. This chapter presents the federation of Fog-Cloud and the way it relate themselves to the IoT requirements. Further, the chapter deals with autonomic resource management with Reinforcement learning (RL) which will forward, the fog computing paradigm, to the future generation expectations.

Chapter 2: A Novel Resource Management Framework for Fog Computing by Using Machine Learning Algorithm

With the development of edge devices and mobile devices, the authenticated fast access for the networks is necessary and important. To make the edge and mobile devices smart, fast and for the better Quality of Service (QoS), fog computing is an efficient way. Fog computing is providing the way for resource provisioning, service providers, high response time, and the best solution for mobile network traffic. In this chapter, the proposed method is for handling the fog resource management using efficient offloading mechanism. Offloading is done based on machine learning prediction technology and also by using the KNN algorithm to identify the nearest fog nodes to offload. The proposed method minimizes the energy consumption, latency and improves the QoS for edge devices, IoT devices, and mobile devices.

Chapter 3: Security Issues in Fog Computing for Internet of Things

The inherent features of Internet of Things (IoT) devices, like limited computational power and storage lead to a novel platform to efficiently process data. Fog Computing came into picture to bridge the gap between IoT devices and data centres. The main purpose of fog computing is to speed-up the computing processing. Cloud Computing is not feasible for many IoT applications, therefore fog computing is a perfect alternative. Fog Computing is suitable for many IoT services as it has many extensive benefits such as reduced latency, decreased bandwidth and enhanced security. However, the characteristics of fog arise new security and privacy issues. The existing security and privacy measures of cloud computing cannot be directly applied on fog computing. This paper gives an overview of current security and privacy concerns, especially for the fog computing. This survey mainly focuses on ongoing research, security challenges and trends in security and privacy issues for fog computing.

Chapter 4: Analysis of Identity Based Cryptography in Internet of Things (IoT)

Fog networking supports the Internet of Things (IoT) concept, in which most of the devices used by humans on a daily basis will be connected to each other. Security issues in fog architecture is still a major research area as the number of security threats increases every day. Identity-Based Encryption (IBE) has a wide range of new cryptographic schemes and protocols which are particularly found to be suitable for light weight architecture such as IoT and wireless sensor networks. This paper focuses on these schemes and protocols in the background of wireless sensor networks. Also, this paper analyses identity-based encryption schemes and the various attacks they are prone to.

Chapter 5: Cloud Security Architecture Based on Fully Homomorphic Encryption

Cloud Computing is a new environment in computer-oriented services. The high costs of network platforms, development in client requirements, data volumes and weights on response time pushed companies to migrate to Cloud Computing providing on demand web facilitated IT Services. Cloud storage empowers users to remotely store their information and delight in the on-demand high quality cloud applications without the affliction of local hardware management and programming administration. In order to solve the problem of data security in cloud computing system, by introducing fully homomorphism encryption algorithm in the cloud computing data security, another sort of information security solution to the insecurity of the cloud computing is proposed and the scenarios of this application is hereafter constructed, This new security arrangement is completely fit for the processing and retrieval of the encrypted data, successfully prompting the wide relevant prospect, the security of data transmission and the stockpiling of the cloud computing.

Chapter 6: Object Detection in Fog Computing Using Machine Learning Algorithms

The moment we live in today demands the convergence of the cloud computing, fog computing, Machine Learning and IoT are the exploration of the new technological solutions. Fog computing is an emerging architecture intended for alleviating the network burdens at the cloud and the core network by moving resource-intensive functionalities such as computation, communication, storage, and analytics closer to the End Users. Machine learning is a subfield of computer science, and is a type of Artificial Intelligence (AI) that provides machines with the ability to learn without explicit programming. In IoT edges has the ability to make decision and take actions autonomously based on algorithmic sensing to acquire sensor data? These embedded capabilities will range across the entire spectrum of algorithmic approaches that is associated with machine learning. Here we explore how machine learning methods have used to deploy the object detection, text detection in an image and incorporated for better fulfillment of requirements in fog computing.

Chapter 7: Distributed Intelligence Platform to the Edge Computing

With the explosion of information, devices and interactions, cloud design on its own cannot handle the flow of data. While the cloud provides us access to compute, storage and even connectivity that we can access easily and cost-effectively, these centralized resources can create delays and performance issues for devices and information that are far from a centralized public cloud or information centre source. Internet of Things-connected devices are a transparent use for edge computing architecture. In this chapter, author discuss about main difference between Edge, Fog and Cloud Computing, its pros and cons and various its applications namely, Smart Cars and Traffic Control in Transportation, Visual and Surveillance Security, Smart ID Card.

Chapter 8: Internet of Things and Fog Computing Applications in Intelligence Transportation Systems

Self-driving vehicles such as Autonomous cars manufactured mostly with Smart sensors and IoT Devices with Artificial Intelligence (AI) techniques. In-vehicle communication most of the cases smart sensors networked with IoT devices to transmit the data in real-time. IoT devices transmit the sensors data to the processing unit to do necessary actions based on sensor output data. The processing unit executes the tasks based on pre-defined instructions given to the processor with embedded and AI coding techniques. Continuous streaming of sensors raw data to the processing unit and for cloud storage is creating a huge load on cloud devices or on servers. In order to reduce the amount of stream data load on the cloud, Fog computing or fogging technology helps a lot. Fogging is nothing but the pre-processing of the data before deploying into the cloud. In fog environment, data optimization and analytical techniques take place as a part of data processing in a data hub on IoT device or in a gateway.

Chapter 9: Agribot

This robotic vehicle is a farming machine of significant power and incredible soil clearing limit. This multipurpose system gives a propel technique to sow, furrow, water and cut the harvests with the least labour and work making it an effective vehicle. The machine will develop the ranch by considering specific line and a section at settled at a fixed distance depending on the crop. Moreover, the vehicle can be controlled through Voice commands connected via Bluetooth medium using an Android smartphone. The entire procedure computation, handling, checking is planned with engines and sensor interfaced with the microcontroller. The major modules of the vehicle are cultivating, sowing seeds, watering, harvesting the crop. The vehicle will cover the field with the help of the motors fixed which is being controlled with the help of the voice commands given by the user. The main motto of this project is to make the vehicle available and should be operated by everyone even without any technical knowledge.

Chapter 10: Towards Efficient Resource Management in Fog Computing – A Survey and Future Directions

Cloud computing is an emerging field with its three key features and its natural favourable circumstances, has few difficulties in the recent years. The gap between the cloud and the end devices must be reduced in latency specific applications i.e. disaster management. Right now, Fog computing is an advanced mechanism to reduce the latency and congestion in IoT networks. It emphasizes processing the data as close as possible to the edge of the networks, instead of sending/receiving the data from the data centre by using large quantity of fog-nodes. The virtualization of these fog-nodes (i.e. nodes are invisible to the users) in numerous locations across the data centres enabled the fog computing more popular. The end users need to purchase the computing resources from the cloud authorities to process their excessive work load. Since, computing resources are heterogeneous, resource constrained and dynamic in nature, allocating these resources to the users becomes an open research issue and must be addressed as the first priority.

Sam Goundar
The University of the South Pacific, Fiji

REFERENCES

Cisco. (2015). *Fog Computing and the Internet of Things: Extend the Cloud to Where the Things Are.* Retrieved from https://www.cisco.com/c/dam/en_us/solutions/trends/iot/docs/computing-overview.pdf

Datta, S. K., Bonnet, C., & Haerri, J. (2015). Fog Computing Architecture to Enable Consumer Centric Internet of Things Services. In *2015 International Symposium on Consumer Electronics (ISCE)* (Pp. 1-2). IEEE. 10.1109/ISCE.2015.7177778

Hu, P., Dhelim, S., Ning, H., & Qiu, T. (2017). Survey on fog computing: Architecture, key technologies, applications and open issues. *Journal of Network and Computer Applications*, *98*, 27–42. doi:10.1016/j.jnca.2017.09.002

Roman, R., Lopez, J., & Mambo, M. (2018). Mobile edge computing, Fog et al.: A survey and analysis of security threats and challenges. *Future Generation Computer Systems*, *78*, 680–698. doi:10.1016/j.future.2016.11.009

Stojmenovic, I., & Wen, S. (2014). The fog computing paradigm: Scenarios and security issues. In *2014 Federated Conference on Computer Science and Information Systems* (pp. 1-8). IEEE. 10.15439/2014F503

Acknowledgment

I would like to especially acknowledge my Fellow Editors (Dr. Bharath Bhushan and Rayani Kumar) for all the hard work they did in managing the chapters of the book. Without them, this book would not have gone to publication. We are proud to present the book on *Architecture and Security Issues of Fog Computing Applications*. We would like to thank all the reviewers that peer reviewed all the chapters in this book. We also would like to thank the admin and editorial support staff of IGI Global Publishers that have ably supported us in getting this issue to press and publication. And finally, we would like to humbly thank all the authors that submitted their chapters to this book. Without your submission, your tireless efforts and contribution, we would not have this book.

For any new book, it takes a lot of time and effort in getting the Editorial Team together. Everyone on the Editorial Team, including the Editor-in-Chief is a volunteer and holds an honorary position. No one is paid. Getting people with expertise and specialist knowledge to volunteer is difficult, especially when they have their full-time jobs. Next was selecting the right people with appropriate skills and specialist expertise in different areas of the fog computing applications, architecture and security to be part of the Review Team.

Every book and publisher has its own chapter acceptance, review and publishing process. IGI Global uses an online editorial system for chapter submissions. Authors are able to submit their chapters directly through the e-Editorial Discovery system. The Editor-in-Chief then does his own review and selects reviewers based on their area of expertise and the research topic of the article. After one round of peer review by more than three reviewers, a number of revisions and reviews, a chapter and subsequently all the chapters are ready to be typeset and published.

I hope everyone will enjoy reading the chapters in this book. I hope it will inspire and encourage readers to start their own research on fog computing. Once again, I congratulate everyone involved in the writing, review, editorial and publication of this book.

Chapter 1
Fog Resource Allocation Through Machine Learning Algorithm

Gowri A. S.
Pondicherry University, India

Shanthi Bala P.
Pondicherry University, India

ABSTRACT

Internet of things (IoT) prevails in almost all the equipment of our daily lives including healthcare units, industrial productions, vehicle, banking or insurance. The unconnected dumb objects have started communicating with each other, thus generating a voluminous amount of data at a greater velocity that are handled by cloud. The requirements of IoT applications like heterogeneity, mobility support, and low latency form a big challenge to the cloud ecosystem. Hence, a decentralized and low latency-oriented computing paradigm like fog computing along with cloud provide better solution. The service quality of any computing model depends on resource management. The resources need to be agile by nature, which clearly demarks virtual container as the best choice. This chapter presents the federation of Fog-Cloud and the way it relates to the IoT requirements. Further, the chapter deals with autonomic resource management with reinforcement learning (RL), which will forward the fog computing paradigm to the future generation expectations.

DOI: 10.4018/978-1-7998-0194-8.ch001

INTRODUCTION

Innovations in the Internet of Things (IoT) open an era for a quality life. The exponential growth in IoT also raises issues on the management of those resources that are used for its computation and storage. One of the main challenges of IoT services is the low latency requirement (Ray, 2018). As of now, the IoT services are either dealt with the cloud or edge computing. Though edge computing provides faster response, it neither permits sharing of data nor allows real-time analytics (due to their limited compute/storage power). The cloud on the other hand, in spite of its capability to support big data analytics, causes an intolerable delay in latency constraint IoT environment. That means cloud computing reduces the possibilities of acting over the situation by the time the data/request reaches the cloud. In real time application like emergency health care or hazardous industrial applications, a small delay may cost a life or some severe catastrophic damages. Therefore, cloud computing is not an advisable solution for IoT applications where low latency is of utmost priority. To overcome the limitations of edge and cloud, as the middle layer, fog computing proves itself as the best solution, especially for delay sensitive applications of enormous IoT devices.

Fog Computing is a distributed computing paradigm that brings cloud services near to the edge network of the IoT devices where the data/request is generated (Iorga et al., 2018). The fog layer as shown in Figure 1 performs the preprocessing of the data that are collected from various edge devices and moves only the necessary information on to the cloud as and when required. The filtered and preprocessed data can be later used by the cloud for historical analytics in order to reveal better insights for business (Aazam, M., & Eui-Nam Huh. 2015). Hence, for delay sensitive applications, timely solution is provided in the fog itself rather than overwhelming the communication network towards cloud. Thus by saving bandwidth, fog reduces the unnecessary overload on the cloud. Besides deciding, which or what type of data/request are to be forwarded to the cloud, dealing the resource management in fog is one of the key tasks as it has a significant impact on the low latency and power conservation.

The existing programming paradigms and management tools are inadequate to handle the complexity, heterogeneity and scalability requirements of the IoT devices dynamically. Apart from automated software-defined solutions, an autonomic system that can manage the resource allocation by itself with intelligence is required. Machine learning techniques like Reinforcement learning (RL) will better suite, to achieve efficient resource management in fogs (Dutreilh, Kirgizov, Melekhova, Malenfant, & Rivierre, 2011). The RL equipped fog control nodes can solve the resource management issues in fog at a paramount level of Quality of service (QoS).

Figure 1. Fog computing paradigm
(Aazam, M., & Eui-Nam Huh. 2015)

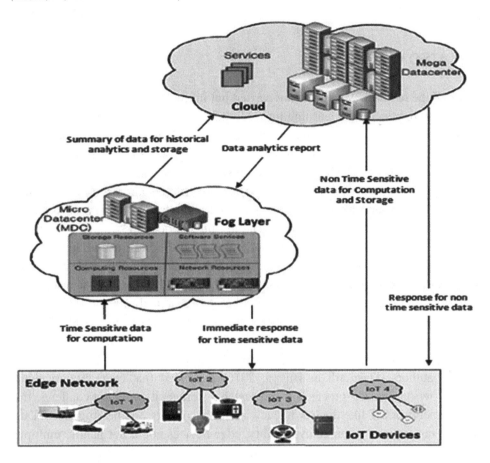

The chapter is organized as follows. The next section discusses the various works related to resource allocation in fog computing. Then the Significance of fog computing briefs the necessity of fog for IoT applications. Followed by it, the various service models, deployment models, characteristics and benefits of fog computing are described. The chapter then gives basic information about virtual containers which is considered as the compute/storage resource of the micro datacenters in fog computing. Then the chapter deals with the fundamental knowledge of autonomic computing and reinforcement learning in the context of resource provision in fog. Next, the chapter introduces the proposed fog-cloud layered architecture which elaborates about the hierarchy in which devices are layered from the end device-fog layer-cloud. Then the proposed work, autonomic resource management combined with reinforcement learning is described in detail with code. Finally, the security and privacy issues of fog computing are discussed followed by a conclusion and future enhancements.

RELATED WORKS

Some of the research works that are carried out in the field of autonomic resource allocation, reinforcement learning for resource provisioning, federation of fog and cloud for efficient resource management are discussed in in this section. The section brings into focus the similarity and conflicts of the proposed work of this chapter with the existing works in the area of fog resource management.

Resource management can be resolved through different approaches. The author discussed the resource allocation strategy carried out for IoT applications in the cloud data center (Singh & Viniotis,2017). The resource allocation strategy was purely designed on the basis of SLA. The work proposed buffering, scheduling and cost limiting strategies to enforce SLA. The work was implemented by a discrete event simulator in C and achieved conformance without dependence on the request arrival pattern. Brogi et al proposed an activity that was designed to show the different deployment models for IoT applications viz, IoT+edge, IoT+cloud, and IoT+fog. The objectives were to constitute hands-on lab for fog computing, to have quick learning rate and limited cost (Brogi, Forti, Ibrahim, & Rinaldi,2018).

The authors (Dastjerdi & Buyya, 2016) described that even though cloud could offer on-demand processing and scalable storage, it could not challenge the requirements of IoT like the low latency, mobility support, and heterogeneity. Due to their constrained resource availability, edge devices could not handle multiple IoT requests resulting in resource contention problem and increased processing delay. The concept of elasticity is emphasized in (Coutinho, Gomes& de Souza, 2015). Elasticity in terms of scaling the resources during allocation is elaborated. The author discussed how autonomic computing is used to implement elasticity in resource provisioning.

The authors (Casalicchio, Menascé, & Aldhalaan, 2013) discussed that resource provisioning can be performed more efficiently with a heuristic algorithm that gives near optimal solution (NOPT). Issues regarding resource management in the IoT ecosystem were discussed in (Flávia C. Delicato, Paulo F. Pires, Thais Batistal, 2017). The main requirements of resource management in the context of IoT were derived. The author proposed monitoring, modeling, discovery, estimation, and allocation as the various activities of resource management.

The authors (Bonomi, Milito, Natarajan, & Zhu, 2014), described fog as a hierarchical and distributed platform for service delivery. The intrinsic features of fog, its integration with cloud were discussed. Use cases that motivated the relevance of fog with IoT and big data were elaborated. The Ferrández et al suggested the development of smart building services through IoT edge and fog computing (Ferrández-Pastor, Mora, Jimeno-Morenilla, & Volckaert, 2018). The fog deployment proved better control over energy management, security system, and climate information system in the smart building service. The work demonstrated how edge and fog paradigms can be integrated through which the benefits can be reinforced.

The hybridization of reinforcement learning (RL) and queuing models for autonomic resource allocation in the cloud platform is explored (Tesauro, Jong, Das, & Bennani,2006). The RL trained the data offline while the queuing model was used to control the system. Autonomic computing was adopted for efficient resource management. The initial bad policy of RL and the methods to overcome it are sketched in detail. Though it resembles the proposed work of this book chapter, it differs in terms of architecture and the technique employed for prediction.

Atlam, Walters, and Wills (2018) highlighted the integration of IoT and fog computing. The author described the architecture of fog that is adaptable to the requirements of IoT. It discussed how fog can support IoT in the arena of smart traffic lights, smart home, wireless sensor networks, health care, and cyber-physical systems. The author Bushan et al., (Bhushan & Reddy, 2018) describes the cloud service distribution as a NP-hard optimization problem with the challenges as the various constraints.The author recommends particle swarm optimization and fruit fly optimization algorithms to evaluate the execution time and error rate.

The authors Khalid et al. compared the traditional cloud with fog computing for a body area network use case in a simulated environment ("Service Architecture Models For Fog Computing," 2017). The result of the work proved that the future of IoT and real-time processing lies in the adoption of fog computing. The author substantiates that adopting fog for IoT can overcome issues that cannot be solved by cloud alone. The standard definition of fog computing, its characteristics, attributes, service models and deployment models were described in Iorga et al. (2018). Apart from edge and cloud, the author compared fog with mist computing and dew computing too.

The Swati et al presented two types of architecture for resource provisioning in fog computing (Agarwal, Yadav & Yadav, 2017). The two layer and three layer fog resource allocation architectures depicted the federation of fog with the cloud to enhance the efficiency in resource provisioning. The comparative analysis proved minimized response time, data transfer cost and VM cost. Whereas the proposed work in this book chapter adopts an advanced technique for resource allocation in terms of machine learning.

The methodology for resource estimation and management was proposed (Aazam & Eui-Nam Huh, 2015). The type of customer, relinquish probability of customer, type of service are some of the parameters taken into account for estimating the resource.

The Federation of IoT and WSN services in the fog is also addressed. The method follows a conventional approach and exhibits a shortage of guarantee about addressing the stochastic issues of IoT. Utilization of fog for optimal resource provision and service placement is substantiated in (Skarlat, Nardelli, Schulte, & Dustdar,2017). Each service request followed sense, process and actuate sequence. The fog service placement problem (FSPP) mapped the IoT applications and computational resources to obtain optimized resource provision. The output was compared among different services in the perspective of response time and deadline distance.

The author analyzed different architectures of IoT (Ray, 2018). It discussed the various device components of IoT at the connectivity level, process level, interface level, storage, and memory level. The study on the architecture and device components exhibits the nature of IoT requirements. It describes the utility factors when IoT applications are incorporated into the cloud platform. A novel concept called "Io<*>" is proposed in the paper. The author discussed the difficulty of connecting numerous things to the cloud. The authors in (La, Ngo, Dinh, Quek, & Shin, 2018) proposed an approach that involved device driven and human-driven intelligence as key drivers to reduce energy consumption and latency in fog computing. The result explored the unexplored potential of intelligence in handling the challenges of fog computing.

A novel fog-cloud resource allocation algorithm based on Gaussian Regression model was introduced ("Rodrigo A. C. da Silva; Nelson L. S. da Fonseca.2018"). The Gaussian model is employed to predict the future demands and to avoid request blocking especially the delay sensitive ones. It was proved that the Gaussian model-based prediction reduced energy consumption, latency and blocking rate. The authors (Zahoor & Mir, 2018) discussed the basic functions of IoT, components that makeup IoT, constraints of IoT in terms of processing, storage, energy, bandwidth, device addressing, management protocols and security. Analysis of resource management was elaborated in the viewpoint of data aggregation protocols, routing approaches, QoS and security issues. The author described how the edge device aggregated the values from IoT devices in a body area network.

The authors discussed the definition of fog computing and some related application scenario (Yi, Li, & Li, 2015). An elaborative survey had been performed that described the issues related to QoS, interfacing, resource management, security, and privacy. The authors introduced a performance model that emphasized to derive an appropriate initialization policy for a good performance start (Dutreilh, Kirgizov, Melekhova, Malenfant, & Rivierre, 2011). The implementation proved the convergence speed up technique to reach the optimal solution faster.

The authors (Xu & Zhu, 2015) have done a detailed survey of the security and privacy issues of fog computing. The security challenges in the context of trust, authentication and privacy issues regarding data, usage, and location are focused elaborately. The author Lee et al. clearly distinguishes the significance of IoT fog from that of IoT cloud. Eventually, the work highlights the security and privacy issues that are faced by the end devices and the fog nodes. The various threats and the remedies to resolve them analyzed in brief (Lee et al., 2015). The paper (Rayani, Bhushan, & Thakare, 2018) focused on token based multilayer authentication mechanism to identify unauthorized access of fog nodes. The honey password scheme aims to avoid DoS attack, surfing attack and password guessing attack.

The paper (Mukherjee et al., 2017) surveys an overview of existing security and privacy issues in fog computing. The author tabulated the different authentication and privacy models with their performance and limitations. The various research challenges with its scope are summarized. The paper provides a state of art survey on the security and privacy issues in fog computing. The author Stojmenovic et al. describes the different types of possible attacks in fog computing. The stealthy features of these attacks are examined in the perspective of CPU and memory consumption in fog device (Stojmenovic & Wen, 2014).

The paper (Stojmenovic et al., 2016) describes the need for fog computing. It highlights the necessity of fog especially in smart traffic lights, connected vehicles, smart grids, WSN (Wireless Sensor Networks), smart building control, cyber-physical systems and SDN (Software-defined Networking) based vehicular networks. The author describes authentication and authorization issues under the fragile connection between end device-fog-cloud. The paper (Alrawais et al., 2017) describes how fog computing plays a vital role to alleviate the security and privacy issues in an IoT environment. The author describes a case study on existing certificate revocation schemes.

Almost all the works discussed so far, describes the significance and characteristics of fog in serving IoT applications. Similar works in the area of fog resource provisioning, clearly emphasize the need for machine learning technique. However, resource provisioning techniques that can scale for the massive IoT request depends on the type of machine learning algorithms used for prediction and task allocation. Though a considerable number of works exists in predicting the future demand for VMs, the combination of machine learning with autonomic computing described in the proposed work of this book chapter is a novel concept in fog.

The following section discusses the factors that motivate to choose fog computing paradigm for IoT applications in terms of its significance. The section also addresses the service models, deployment models of fog computing followed by its characteristics and benefits.

SIGNIFICANCE OF FOG

The existing cloud models have certain difficulties to handle the volume, velocity, and variety of data that IoT devices generate. Along with the diverse types of devices, the issues of heterogeneity, mobility support, and context awareness also arises with its negative impact. Cloud servers can communicate with IP only, not with numerous other protocols used by the IoT devices. Further, the deployment of the ubiquitous and pervasive computing paradigm, which needs computing to be brought to the data source, have triggered the advancements in the Internet of Everything (IoE) applications. The explosion of mobile devices, smart sensors have driven the necessity of providing solutions with low latency and context awareness which are difficult constraints for the existing cloud models to deal with. Hence a distributed computing paradigm like fog computing that addresses the IoT constraints with ease is inevitable (Atlam, Walters, & Wills, 2018). At the same time, the inherent limitations of fog cannot replace cloud. But the integration of fog with cloud computing will resolve the technological gaps thereby enhancing the Quality of Experience (QoE) to the end users.

Fog Computing: An Extension of Cloud for the IoT Services

Fog computing can be defined as a layered model where thousands and millions of heterogeneous, wireless, autonomous, decentralized computing devices communicate, process and store data near to the devices that produce those data. In this context, any device with the capacity of computing, storage, and connectivity above the edge network can be called as Fog nodes. The devices can be a gateway, router, switch, access points, base stations or high-end devices like cloudlets or microdata centers. In this chapter, microdata centers are considered as the fog nodes for which the resource allocation is dealt with.

While there exist similar concepts like Mobile Edge computing (MEC), Mobile Cloud Computing (MCC), Mist computing or Dew computing, among all, fog computing proves itself a more promising computing paradigm for IoT applications. Just like cloud, fog computing is also supported by various service models and deployment models.

Fog Service Models

Infrastructure as a Service (IaaS)

The real-time nature of the IoT applications that are geographically dispersed, demand fog infrastructure to provide run-time decision making and dynamic resource management (Singh & Viniotis, 2017). The fog based infrastructure service should also tackle the requirements of different stakeholders of the current IoT usage. Consideration has to be given to both the time critical events and data analytic bulk storage events when customizing fog based IaaS. This necessitates the fog based IaaS to associate with the cloud as shown in the Figure 2.

The fog based infrastructure as a service would provide real-time processing with transient storage for the hot data whereas the cloud-based infrastructure as a service ensures bulk data processing and long term storage for historical analysis (Bhushan & Reddy, 2018). A hot data depicts the property that is time critical and mobile, detour of which either leads to catastrophic failures or the data become stale and lose its value for further usage in that specific scenario. Those data whose value gets diminished as the time elapses are called cold data. Such cold data still have their importance for historical analytics and hence needs to be stored in long term storage such as cloud datacenter.

The fog based IaaS is made up of devices that constitute transient storage device and resource-constrained processing elements like virtual containers, virtual servers, and micro datacenters (Aazam, M., & Eui-Nam Huh. 2015). The cloud infrastructure is made up of high-end host servers, virtual machines and virtual containers that form the large scale mega-datacenter. The IoT applications that demand mobility and low latency would be served within the fog based IaaS layer whereas the resource-intensive applications that are not time critical would be better served in the cloud-based IaaS.

Platform as a Service (PaaS)

The main job of PaaS is providing a packed environment of Os, compiler, web servers, database servers, IDE and software that are specific to the development of applications. As far as fog computing is concerned, PaaS would support, both the real-time application and analytical type of applications. The PaaS for fog would ensure that the flexibility is provided to the application developers to build real-time app modules using fog based PaaS and analytical app modules using cloud-based PaaS.

Figure 2. Fog IaaS in association with cloud

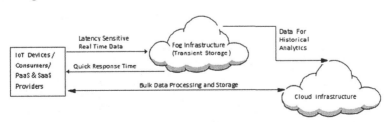

Figure 3 shows how the application developers make use of both the fog and the cloud-based PaaS to construct their respective modules. As per the PaaS architecture (Adnan Khalid, Muhammad Shahbaz, 2017), the app developers or the PaaS users would build the real-time processing module at the fog layer and analytical processing modules in the cloud layer. The integration of the PaaS from both the fog and cloud layer will enable to build any type of applications that may partially require both fog and cloud-based PaaS.

Software as a Service (SaaS)

The essence of SaaS lies in providing the required software assistance to the application users and software vendors. However, as far as a distributed environment like the fog is concerned, software (SW) support would be provided to the two different users at two different levels, one for the cloud-dependent software developers and another to the fog application vendors as shown in the Figure 4

The application providers and the software vendors would be able to avail the real-time application module through the fog based SaaS portals. The application modules can either be downloaded from the SaaS of Fog layer or the portal can be hired by the respective fog devices.

Figure 3. Fog PaaS in association with cloud

Figure 4. Fog SaaS in association with cloud

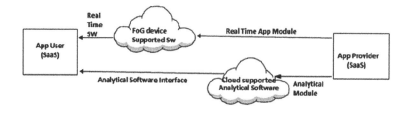

Fog Deployment Models

The deployment of fog nodes are more domains specific and depend on the type of use case scenario. With IoT, most of the application expects, quick processing and instant response rather than longtime analytics. Processing needs to be done near the edge where the data originated thus saving the network traffic spent on transportation of the data (Bonomi, Milito, Zhu & Addepalli, 2012). One of the main parameters that define the deployment of fog nodes is the time limit permitted between the event and the action to be taken. The deployment of fog nodes at various support layers of IoT purely depends on the type of applications. Based on the application's latency requirement, deployment of fog nodes at various layers of IoT are shown in the Table 1.

1. **High Time-Sensitive Apps (Type1):** The applications that require a response in sub-milliseconds or the applications from certain geographic locations where cloud access is tedious or almost impossible are categorized in type1. Also, there are applications where neither it is practically feasible to transport bulk amount of data from thousands of edge devices to the cloud nor it is necessary because many time critical event analysis do not require cloud scale processing or storage. For such scenarios, fog node alone fits. Hence fog nodes are deployed at every layer of the IoT as depicted in the Table 1.

    For example, such high time-sensitive app includes health care units that may cost life with the delay in response, a nuclear reactor unit or industrial units where pressure monitoring and controlling is time critical to avoid disasters, a military combat system in a remote area.

2. **Medium Time-Sensitive Apps (Type2):** The applications which can wait for the response in terms of minutes. This includes scenarios where pre-processing is performed in the fog nodes and analytical results are awaited from cloud to take further action.

    Use cases like commercial marketing, stock exchange, and retail business come under this type of medium time-sensitive apps which includes the partial deployment of both the fog nodes and cloud infrastructure.

3. **Less Time-Sensitive Apps (Type3):** The applications which need more operational and business control over the scenario and that can tolerate response time in terms of hours. This requires the deployment of fog nodes for time-

Table 1. Layered view of IoT depicting the deployment of fog nodes at various levels

IoT layers	Type1	Type2	Type3	Type4
Business support	Fog nodes	cloud	cloud	cloud
Operational support	Fog nodes	Fog	cloud	cloud
Monitoring and control	Fog nodes	Fog	Fog	cloud
Sensors & Actuators	IoT / IoE devices			

sensitive computations and deployment of clouds for operational cum business related management information processing.

Use case scenarios like a content delivery network, live telecasting, etc fits better in this type.

4. **Time-Insensitive Apps (Type4):** The applications which need insight on business analytics and data visualization depends more on the cloud at every level of the IoT layer rather than fog nodes. These are the environments where the deployment of fog nodes is neither economical nor feasible.

Examples like metrological whether monitoring stations, oceanography research projects, etc.

Like a cloud, fog computing also comes with deployment models like private fogs, community fogs, public fogs, and hybrid fogs. The different vendors who provide Fog as a Service (FaaS) are named as Fog Service Providers (FSP). Figure 5. shows the different deployment models of FaaS (Francisco-Javier et al., 2018).

1. **Private Fog**: The fog infrastructure owned by a single organization either on premise or off premise and that provides services to all its branches across a particular geographical area are called as private fog. High security is of utmost priority of private fog as they maintain their own firewall, Intrusion detection systems (IDS), etc. Thus the organization that provides private fog preserves confidentiality, especially of both the data and business details of the customers.

Figure 5. Fog deployment models

For example, a public sector bank owning its own microdata center and catering service to all its branches in a city can be considered as a private fog provider to its branches.

2. **Community Fog**: The fog infrastructure that serves for the exclusive use of a group of business, sharing common mission and policies. These business vendors are individually small enough to invest in capital expenditure (CapEx) and the maintenance i.e. operational expenditure (Opex) of the fog infrastructure. Hence they group together to own and maintain the fog infrastructure that serves their community goals. Like private fogs, community fog also preserves the privacy of the data, software and hardware infrastructure, but with community mission.

Examples like, a set of private sector banks join together to provide mobile banking access to its customers within a city. The microdata center established and maintained by the private banks serves as community fog.

3. **Public Fog**: The fog nodes that serves for the use of the general public. They are owned and operated by academic, government or combination of them over a geographical area. Such public fogs are preferred when security or privacy is not a matter of primary importance.

Examples like the local cable operators providing data center facility to their locality.

4. **Hybrid Fog**: The hybrid fog can be described as a one in which the private or community fog nodes hires the public fog nodes for a specific amount of time in order to compensate the downtime or load balance problems in their own infrastructure.

Essential Characteristics Associated With Fog Computing

1. **Minimal Latency**: While dealing with reactors, electrical furnaces, automobile braking system, medical diagnosis, grid sensors and other Industrial environments, every millisecond and sub-second matters. Performing computation closer to the device that produces the data shall have a difference between avoiding the disaster and cascading the system failures.
2. **Location Awareness**: Fog computing is able to provide a solution in minimal latency, as the fog nodes are aware of their geographical location from the edge devices that requests the service.
3. **Context Awareness**: As the IoT device are not protocol specific, the fog nodes take care of grouping similar requests from edge networks.
4. **Mobility Support**: The aggregate fog nodes provide high-quality stream services to the devices on the move through access points and proxies along highway tracks.
5. **Geographical Distribution**: Fog computing extends seamless support to the huge number of IoT devices that are geographically distributed across a long landscape.
6. **Heterogeneity**: The different types of edge networks with countless protocols are supported by the fog nodes through various network communication capabilities.
7. **Interoperability**: The fog nodes hold the ability to cooperate with different Internet Service Providers and are able to federate across domains.
8. **Real-time Interaction**: Fog computing best suits for real-time applications, unlike other computing paradigms.
9. **Scalability**: The technological advancements in virtualization, microdata centers and the inherent property of the aggregate fog nodes to switch over to any type of serving machines, have made scalability a trivial matter of concern to fog computing.
10. **Privacy and Security**: With fog computing offering private and community fogs, well protected with firewalls and legacy security systems, the consumers feel at ease using fog computing, as it provides transparency of where and with whom their data resides.

Benefits of fog computing:

1. Deeper analytical insights with utmost speed response.
2. Better business agility
3. Distance and location-aware service
4. Low operation cost

5.   Better security

These benefits of fog, spiced with its characteristics, forms the crust of fog computing in addressing the IoT applications of this generation. Autonomic resource allocation with machine learning in fog being a novel approach, it is important to know their fundamental concepts. The relevance of autonomic computing and reinforcement learning in fog computing paradigm also needs a focus. The next section proceeds with the background knowledge about virtual containers (the compute resource of fog), followed by autonomic computing and reinforcement machine learning concepts in the perception of resource management in fog.

Virtual Containers

The software executed on the fog nodes exhibits the purpose of the application for which it is intended. The resources used by the software architects for application development, computation, communication, and storage have a greater impact on the QoS constraints of fog (Baresi, Guinea, Quattrocchi, & Tamburri, 2016). The robust deployments of fog node have to ensure a seamless difference between the fog node, fog platform, and the fog software. This can be achieved by facilitating virtual containers as the system resource for application development and execution. Virtual containers are highly distributed, lightweight technology offering isolation at application and system level which are the essential features required in a fog environment.

The virtual containers are a lightweight, stand-alone, executable package of application software that includes all the components needed to run it viz., code, system tools, runtime binaries, system libraries, etc, (Singh & Singh, 2016). In other words, containerization is an isolated, platform-independent software environment, portable enough to be fetched and run at various locations in the network. The innate nature of containers supports the essentialities to address IoT application requests in fog.

Figuer 6 shows different versions of invoking containers that can vary depending upon the application requirement. Containers allow multiple applications to run in a single physical host or across multiple virtual machines. This capability of elastic compute environment is very much needed for fog computing.

Resource Provisioning Based on Autonomic Computing

The ongoing proliferation of IoT services in scale, complexity, and connectivity has driven the necessity of developing computing systems that are capable of managing themselves (Casalicchio, Menascé & Aldhalaan, 2013). The delay to process the

Figure 6. (a) Containers within VM (b) Light weight VMs (c) Unikernels

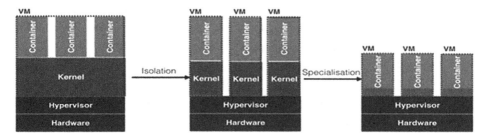

unlimited amount of data generated from the Internet of Everything (IoE) is due to the conventional predefined type of programming style. Usually, the legacy programming approach would specify, only a broad high-level objective as input to the system's management algorithms. In the old fashioned programming approach, once the system starts functioning, the algorithms would continuously sense the state and execute the appropriate actions that could optimally achieve the high-level objective. Those algorithms were programmed to work according to the predetermined case-based reasoning method and fail gradually for the unpredictable changes in the workload. Hence a system like autonomic computing that can manage the heterogeneity of IoT applications dynamically is the right solution for a fog environment.

Autonomic computing in fog refers to the self-managing characteristics of distributed resources that can adapt to the unpredictable workload changes hiding the complexity from the users. One of the goals of autonomic computing is to minimize the degree of human intervention in managing distributed resources. Hence the autonomic computing module acts as the right choice for the intrinsic nature of the distributed resources in fog computing. The autonomic computing model traces the steps of Probe, Analyze, Plan and Execute (PAPE) control loop structure as shown in the Figure 7 (Bonomi, Milito, Natarajan, & Zhu, 2014).

These phases viz., Probe, Analyze, Plan and Execute are repeated in an orderly fashion at regular intervals of time. It probes the state of the system (user requests and resource availability) through the sensors, analyzes the amount and type of requests, plans the required resource management decision and executes the decision through the actuators. The central log repository saves the log information about each and every phase and the respective decisions taken in achieving the objective at various point of time for future reference.

Figure 7. Autonomic computing model for fog resource management

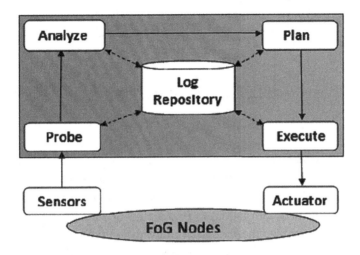

Resource Provisioning Based on Reinforcement Learning

The rapid increase in human to machine and machine to machine communication has led to the development of computing systems that needs to make intelligent decisions at a fast rate. Such intelligent computing systems need algorithms that can understand and act according to the stochastic behavior of IoT applications. If the algorithms are predefined as done in traditional programming style, the software cannot withstand the unpredictable and heterogeneous nature of application requirements (Dutreilh & Kirgizov, 2018). Therefore, instead of coding the system what to do and when to do it, make the machine (system) to learn itself and decide about the timely action that it has to take.

In general, machine learning is about the study and construction of systems that can learn to take decisions on its own. The system can generate accurate decisions only by experience. Experience leads to knowledge. With knowledge, the system can take an accurate decision in the long run. Experience can be accumulated by learning the environment. The system learns the environment, every time as it receives positive or negative rewards as feedback when a decision is taken. Thus, based on the reward, the system will learn, refine and adapt itself in due course of time, according to the dynamic requests of the application. This is the concept behind reinforcement machine learning that can suite very well for the autonomic resource allocation in the fog-cloud service model.

In the case of RL, as shown in the Figure 8, Learning takes place as a result of interaction between an agent and the environment (system). At the earlier stage, the agent acts on its environment receive some feedback (reward) for its action but

Figure 8. Reinforcement learning model
(Bahrpeyma, Haghighi, & Zakerolhosseini, 2015)

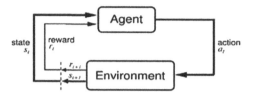

it is not aware of which action is correct to achieve the goal (Tesauro, Jong, Das & Bennani, 2006). Only by experience, it learns to take an optimal decision. To learn from experience, the agent decomposes the reward component for evaluation. The evaluation is performed with a goal to find an optimal policy, for mapping states to actions and to maximize the measure of reward in the long run. The perception received by an agent should be used not only for acting but also for improving the agent's ability to behave optimally in the future to achieve the goal.

By contemporary, reinforcement learning is a Markov Decision Process (MDP) which describes that the current state of the environment (system) depends on the last state and the action taken on it. The MDP model is defined as STAR, where S- is the set of states, T- is the set of probabilistic transition from current state S to the next state S', on the action a_t, A- is the set of actions and R- is the set of feedback reward for the action a_t on state s.

Reinforcement learning can be portrayed as a collection of trial and error method by which a learner agent learns to make good decisions through a sequence of interactions with a system or an environment. Each interaction involves (i) observing the system's current state s_t at time t, (ii) take some legal action a_t in-state s_t to derive the new state s_{t+1} and finally (iii) receiving a reward r_t, a numerical value that the agent would like to maximize by taking better decision from its experience in long term.

The reinforcement learning based RL agent is implemented as the main part of the planner phase of the PAPE control loop. It takes action dynamically to change the amount of provisioned resources with respect to the current state of the system. The Q-learning algorithm which is a model-free version of the RL is used to implement the RL agent. The term model free refers to the algorithmic technique that does not need a prior trained model to take dynamic decisions. The Q-learning algorithm is expressed by the Q-function Q(s, a) where at time 't' an action a_t is taken on the current state s_t which will lead to the next state s_{t+1}. Υ is the discount factor. This Q-function is updated by the equation(1).

$$Q\ (s_t, a_t) = r(s, a) + \Upsilon \max a_{t+1}\ Q(s_{t+1}, a_{t+1}) \tag{1}$$

Figure 9. Layered architecture of fog-cloud eco system

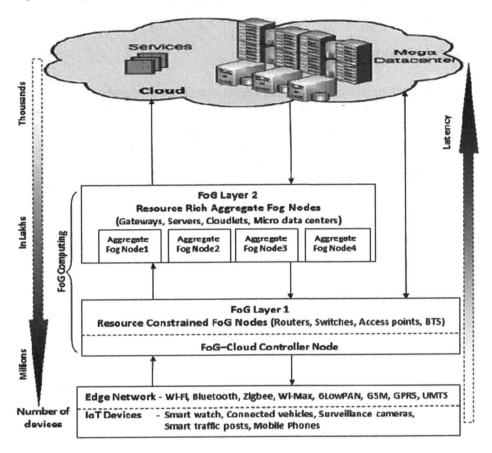

The forthcoming section presents a layered architecture for fog-cloud computing paradigm. It discusses the role performed by each layer of the fog-cloud. The difference between the fog layers and cloud are compared in terms of technical parameters. The section further deals with the working concept of resource management framework which is designed exclusively for fog-cloud computing paradigm.

Fog Cloud Layered Architecture

The layered architecture of fog-cloud ecosystem serving the edge devices is depicted in Figure 9. The fog nodes are aware of their geographical location within context. The Fog computing layer is sub layered as resource-rich aggregate fog nodes and resource-constrained fog nodes (Swati Agarwal, Shashank Yadav, Arun Kumar Yadav, 2017). Devices like servers, virtual containers, cloudlets, and micro datacenters form the resource-rich fog nodes whereas devices like switches, routers, surveillance cameras, and access points are categorized as resource constrained fog nodes.

Request Response Service

As and when the requirement arises, the aggregate fog nodes forms cluster with its counterparts, to extend its resource capacity. The number of IoT devices serviced decreases towards the clouds, unlike the latency increases as such. But, the Fog layer is capable of providing service to a huge number of IoT devices with minimal latency and hence termed as Fog as a Service (FaaS) model. The FaaS model deals with the different type of application request that is either time sensitive, resource intensive or the combination of both time and resource.

1. Low time sensitive and low resource intensive -- service at aggregate fog layer2
2. Low time sensitive and medium-resource intensive – service at aggregate fog layer 2
3. Low time sensitive and high resource intensive – service in the cloud
4. Medium Time sensitive and low resource intensive – service at aggregate fog layer 2
5. Medium Time sensitive and medium-resource intensive – service at fog layer 2
6. Medium Time sensitive and high resource intensive -- service at cloud
7. High time sensitive and low resource intensive applications -- service at fog layer 1
8. High time sensitive and medium resource-intensive applications – service at aggregate fog layer 2
9. High time sensitive and high resource intensive applications – service at aggregate fog layer 2

The choice of servicing layer for the request that arrives is depicted in Table 2. The range of Low, Medium, and High can be scaled for both time and resource. In terms of time sensitiveness, high refers to the response time slice between sub-milliseconds to seconds, medium sensitive refers to the response time between seconds to minutes and low sensitive refers to the time slice between minutes to less than an hour. In terms of resource intensiveness, high and medium refers to the resource-rich device layer and low refers to the resource-constrained (small capability) device layer. The notations F1 and F2 refer to the fog layer1 and fog layer2 respectively.

The comparison provided in Table 3 can clearly explain the performance quality of each layer with its own pros and cons[1]. It depicts the necessity of fog computing along with cloud infrastructure.

Table 2. Service layer

Time Sensitive \ Resource Intensive	Low	Medium	High
Low	F2	F2	cloud
Medium	F2	F2	cloud
High	F1	F2	F2

Autonomic Resource Management Framework

The autonomic resource management framework of fog computing shown in Figure 10 is a layered model denoted as Fog as a Service (FaaS). The framework comprises of three layers namely fog SaaS (Software as a Service), fog PaaS (Platform as a Service) and fog IaaS (Infrastructure as a Service). The user (IoT devices or end users) from IoE and edge networks generate their requests. The fog SaaS is capable of providing the required software services to the users (Yi, S., Li, C., & Li, Q. 2015). The fog SaaS layer hosts app portals and application programming interface for the different real-time applications. The SaaS layer avails the required platform services from the fog PaaS and resources from the IaaS layer.

The fog PaaS layer is responsible for implementing the autonomic resource allocation through the PAPE control loop. The fog-cloud controller (FCC) in the PaaS layer plays a vital role in directing the request to one of the appropriate fog service layer either F1 or F2. To achieve efficient resource allocation, it is essential to have a component that anticipates the amount and type of incoming requests in advance. Such issues are taken care of by the autonomic resource management component incorporated in the FCC. It takes care of the overall resource management in an autonomic fashion.

The fog IaaS layer is the micro data center that houses the physical servers. The physical servers host virtual containers as the resource for storage and computations. The fog IaaS layer is categorized into two resource pool for faster and efficient management. Resource pool-1 (rp1) hosts physical servers that are resource constrained while the resource pool-2 (rp2) houses resource-rich physical machines. Virtual containers are instantiated in these physical servers as and when required.

The autonomic resource management is a software component (ARMC) that executes the PAPE (Probe, Analyze, Plan, Execute) loop with sensors and Actuators. As the first step, the ARMC probes the incoming service requirements, analyzes the

Table 3. Comparison between fog layer and cloud

Sl. No.	Parameters	Fog Nodes near to the IoT devices (F1 layer)	Aggregate Fog nodes (F2 layer)	Cloud
1	Latency	Milliseconds to sub-second	Seconds to Minutes	Minutes, less than hours
2	Delay Jitter	Low	Medium	High
3	Location of service	At the edge of the local network (Intranet)	Just above the local network	In the Internet
4	Devices Involved	Embedded-devices, sensors.	Gateway, servers, VCs.	Datacenters (servers)
5	The distance between client and server	One Hop	Few Hops	Multiple Hops
6	Duration of data storage	Transient- few hours	Short duration- long hours	Months and years
7	Location awareness	Yes	Yes	No
8	Content generators	IoT devices	IoT devices	Human
9	Target Users	Wireless devices with low transmission range –shopping malls, restaurants.	Wireless devices with higher transmission range- mobile users, connected cars	Common Internet users
10	Management Control	Distributed	Distributed / hierarchical	Centralized / partially Hierarchical
11	Support for Mobility	Supported (lispmob)	Supported	Limited
12	Service Type	Localized information services linked to deployment locations	Localized information services linked to deployment locations	WWW
13	Real-time Interactions	Supported	Supported	Partially Supported
14	Transfer Protocol supported	6lowpan, zigbee	MQTT,COAP	HTTP
15	Geo-Distribution	Distributed –within the restricted geographical area	Distributed	Centralized
16	Invocation			REST API
17	The attack on data enroute	Very low probability	Low probability	High probability
18	Security and Privacy	Can be defined	Can be defined	Cannot be defined
19	Last mile connectivity	Wireless	Wireless	Leased line/wireless
20	Application Examples	Haptic, Telemedicine, Industrial productions, Chemical reactors, M2M -communication	Voluminous - Analytics, Augmented-reality, surveillance-cameras, Metrological, Smart farming.	Big data analytics, Graphical dashboards.

metrics, plans for the correct actions to be taken and executes them. The following section discusses the functions carried out in the different phases of the PAPE control loop.

Probe Phase

The probe phase gathers information from user sensors and resource sensors. The user sensor gathers information like a number of service requests (nsr), type of service requests (TOSR), type of devices and networks from which the requests arrive and request arrival rate. This information forms the input to the service requirement component. The role of the resource sensor is to collect the computational metrics

Figure 10. The fog-cloud resource management framework

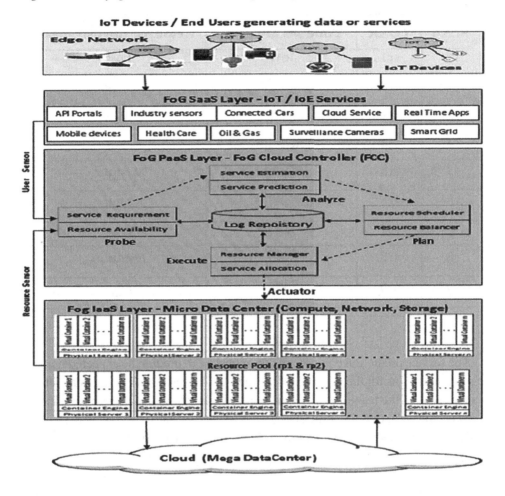

like amount of the resources (virtual containers) available, number of virtual container (VC) in use, number of free VCs and configuration of those resources. These technical details are fed to the resource availability component for further processing.

Analyzer Phase

Based on the information collected in the probe phase, the analyzer performs estimation and prediction. The service estimation component computes the number of service requests that arrive in each type of service requests at time t. The type of service requests (TOSR) that arrive is classified into nine types as shown in Table 4. Accordingly, the amount of resource required from the resource pool at time t is calculated.

Table 4. Type of service requests

Sl.No	TOSR	Time sensitiveness	Resource Intensiveness
1	sr1	low	Low
2	sr2	low	Medium
3	sr3	low	high
4	sr4	medium	Low
5	sr5	medium	Medium
6	sr6	medium	high
7	sr7	high	Low
8	sr8	high	Medium
9	sr9	high	high

The service prediction component is responsible to predict the expected number of service requests for the next time interval t+1 according to which the planner can plan for scaling the resource. The statistical tool called the linear regression model (lrm) is employed to predict the service request arrival rate psr_i. The general form of the linear regression statistical model for the fog service request sr_i at the time t' is given by equation (2).

$$Y_{t+1} = a\,X_t + b \tag{2}$$

Where X_t is the indices of the sample service request (observation), Y_{t+1} is the number of expected service request sr_i, t is the value of the timestamp at the moment that each request was taken for the experiment and n is the total number of service requests received. The value of a and b are calculated by solving the linear regression equation based on the ordinary least squares as given by equation (3) and (4).

$$a = \frac{\sum X_t^2 \sum Y_t - \sum X_t \sum X_t Y_t}{n\sum X_t^2 - (\sum X_t)^2} \tag{3}$$

$$b = n\sum X_t Y_t - \sum X_t \sum Y_t$$

$$n\sum X_t^2 - (\sum X_t)^2 \tag{4}$$

Information from each of the phase is updated periodically in the log repository (the database structure) for future reference and analytics.

Planner Phase

The estimated and predicated information from the analyzer phase forms the input to the planner phase. The planner phase develops a plan of action by employing reinforcement learning (RL) technique. It takes care of the following responsibilities. First, depending upon the type of service request (TOSR) as listed in the Table 5, the planner phase forwards the request to the appropriate resource pool (either rp1 or rp2 or cloud) through the resource scheduler.

The decision to forward the request to the appropriate resource pool in the fog IaaS layer depends on the time sensitiveness of the request, resource intensiveness, type of device requesting the service, frequency of such request and amount of resources required for such request. Along with these details, the reinforcement learning algorithm takes into account the current state of the resource availability at each fog IaaS layer to take decisions.

Table 5. Mapping of TOSR with resource pool

TOSR	Servicing Layer	Resource pool
sr1	F2	rp2
sr2	F2	rp2
sr3	cloud	cloud
sr4	F2	rp2
sr5	F2	rp2
sr6	cloud	cloud
sr7	F!	rp1
sr8	F2	rp2
sr9	F2	rp2

Table 6. State-action for scaling decision

	at time 't', $nsr > rp$ at 't+1' $psr_i > sr_{i(t)}$	at time 't', $nsr = rp$ at 't+1' $psr_i = sr_{i(t)}$	at time 't', $nsr < rp$ at 't+1' $psr_i < sr_{i(t)}$
State	Over utilization	Normal utilization	Underutilization
Action (Forwarding the request to the specific layer)	Scale-out (increase the required number of VCs from the resource pool to the IaaS)	No-op (no operation)	Scale in (release the excess VCs from IaaS, back to the resource pool)

Secondly, the RL agent incorporated in the resource balancer compares the number of requests arrived at a time 't' and the number of free VCs in the respective fog resource pool, then it classifies the state of the current system as either over-utilized or under-utilized. If the state is found to be over utilized then more containers need to be added (scale out) to the infrastructure layer from the reserved resource pool. On the other hand, if the state found to be underutilized, it is assumed that there exist excess resources that are not utilized; hence those resources need to be released back to the resource pool (scale-in). In case neither of the two states, the system resumes its normal operation.

Given the prediction about the expected number of service requests at time t+1, the RL agent decides whether the next state of the system will go overutilized or underutilized. Then the agent recommends for the appropriate action to be taken either to scale-out or scale-in or no-operation depending upon the requirement of resources and its future availability.

Execution Phase

In this phase, the decision made about the workload-resource scheduling and scaling (balancer) of resources in the planner phase is implemented into action. Depending upon the decision made either to scale-in/scale-out/ no-op the resource manager invokes/release the required number of virtual containers (resources) in the fog IaaS layer. It keeps tracks of the number of containers that are in use (working) and available (free). The number of physical servers and the containers invoked in them is also maintained by the resource manager. Then the resource allocator dispatches the service requests at a time 't' to the suitable virtual containers according to the best-fit algorithm after sorting the service requests in ascending order of time sensitiveness. The processes that occur in all the phases are updated in the log repository for historical analysis and for the reference of future iterations.

Pseudo Code:

Pseudo Code for Autonomic Resource Management in Fog

```
{
      initialize n     //  Boot a random number of  virtual
containers in the micro data center
      repeat for every time interval 't'
      begin
         read tnor                     //  total number of
requests received
            for (every set of fog service requests at time 't')
      begin                           // calls the PAPE
                  probe(sr_i)
                     analyze(sr_i)
                     plan(r_i)
                  execute(sr_i)
      end for
      t=t+1
      end repeat
}
```

Pseudocode for the Probe Phase in PAPE

```
probe (sr_i)
begin
  probe service requirements()    // collects type of service
requests in terms of time-sensitive and resource intensiveness
      {
      app_portal = type.service(sr_i)    // depending upon the app
portal from which the request is invoked, the service
                  request sr_i is categorized either as low
time sensitive, medium or high
                  sensitive  request.
            if sr_i.app_portal = app1                 // app1
represents cloud service api that is not time critical,  like
```

```
web
                sr_i.timesensitive = low              //
services, ecommerce transactions, etc..
        elseif sr_i.app_portal = app2         //   app2
represents real time application portals that are less time
critical
                sr_i.timesensitive = medium
    else
   sr_i.timesensitive = high         // any application service
requests other than app1 and app2 are
           endif
//  considered as highly time critical requests and need to be
addressed


//   in  sub seconds
        device_nw = network.service(sr_i)      // depending upon
the network from which the request is invoked, the service
                        request sr_i is categorized either as
low resource intensive, medium or high
                            intensive request.
        if sr_i.device_nw = lowtrans  // lowtrans  refers to
the short transmission range networks like Bluetooth, wifi,
Zigbee
                sr_i.resourceintensive = low
   elseif sr_i.device_nw = midtrans     // midtrans  refers to
the medium transmission range networks like Wimax,

6lowpan,etc.,
                sr_i.resourceintensive = medium
    else
       sr_i.resourceintensive = high    // any application
service requests other than low and medium-resource type are
   endif
considered as high-end resource requests.


        }          // probe service requirements

   probe resource_availability()
    {   // the inputs about the number of available containers,
used containers are read from the load resource manager that
```

takes care
     of the resources in the resource pool.
  read tnc_rp1   *// total number of containers*
in resource pool1
    read tnc_rp2   *// total number of*
containers in resource pool2
     read rp1_count   *// number*
of containers in use in resource pool1
    read rp2_count   *// number of*
containers in use in resource pool2

    rp1_free = tnc_rp1-rp1_count   // number of
containers available in resource pool1
    rp2_free = tnc_rp2-rp2_count   // number of
containers available in resource pool2
  }
end   *// pseudocode for probe phase ends*

Pseudocode for Analyze Phase in PAPE

{ *// estimate the number of resources (virtual containers)*
needed to serve the arrived service request at time 't'
  // predicts the expected number of service requests at time
't+1'
  // employs linear curve fitting regression model for
prediction.
   Input: service request arrival rate at time 't'
  Output: psr - the predicted number of service requests at a
time 't+1' (expected)
begin
   if sr_i = sr1   *// counts the*
number of requests belonging to specific service type
     sr1count ++   *// type of*
service request sr1 to sr9 mentioned in table 4
   elseif sr_i = sr2
    sr2count ++
   elseif sr_i = sr3
    sr3count ++

29

```
        elseif sr_i = sr4
           sr4count ++
        elseif sr_i = sr5
           sr5count ++
        elseif sr_i = sr6
           sr6count ++
        elseif sr_i = sr7
           sr7count ++
        elseif sr_i = sr8
           sr8count ++
        else
           sr9count ++
        endif
        oldtrans(sr_i)= read.logrecord(sr_i)        // get the
old request arrival rate from log repository
            compute value of a and b from the equation (3) and
(4)
        psr_i =  Y_{t+1}                                     //
predict the number of expected service requests from the
equation (2)
            return psr_i
end
}
```

Pseudocode for Plan Phase in PAPE

```
begin
   input: psr_i,  sr_{i(t)}              //  psr_i - predicted number
of service request,  sr_i - actual number of service requests
arrived at time 't'
   output: Select action        //   forward the request to
either resource pool1 or resource pool2 of the fog IaaS and
scale-in/scale-out/no-op
   Initialization: The Q-values table of pairs (s,a) by zero
   while (t<300)     // the time interval for  300 seconds
   begin
      if (sr_{i(t)} = = sr7) then                      // sr7 is
highly time sensitive service request
```

```
            {    nsr= sr7count
// get the count of service request7
        rp = rp1_free
           resource_scheduler(nsr, rp)            // forward the
request to rp1 which is resource pool1
            }
          elseif (sr_{i(t)} = = sr3) or (sr_{i(t)} = = sr6)
//  sr3 and sr6 are highly resource intensive service request
            {    nsr = max(sr3count, sr6count)
        rp = rpcloud
           resource_scheduler(nsr,rp)                    //
forward the request to  rpcloud – cloud resource pool
            }
      else
      {    nsr = max(sr1count, sr2count, sr4count, sr5count,
sr8count, sr9count)
         rp = rp2_free
           resource_scheduler(nsr,rp)          //   forward all
other requests to  rp2 – resource pool2  for fog layer F2
      }
      endif
    end while
    if (psr_i > sr_{i(t)}) then                        // number of
expected request is greater than current request rate
           nxtstate = over-utilization        //  the next
state of the system is going to be over utilized & needs more
resources
       elseif  (psr_i < sr_{i(t)})                          //  number
of expected request is lesser than current request rate
           next state = under-utilization   //  the next
state of the system is going to be underutilized & needs fewer
resources
    else
       nxtstate = normal-utilization    //  number of expected
request is equal to the current request rate
       endif
    selected action(psr_i) =lookup(nxtstate, Q-value table)
    return selected action(psr_i)
 end    // plan phase ends
 resource_scheduler(nsr,rp)
```

```
  {
    if (nsr > rp) then                                    //
number of  service request arrived  is greater than number of
free containers
            currstate = over-utilization        // additional
containers need to be added from reserved resource pool
        elseif (nsr < rp)                                 //
number of service request arrived  is smaller than number of
free containers
          currstate = under-utilization        // excess
containers need to be released from the resource pool
    else                                                  //
number of service request arrived is equal than number of free
containers
          currstate = normal-utilization    // no changes
required
    endif
    choose an action (scale-in,scale-out,no-op) based on the
state-action table
    perform the action a_t and receive the feedback reward r_{t+1} to
reach the new state s_{t+1}
    update the Q-value table using equation 1
    s_t=s_{t+1}
  }
```

Pseudocode for Execution Phase in the PAPE

```
begin
 input: selected action  (scale-in or scale-out or no-op)
if (selected action = scale-out) then
    create new VCs from the resource pool and add them to the
usage // VCs - virtual containers
    else if (selected action = scale-in) then
      release the unused VCs to the resource pool
  else
      no-operation     // the number of the virtual containers
is maintained as it is currently existing
    endif
```

```
        service-allocator()              // distribution of
requests to the virtual containers in rp1/rp2 /cloud on best
fit strategy
end
```

Pseudocode for Reinforcement Algorithm (Q-Learning)

```
begin
    initialize the q-values table of pairs(s, a) arbitrarily
    repeat
        observe the current state s_t
        choose the action based on the given function
        perform an action a, receive the feedback reward r to
reach the next state s_{t+1}
        update the cumulative reward (q-value)
        s_t=s_{t+1}
    until the end of the time interval         // 300 seconds
end
```

Procedure for Best Fit Strategy Employed in Service Allocator

```
begin
  read noc, nsr      // Get number of free containers and
number of  service requests
    sortdown(nfc)    // Sort the virtual containers in
descending order of their compute capacity (MIPS)
    sortup(nsr)        //        Sort the service requests in
ascending order of their time sensitiveness
    allocate(VC,sr)  //            Start picking each service
request and find the suitable VC that can be assigned the
service request and
                                 Deploy the service
request on to the virtual container and get executed.
    return service response    // Return the service response.
end
```

The pseudo code emphasizes the resource allocation which can be implemented in iFogsim tool. The code can be tested for various real-time datasets that are specific to IoT applications. The concept shall prove that the intelligence enabled fog computing paradigm to outshine the cloud in terms of performance. Low latency with mobility support is the highlight of the Fog-Cloud federation. The combination of fog and cloud can solve many unpredictable issues. The autonomic resource provision with machine learning techniques in fog brings out a viable solution for real-time applications of IoT.

Fog computing allows applications to run close to the data where it is generated. The fog nodes are accessed by a large number of IoT devices. An IoT device that requests a service, communicates with the fog network. The fog node decides whether to process the data with its available resources and send it to the cloud if it involves more computation power. Hence the security and privacy of the data along with its communication network is an inevitable part of the fog computing. The following section presents a panorama of security and privacy problems in fog computing along with the existing technologies that resolve the issues.

Security and Privacy Issues of Fog Computing

In the near future, it is expected that the IoTs will establish its utility in most part of our daily life. Consequently, personal information of people, their interests, likes, dislikes, habits, location, trajectory path, and the lifestyle will depend on the IoT. As the IoT devices depends on fog nodes for storage, computation, and communication, the fog nodes are more susceptible to security threats than the cloud.

The security and privacy mechanisms followed in the cloud, as it is cannot be used in fog computing due to its demand for requirements like mobility support, low latency, heterogeneity, and large scale geographic distribution. At the same time, lack of proper security and privacy preserving mechanisms (Xu & Zhu, 2015) will make fog computing unacceptable despite its usefulness.

Security and privacy of fog computing have to be considered in two point of view. One way is the mechanisms to mitigate the issues and threats faced by fog nodes and the other way is the techniques by which fog computing leverage in resolving security and privacy issues of IoT devices. In this section, the security and privacy issues of fog computing are analyzed in both the views interchangeably in the perspective of Trust, Access control, Intrusion detection system, data, and location privacy. These issues are addressed between IoT device and fog nodes, within fog nodes, and between fog node and cloud.

Trust Model

Trust is the degree of reliability of an entity. In fog computing trust is ensured as a two-way model (Lee, Kim, Ha, Rajput, & Oh, 2015). The trust over the fog nodes depends on the fog service providers. The fog service providers (FSP) can be either an ISP (Internet Service Provider) or a local private cloud provider or a CSP (cloud service provider) who converts the existing infrastructure into fog service thus making more profit. Among different trust models, opinion based trust management well suits for fog computing (Xu & Zhu, 2015). However several factors that are used to measure the trust are taken into account in designing a trust model.

Access Control

Access control of an entity constitutes Authentication, Authorization, and Accounting (AAA)[2]. Authentication refers to proving one's identity whereas authorization refers to the control who provides the right to access an entity. Accounting refers to the bookkeeping and tracking mechanism that is vital in a security scheme to detect intrusion behavior. The IoT devices that request for services are heterogeneous in nature and fragile to threats. If the IoT devices carry wrong information, it causes serious problems and leads to a lot of damage (Lee et al., 2015). Any device that requests a fog service has to authenticate itself to the fog node. This will ensure that only authorized devices access the fog network. The device can be an IoT device or the network devices that are used for data communication between various layers of fog framework (Rayani, Bhushan, & Thakare, 2018). Similarly, since the fog nodes collaborate with cloud, only those fog nodes that are approved by the cloud can be a part of the fog framework. Hence fog nodes also should be checked for its integrity.

Conventional PKI (public key) authentication schemes do not scale the massive end devices (IoT) (Alrawais, Alhothaily, Hu, & Cheng, 2017). The encryption and decryption processes impose huge storage and computation burden on both the IoT devices and the fog nodes. Therefore biometric authentication schemes like finger print, key stroke, and face authentication fit best for fog computing (Mukherjee et al., 2017). Unlike these techniques, a third party certifying authority (CA) can alleviate the resource constraints problems of IoT devices (Alrawais et al., 2017). In this technique, any IoT device that need to authenticate itself to the fog node get it done through a CA. On the other hand, fog nodes are authenticated by a fog node that takes the authorization responsibility to check the integrity of other nodes in its geographic area. To reduce the storage and computation burden, fog nodes are authenticated either by the cloud or a CA in most of the scenario (Lee et al., 2015).

Intrusion Detection Systems (IDS)

In general Intrusion detection system is meant to detect the threats caused by insider attack on data, hardware and software. IDS is known for its mitigation against DoS attacks. With respect to the fog environment, IDS detect malicious IoT devices and notify others to take proper action(Alrawais et al., 2017). The IDS analyze the user login information for the intrusion of the unauthorized/malicious entity that can corrupt the data and the network.

In fog computing, intrusion detection is carried out either signature-based or anomaly based. In the signature-based method, the observed pattern of workflow is compared with the existing database of misbehavior. In anomaly based method the observed behavior pattern is checked against expected behavior (Stojmenovic & Wen, 2014). A virus or a malware can propagate from an end device to any part of the fog-cloud framework. Hence incorporating IDS in the fog nodes provides additional protection on both cloud and IoT devices.

Privacy Preservation

Privacy preservation refers to the protection mechanism against the leakage of private information such as data, location, and usage pattern (Alrawais et al., 2017). Fog computing is a distributed environment where the data is scattered across the geographically dispersed fog nodes. Once a less secured fog node is compromised, the privacy of the user data is lost (Mukherjee et al., 2017). The increased communication between the different layers of fog framework is a high source of data leakage.

Data Privacy

In fog computing, the fog nodes are exposed to a massive amount of data from end devices. Most of the data are sensitive, concerning the identity of the user, usage utilities and private information (Mukherjee et al., 2017). Data leakage can happen at any level viz., storage, computation and communication (the network). Hence privacy preservation of data in fog computing is a critical challenge.

Conventional protection mechanisms like encryption/decryption techniques consume a specific amount of storage and computation resources. Due to this reason, it is highly impractical for IoT devices to adopt encryption/decryption (Alrawais et al., 2017). On the other side, the resource-constrained fog nodes too cannot be overloaded in its effort to address the massive scale of IoT devices. Homomorphic functions and differential privacy are some of the privacy-preserving techniques employed in a fog computing environment.

Location and Usage Privacy

The end devices offload a large amount of data to the nearby fog nodes. The place of the devices can be linked to the owner (Mukherjee et al., 2017). The fog nodes can infer the location identity, mobility habit, and trajectory of the devices by analyzing their pattern. As long as the device is held by the person or important object the location privacy of the end user is at risk (Xu & Zhu, 2015). Choosing different fog nodes every time and identity obfuscation are some of the techniques used in fog computing for preserving location privacy.

Along with the request, the user data is also revealed when end devices communicate with fog nodes (Mukherjee et al., 2017). When smart home equipment refers the fog nodes for processing, an adversary can reveal the end user's details like preferred TV channels, items preserved in the fridge, the browsing habits, shopping frequency through e-carts, etc., leakage of such usage pattern is a high threat to the privacy of the end user. Such problems are eliminated by partitioning the task among different fog nodes (Stojmenovic, Wen, Huang, & Luan, 2016) (Xu & Zhu, 2015).

In fog computing, it is hard to design security and privacy policies that span across end device-fog-cloud environment with restricted resource facility. Efforts are taken to develop lightweight security algorithms that can work in large scale, widely geo-distributed and mobile environments (Alrawais et al., 2017).

CONCLUSION AND FUTURE ENHANCEMENTS

The chapter contributes a novel proposal for an efficient resource allocation in fog architecture that can reduce the cost of the Fog Service Providers thereby minimizing the price to the service consumers. The Fog-Cloud federation minimizes the network traffic towards the cloud as most of the workloads are processed in the aggregate fog nodes. Moreover, the latency-intolerant applications from the massive number of IoT devices are well addressed by fog than the cloud. The combination of autonomic computing and reinforcement learning in resource allocation guarantees a high quality of service to the end user. This hybrid resource allocation approach exhibits the benefit of RL's ability to learn in a model-free environment. The recommended architecture adapts to the unpredictable workload spikes and deals with the undesirable states of the system dynamically. Thus, the reinforcement learning supported autonomic resource provisioning unveils the potential of fog computing to its fullest.

The future work extends to adopting deep reinforcement learning (DRL) algorithms for resource management. The DRL techniques are expected to address harsh real-time environments like railway track monitoring, underwater communication where mobility of end devices and low latency are unavoidable. Devising a separate strategy for Independent fog devices and interconnected fog devices can improve efficiency better. The independent fog devices directly deal with cloud while the interconnected fog devices collate among one another. Augmented reality, WSNs (Wireless Sensor Networks), Cyber-physical systems and software-defined networking are some of the scopes for which fog computing needs to facilitate resources efficiently.

REFERENCES

Aazam, M., & Huh. (2015). Dynamic resource provisioning through Fog micro datacenter. *2015 IEEE International Conference on Pervasive Computing and Communication Workshops*. 10.1109/PERCOMW.2015.7134002

Agarwal, S., Yadav, S., & Yadav, A. K. (2017). An Efficient Architecture for Resource Provisioning in Fog Computing. *International Journal of Science and Research, 6*(1), 2065–2069.

Alrawais, A., Alhothaily, A., Hu, C., & Cheng, X. (2017). Fog Computing for the Internet of Things: Security and Privacy Issues. *IEEE Internet Computing, 21*(2), 34–42. doi:10.1109/MIC.2017.37

Atlam, H., Walters, R., & Wills, G. (2018). Fog Computing and the Internet of Things: A Review. *Big Data and Cognitive Computing, 2*(2), 10. doi:10.3390/bdcc2020010

Bahrpeyma, F., Haghighi, H., & Zakerolhosseini, A. (2015). An adaptive RL based approach for dynamic resource provisioning in Cloud virtualized data centers. *Computing, 97*(12), 1209–1234. doi:10.100700607-015-0455-8

Baresi, L., Guinea, S., Quattrocchi, G., & Tamburri, D. A. (2016). MicroCloud: A Container-Based Solution for Efficient Resource Management in the Cloud. In *2016 IEEE International Conference on Smart Cloud (SmartCloud)* (pp. 218–223). New York: IEEE. 10.1109/SmartCloud.2016.42

Bhushan, S. B., & Reddy, P. C. H. (2018). A Hybrid Meta-Heuristic Approach for QoS-Aware Cloud Service Composition. *International Journal of Web Services Research, 15*(2), 1–20. doi:10.4018/IJWSR.2018040101

Bonomi, F., Milito, R., Natarajan, P., & Zhu, J. (2014). Fog Computing: A Platform for Internet of Things and Analytics. In N. Bessis & C. Dobre (Eds.), *Big Data and Internet of Things: A Roadmap for Smart Environments* (Vol. 546, pp. 169–186). Cham: Springer International Publishing. doi:10.1007/978-3-319-05029-4_7

Brogi, A., Forti, S., Ibrahim, A., & Rinaldi, L. (2018). Bonsai in the Fog: An active learning lab with Fog computing. In *2018 Third International Conference on Fog and Mobile Edge Computing (FMEC)* (pp. 79–86). Barcelona: IEEE. 10.1109/FMEC.2018.8364048

Casalicchio, E., Menascé, D. A., & Aldhalaan, A. (2013). Autonomic resource provisioning in cloud systems with availability goals. In *Proceedings of the 2013 ACM Cloud and Autonomic Computing Conference on - CAC '13* (p. 1). Miami, FL: ACM Press. 10.1145/2494621.2494623

Coutinho, E. F., Gomes, D. G., & de Souza, J. N. (2015). An Autonomic Computing-based architecture for cloud computing elasticity. In *2015 Latin American Network Operations and Management Symposium (LANOMS)* (pp. 111–112). Joao Pessoa, Brazil: IEEE. 10.1109/LANOMS.2015.7332681

da Silva, R. A. C., & da Fonseca, N. L. S. (2018) Resource Allocation Mechanism for a Fog-Cloud Infrastructure. In *2018 IEEE International Conference on Communications (ICC)*, Kansas City, MO. 10.1109/ICC.2018.8422237

Dastjerdi, A. V., & Buyya, R. (2016). Fog Computing: Helping the Internet of Things Realize Its Potential. *Computer*, *49*(8), 112–116. doi:10.1109/MC.2016.245

Delicato, F. C., Pires, P. F., & Batistal, T. (2017). *Resource Management for the Internet of Things*. SpringerBriefs in Computer Science. doi:10.1007/978-3-319-54247-8

Dutreilh, X., Kirgizov, S., Melekhova, O., Malenfant, J., & Rivierre, N. (2011). *Using Reinforcement Learning for Autonomic Resource Allocation in Clouds: Towards a Fully Automated Workflow*. Academic Press.

Ferrández-Pastor, F.-J., Mora, H., Jimeno-Morenilla, A., & Volckaert, B. (2018). Deployment of IoT Edge and Fog Computing Technologies to Develop Smart Building Services. *Sustainability, MDPI, Open Access Journal*, *10*(11), 1–23.

Iorga, M., Feldman, L., Barton, R., Martin, M. J., Goren, N., & Mahmoudi, C. (2018). *Fog computing conceptual model (No. NIST SP 500-325)*. Gaithersburg, MD: National Institute of Standards and Technology. doi:10.6028/NIST.SP.500-325

Khalid & Shahbaz. (2017). Service Architecture Models For Fog Computing: A Remedy for Latency Issues in Data Access from Clouds. *KSII Transactions on Internet and Information Systems, 11*(5).

La, Q. D., Ngo, M. V., Dinh, T. Q., Quek, T. Q. S., & Shin, H. (2018). *Enabling intelligence in fog computing to achieve energy and latency reduction.* Digital Communications and Networks.

Lee, K., Kim, D., Ha, D., Rajput, U., & Oh, H. (2015). On security and privacy issues of fog computing supported Internet of Things environment. *2015 6th International Conference on the Network of the Future (NOF)*, 1–3.

Mukherjee, M., Matam, R., Shu, L., Maglaras, L., Ferrag, M. A., Choudhury, N., & Kumar, V. (2017). Security and Privacy in Fog Computing: Challenges. *IEEE Access: Practical Innovations, Open Solutions, 5*, 19293–19304. doi:10.1109/ACCESS.2017.2749422

Ray, P. P. (2018). A survey on the Internet of Things architectures. *Journal of King Saud University - Computer and Information Sciences, 30*(3), 291–319.

Rayani, P. K., Bhushan, B., & Thakare, V. R. (2018). Multi-Layer Token Based Authentication Through Honey Password in Fog Computing. *International Journal of Fog Computing, 1*(1), 50–62. doi:10.4018/IJFC.2018010104

Singh, A., & Viniotis, Y. (2017). Resource allocation for IoT applications in cloud environments. In *2017 International Conference on Computing, Networking and Communications (ICNC)* (pp. 719–723). Silicon Valley, CA: IEEE. 10.1109/ICCNC.2017.7876218

Singh, S., & Singh, N. (2016). Containers & Docker: Emerging roles & future of Cloud technology. In *2016 2nd International Conference on Applied and Theoretical Computing and Communication Technology (iCATccT)* (pp. 804–807). Bangalore, India: IEEE.

Skarlat, O., Nardelli, M., Schulte, S., & Dustdar, S. (2017). Towards QoS-Aware Fog Service Placement. In *2017 IEEE 1st International Conference on Fog and Edge Computing (ICFEC)* (pp. 89–96). Madrid, Spain: IEEE. 10.1109/ICFEC.2017.12

Stojmenovic, I., & Wen, S. (2014, September 29). *The Fog Computing Paradigm: Scenarios and Security Issues.* Academic Press.

Stojmenovic, I., Wen, S., Huang, X., & Luan, H. (2016). An overview of Fog computing and its security issues: An overview of fog computing and its security issues. *Concurrency and Computation, 28*(10), 2991–3005. doi:10.1002/cpe.3485

Tesauro, G., Jong, N. K., Das, R., & Bennani, M. N. (2006). A Hybrid Reinforcement Learning Approach to Autonomic Resource Allocation. In *2006 IEEE International Conference on Autonomic Computing* (pp. 65–73). Dublin, Ireland: IEEE. 10.1109/ICAC.2006.1662383

Xu, K., & Zhu, H. (Eds.). (2015). *Wireless Algorithms*. Systems, and Applications. doi:10.1007/978-3-319-21837-3

Yi, S., Li, C., & Li, Q. (2015). A Survey of Fog Computing: Concepts, Applications, and Issues. In *Proceedings of the 2015 Workshop on Mobile Big Data - Mobidata '15* (pp. 37–42). Hangzhou, China: ACM Press. 10.1145/2757384.2757397

Zahoor, S., & Mir, R. N. (2018). Resource management in the pervasive Internet of Things: A survey. *Journal of King Saud University - Computer and Information Sciences*.

ENDNOTES

[1]   https://www.nebbiolo.tech/ whitepaper-fog-vs-edge.pdf
[2]   OpenFog_Reference_Architecture_2_09_17-FINAL.pdf

Chapter 2
A Novel Resource Management Framework for Fog Computing by Using Machine Learning Algorithm

Shanthi Thangam Manukumar

ⓘD https://orcid.org/0000-0001-5026-4889
Anna University, India

Vijayalakshmi Muthuswamy
Amity University, India

ABSTRACT

With the development of edge devices and mobile devices, the authenticated fast access for the networks is necessary and important. To make the edge and mobile devices smart, fast, and for the better quality of service (QoS), fog computing is an efficient way. Fog computing is providing the way for resource provisioning, service providers, high response time, and the best solution for mobile network traffic. In this chapter, the proposed method is for handling the fog resource management using efficient offloading mechanism. Offloading is done based on machine learning prediction technology and also by using the KNN algorithm to identify the nearest fog nodes to offload. The proposed method minimizes the energy consumption, latency and improves the QoS for edge devices, IoT devices, and mobile devices.

DOI: 10.4018/978-1-7998-0194-8.ch002

INTRODUCTION

In this era, the most upcoming technique is the edge devices IoT and mobile device users are increasing in drastic manner. By this same speed, the high complexity real time applications and data intensive applications gadgets such as Virtual Reality, Augmented Reality, Drones are developed. The resources limitations, energy consumption, mobile network traffic, high computation and storage are the main difficulties facing by the user. It is very difficult to solve these limitations with cloud computing model to support the cloud, a new concept to deploy task and storage, edge computing, fog computing, mobile edge computing are introduced.

To overcome the challenges and to support the cloud fog computing is proposed by Cisco, virtual platform provides storage, computation, network services and plays its role between the end devices and cloud (Bonomi et al., 2012). A decentralized networks which performs actions as cloud server but it relays on the cloud computing for high computation (Mahmud & Buyya, 2017). It performs wonders for edge devices, IoT devices and mobile devices due its low latency for real time applications and low mobile network traffic. In fog computing, main challenge is resource allocation and heterogeneous devices.

Offloading (Hyytia, Spyropoulos & Ott, 2015) is the way of transferring the task from the edge device to the fog nodes or to the cloud. Due to large complex applications and lack of resource its task or the part of the task offloaded is to the cloud or to the fog node to overcome the above mentioned challenges. Offloading decision is made based on the prediction technology and KNN algorithms to provide the best resource management for fog nodes. The important of fog computing and its characteristics are represented the energy minimization IoT devices resource management is discussed (Dastjerdi & Buyya, 2017).

Machine learning is way to increase the intelligence of the system and it is important to analyze. It is the way of learning the system for high computational real time applications (Angra & Ahuja, 2017). Detailed learning process about the data to understand and to classify accordingly will lead to improve the knowledge about the data (Mitchell, 1997). Machine learning algorithms applied to large data set to learn the data. Machine learning algorithm is used to improve problem solving with the prior knowledge about the data. It leads the dataset to train according to the learned information and it will find the way to reduce the problem and improves its performance. There some challenges in the machine learning while using in the data like how much data need to learn?, what algorithm is fit for this data? etc.,

The proposed method of this system used the machine learning algorithm KNN for resource allocation in fog nodes. It will show the nearest fog node to the user by using the machine learning KNN algorithm for efficient offloading and resource management. K- Nearest Neighbors (KNN) (Parsian, 1015) is the machine learning classification algorithm, here *K* is a numerical value always greater than 0.

KNN algorithm is used to find out the nearest data points in the dataset using the standard Euclidean distance. The (KNN) is a non-parametric method used for classification, to calculate the accuracy and for the validation of the KNN classification confusion matrix and the statistical method likelihood-ration is also used (Huang et al., 2013).

This chapter covers the introduction about this proposed work with brief discussion. It also includes about the new techniques, machine learning algorithms how it supports to this proposed system and also about the issues and challenges with the technique. In related works it shows analyse and survey about how the fog computing works and its issues, how the machine learning technique and KNN is useful for making decision and its challenges. In this related work, the discussion about offloading and its challenges are in wide manner. In the proposed work part it shows how to find the execution location and how KNN is works with this proposed system.

In the experimental result part, shows how the implementation takes part, how the task identify its execution location and it also gives how to evaluate and performance accuracy in classification is done, how R programming is used for statistical learning and how this proposed system implemented using R. In the last section, discussed about what this proposed system achieves, how the resource managed in the complex application and it shows the latency and high resource utilization, future work is also discussed related to this proposed system.

RELATED WORKS

Redowan Mahmud and R. Buyya (2017) provide a detailed fog taxonomy, survey and challenges facing in cloud computing and the how the fog computing techniques is supported. In addition to that, discussed about how the fog computing is acts an intermediate between the cloud and IoT devices, high computation mobile applications. They also tell how the fog computing technique works and its current research challenges. Luis M. Vaquero and Luis Rodero-Merino (2014) proposed the fog with a comprehensive definition. They discussed about the device ubiquity as the main and addressed how the fog connects with mobile devices and other IoT/sensor devices and challenges on services and network management in fog applications. Ben Zhang et al. (2015) discussed about why moving from the cloud to fog and tell us about how the cloud is not enough and how to change from cloud computing to fog computing. They argued that the level of abstraction to a data-centric design and showed the information how IoT is protected and much better computation performance in the fog than cloud. Ashkan Yousefpour et al. (2018) showed a complete survey about fog computing and its research topics and tutorial on fog computing and its paradigms. Chenn-Jung Huang et al. (2013) proposed machine learning prediction mechanism realized by using Support Vector Regressions (SVRs) to find the low latency time and the resources allocation. A. Singh et al. (2016) reviewed about the machine learning supervised algorithm to predict the future instances, to classify, and for clustering and discussed about the speed of the learning, complexity of the applications. Mario Bkassiny et al. (2013) reviewed the learning problem in cognitive radios and feature classification and decision making are done using the learning algorithms. Deng et al. (2016) proposed the investigation between power consumption and transmission delay in the fog to cloud computing system. They suggested the workload allocation problem between the fog and cloud to achieve the minimum delay and power consumption. Muhammad Aamir Nadeem et al. (2016) provide the survey about the fog computing emerging paradigm and issues and the challenges of the fog architecture is mentioned. Pengfei Hu et al. (2017) presented the hierarchical architecture of fog computing its characteristics and comparison with cloud computing and edge computing. They analyzed the key technologies like computing, communication and storage technologies, naming, resource management, security, privacy protection and also considers the bandwidth, latency to improve the performance of fog and cloud computing. Katrina Wakefield (n.d.) discussed about predicting models and machine learning algorithm, it also gives the information about the how to use the prediction technology and how machine learning algorithms are powerful for the prediction. Eren Balevi and Richard D. Gitlin (2018) determine the optimum number of normal nodes is changes to fog nodes with more computational capabilities to increase the data rate and to minimize the transmission delay. Changsheng You et al. (2018) studied the energy efficient resource management policies for asynchronous mobile edge computation offloading and determines by using the deadlines and also by considering arrival time of heterogeneous input data. By considering the arrival and deadlines and minimum mobile energy consumption in achieved. Yueyue Dai et al. (2018) proposed joint computation offloading and user association to provide the better offloading decision and for minimizing the overall energy consumption.

The motivation for this method is to improve the resource allocation in the fog nodes and to achieve the Quality of Service (QoS) by providing the services from the nearest fog nodes to the user. Tom M. Mitchell (1997) described the instance-based learning methods the KNN algorithm a machine learning techniques which are defined using the Euclidean distance. Learning in this algorithm simply provides the training dataset in the sorted manner, K is numerical value which is always greater than 0. The KNN algorithm is efficient memory indexing algorithm, and the distance- weighted KNN is effective inductive inference method for many practical problems. It is good and effective to noisy training data and also for large dataset of training data.

PROPOSED METHOD

The proposed method is to improve the resource allocation in the fog nodes and to achieve the Quality of Service (QoS) by providing the services from the nearest fog nodes to the user also by reducing the delay and improving resource. To improve the offloading mechanism, machine learning algorithm is used for predicting the fog nodes. KNN algorithm is used to find and to analyze the fog nodes which are available and provides accurate resource provider for the task so that it will improve the quality and minimizes the delay and latency (Saed Sayad, n.d.). KNN algorithm is simple that stores all the cases and classifies new cases based on the learned class and distance measured based on the similarity of the dataset and it is used in the statistical evaluation.

In this proposed system the task are offloaded either in the cloud side or in the fog side from the edge devices, IoT/sensor devices and mobile devices to avoid the resource constraints. In this system there is a resource provider pool which is having number resources provider such as resource provider 1; resource provider 2 up to resource provider N depends upon resource available. When the needed resource is not available in the resource pool and in the smart devices then the system will dynamically decide to offload the task and the decision making is need to decide which part of the task is offloaded to the cloud or to the fog. Here in the system the pools of resource are provided based on the availability and need. The prediction of the fog nodes and available resources is achieved by using the machine learning engines.

The offloading decision is made based on the machine learning KNN algorithm classification prediction technique. The KNN algorithm (Wikipedia, n.d.; Singh, Thakur & Sharma, 2016; Bkassiny, Li & Jayaweera, 2013) is used to learn about the fog node dataset which contains the details about fog node depends upon the price, CPU utilization, RAM, instance, queue length and it describes the detail about whether the fog node service is available or not. If the fog service is not available then tasks are offloaded to the cloud side for execution. The decision making using the machine learning algorithm reduces the power consumption and the task execution time is reduced. Here the Figure 1 shows system architecture for resource allocation in fog computing.

Figure 1. System architecture for resource allocation in fog computing

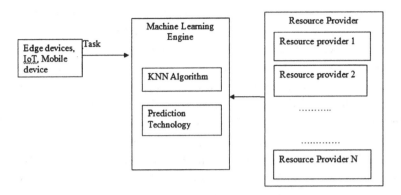

Algorithm

```
Input: Tasks T currently need to execute with their decision
Output: Updation of the execution location
Identify the resource need r_i, resource availability r_a
for all methods do
        if r_i==availability then execute local
        else search(r_i) then
        make decision d and check to execute in remote
                        if d==cloud then execute
                        else execute in fog then
                        update ri
        end
        end
end
```

The algorithm shows that if the task is currently needed to execute with the decision as input and update of the execution location whether in local, or either in the cloud side or in the fog side. While executing the task, it should identify the resource which is needed to execute the task. In all the methods it needs to check whether the resource available or not, if not need to take decision for the offloading location.

EXPERIMENTAL RESULTS

The implementation of the offloading decision making system is done using RStudio. Paul Teetor (2011) explained about the R programming getting started, data structures, probability and how to initialize the variables, and to load the dataset and export the dataset implementation. It also shows how the R programming is used in statistical computing. R studio (Teetor, 2011; James et al., 2013) is one of the best tools for statistics; it is free, open source using R programming. Gareth James et al. (2013) discussed about statistical learning which refers to the tools for understanding the complex dataset and it supports for the machine learning algorithms. This system uses KNN algorithm to make decision based on the availability of the fog service among the nearest fog. In the fog node data 50 patterns are classified two classes, each node has 6 numerical properties. This algorithm implemented using the RStudio; the decision to implement a particular task either in the cloud side or in the fog node is based on the availability of fog services, this decision is purely based on the accuracy and the prediction of the fog nodes.

In this system, the execution of task in smart devices are maintained and monitored, when there is high computation task is performed. If there is lack of the resource in smart device side then it will look out for the resource provider and check whether the resource is available in the resource pool. If the required resource is not available then the machine learning engine will pays it attention to make decision and to find the fog nodes to execute.

Resource management is done by using accuracy, prediction given by KNN algorithm which reduces the delay and response time. Figure 2 describes about the service availability prediction by using KNN algorithm it classified as yes or no. Based on the accuracy the selection of fog service is done to implement the task in the fog. Figure 3 describes the confusion matrix and the statistics about the data

Figure 2. Service availability prediction by using KNN algorithm

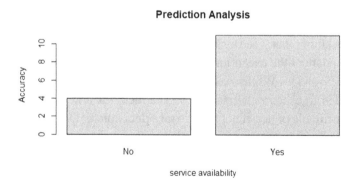

Figure 3. Confusion matrix and statistics

```
Confusion Matrix and Statistics

                Reference
Prediction  No  Yes
       No   4    0
      Yes   3    8

                 Accuracy : 0.8
                   95% CI : (0.5191, 0.9567)
      No Information Rate : 0.5333
      P-Value [Acc > NIR] : 0.03209

                    Kappa : 0.5872
  Mcnemar's Test P-Value : 0.24821

              Sensitivity : 0.5714
              Specificity : 1.0000
           Pos Pred Value : 1.0000
           Neg Pred Value : 0.7273
               Prevalence : 0.4667
           Detection Rate : 0.2667
     Detection Prevalence : 0.2667
        Balanced Accuracy : 0.7857

         'Positive' Class : No
```

set. Figure 4 shows the response time of the task due to the decision prediction and implementing the task as per its requirements.

Figure 4. Response time of the task due to the decision prediction

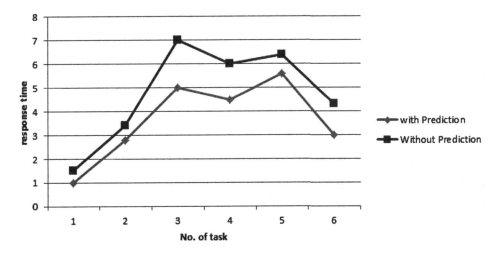

The validation and the estimation for performance accuracy of the classification machine learning KNN algorithm is validated using confusion matrix. For estimating performance for classification (Kuhn, 2013) a confusion matrix is a cross-tabulation of the observed and the predicted classes. R functions for confusion matrix are in the caret package. The performance accuracy of this proposed system is 80% and this system provides better performance by using the fog computing nodes and the high end resource provider cloud.

CONCLUSION

This system achieves the efficient resource allocation by using the machine learning techniques. It improves the QoS, response time and reduced the delay by using the nearest fog nodes for task allocation. In this system machine learning plays a vital role in classification and decision making which provides efficient offloading decision to achieve the execution of task with low latency, high resource utilization.

In future, very large dataset is learned using deep learning techniques and planned to include, achieving the improved resource allocation in the fog side as well as in the smart device side, or in the IoT/sensor nodes. Energy consumption and battery power consumption also measure and minimized to achieve green computing based smart device. Location based smart devices and fog nodes or the cloud are analyzed to provide resource in the efficient resource management.

ACKNOWLEDGMENT

This work is funded by the Ministry of Electronics and Information Technology has initiated "Visvesvaraya PhD Scheme for Electronics and Information Technology (IT)", India.

REFERENCES

Angra, S., & Ahuja, S. (2017). Machine learning and its applications: A review. *2017 International Conference on Big Data Analytics and Computational Intelligence (ICBDAC)*, 57-60. 10.1109/ICBDACI.2017.8070809

Balevi & Gitlin. (2018). Optimizing the Number of Fog Nodes for Cloud-Fog-Thing Networks. *IEEE Access, 6*, 11173-11183.

Ben Zhang, Kolb, Chan, Lutz, Allman, Wawrzynek, … Kubiatowicz. (2015). The cloud is not enough: Saving iot from the cloud. *HotStorage*.

Bkassiny, M., Li, Y., & Jayaweera, S. K. (2013). A Survey on Machine-Learning Techniques in Cognitive Radios. *IEEE Communications Surveys and Tutorials*, *15*(3), 1136–1158. doi:10.1109/SURV.2012.100412.00017

Bonomi, F., Milito, R., Zhu, J., & Addepalli, S. (2012). Fog computing and its role in the internet of things. *Proceedings of the first edition of the MCC workshop on Mobile cloud computing*, 13–16. 10.1145/2342509.2342513

Dai, Y., Du Xu, S. M., & Zhang, Y. (2018). Joint Computation Offloading and User Association in Multi-Task Mobile Edge Computing. *IEEE Transactions on Vehicular Technology*, *67*(12), 12313–12325. doi:10.1109/TVT.2018.2876804

Dastjerdi, A. V., & Buyya, R. (2017). Fog computing: Helping the internet of things realize its potential. *Computer*, *49*(8), 112–116. doi:10.1109/MC.2016.245

Deng, R., Lu, R., Lai, C., & Luan, H. (2016). *Optimal Workload Allocation in Fog-Cloud Computing Towards Balanced Delay and Power Consumption. IEEE Internet of Things Journal*.

Hu, Dhelim, Ning, & Qiu. (2017). Survey on fog computing: architecture, key technologies, applications and open issues. *Journal of Network and Computer Applications*.

Huang, Wang, & Guan, Chen, & Jian. (2013). Applications of Machine Learning to Resource Management in Cloud Computing. *International Journal of Modeling and Optimization*, *3*(2).

Hyytia, Spyropoulos, & Ott. (2015). Offload (only) the right jobs: Robust offloading using the Markov decision processes. *World of Wireless, Mobile and Multimedia Networks (WoWMoM), 2015 IEEE 16th International Symposium*, 1–9.

James, G. (2013). *An Introduction to Statistical Learning with Applications in R. In Springer Texts in Statistics*. Springer.

Kuhn, M. (2013). *Predictive Modeling with R and the caret Package useR!* Retrieved from https://www.r-project.org/nosvn/conferences/useR- 2013/Tutorials/kuhn/user_caret_2up.pdf

Mahmud, R., & Buyya, R. (2017). Fog computing: A taxonomy, survey and future directions. In *Internet of Everything*. Springer.

Mahmud, R., Kotagiri, R., & Buyya, R. (2018). Fog Computing: A Taxonomy, Survey and Future Directions. In B. Di Martino, K. C. Li, L. Yang, & A. Esposito (Eds.), *Internet of Everything. Internet of Things (Technology, Communications and Computing)* (pp. 103–130). Singapore: Springer. doi:10.1007/978-981-10-5861-5_5

Mitchell. (1997). *Machine Learning*. McGraw-Hill Science/Engineering/Math.

Nadeem. (2016). *Fog Computing: An Emerging Paradigm*. IEEE Xplorer.

Parsian. (2015). *Data Algorithms*. O'Reilly Media, Inc.

Sayed, S. (n.d.). K nearest neighbors – classification. *Saed Sayed*. Retrieved from: https://www.saedsayad.com/k_nearest_neighbors.htm

Singh, A., Thakur, N., & Sharma, A. (2016). A review of supervised machine learning algorithms. *2016 3rd International Conference on Computing for Sustainable Global Development (INDIACom)*, 1310-1315.

Teetor, P. (2011). R Cookbook. O'Reilly Media, Inc.

Vaquero, L. M., & Rodero-Merino, L. (2014). Finding your way in the fog: Towards a comprehensive definition of fog computing. *Computer Communication Review*, *44*(5), 27–32. doi:10.1145/2677046.2677052

Wakefield, K. (n.d.). Predictive analytics and machine learning. *Sas*. Retrieved from: https://www.sas.com/en_gb/insights/articles/analytics/a-guide-to-predictive-analytics-and-machine-learning.html

Wikipedia. (n.d.). K nearest neighbors algorithm. *Wikipedia*. Retrieved from: https://en.wikipedia.org/wiki/K-nearest_neighbors_algorithm

You, C., Zeng, Y., Zhang, R., & Huang, K. (2018). Asynchronous Mobile-Edge Computation Offloading: Energy-Efficient Resource Management. *IEEE Transactions on Wireless Communications*, *17*(11), 7590–7605. doi:10.1109/TWC.2018.2868710

Yousefpour, Fung, Nguyen, Kadiyala, Jalali, Niakanlahiji, … Jue. (2018). *All one needs to know about fog computing and related edge computing paradigms: A complete survey*. CoRR, abs/1808.05283

Chapter 3
Security Issues in Fog Computing for Internet of Things

D. N. Kartheek
Sree Vidyanikethan Engineering College, India

Bharath Bhushan
Sree Vidyanikethan Engineering College, India

ABSTRACT

The inherent features of internet of things (IoT) devices, like limited computational power and storage, lead to a novel platform to efficiently process data. Fog computing came into picture to bridge the gap between IoT devices and data centres. The main purpose of fog computing is to speed up the computing processing. Cloud computing is not feasible for many IoT applications; therefore, fog computing is a perfect alternative. Fog computing is suitable for many IoT services as it has many extensive benefits such as reduced latency, decreased bandwidth, and enhanced security. However, the characteristics of fog raise new security and privacy issues. The existing security and privacy measures of cloud computing cannot be directly applied to fog computing. This chapter gives an overview of current security and privacy concerns, especially for the fog computing. This survey mainly focuses on ongoing research, security challenges, and trends in security and privacy issues for fog computing.

DOI: 10.4018/978-1-7998-0194-8.ch003

INTRODUCTION

The Internet of Things (IoT) is one of the trending innovations that has the potential to provide enormous benefits to the society. The development of the IoT is reaching a stage at which many of the things around us will be able to connect to the Internet to communicate with each other (Atlam et al., 2017). During the inception, the IoT was intended to reduce human efforts and use different types of actuators and sensors to collect data from the environment and allow automatic storage and processing of these data (Giang et al., 2014; Atlan et al., 2018).

IoT market is expected to grow from more than 15 billion devices three years ago to more than 75 billion in 2025 (Friedman, 2018). IoT requires a robust technological foundation for its swift development and acceptance from the scientific community. Hence, the fog computing is a very strong candidate to provide this foundation for IoT. Because of several advantages, fog computing is expected to be one of the main backbone of the IoT in terms of computational support.

As shown in Figure 1, from a conceptual point of view, we are predicting fog computing to serve as an intermediate level of service for seamlessly handshaking the protocols of cloud computing and IoT. This will bring many benefits: 1) Cloud Computing servers are super fast in contrast to the IoT devices. Fog computing devices will provide an interface between the two far set of devices. 2) This intermediate layer of fog computing will allow several fixes (such as patch updates, etc.) to be done easier. Instead of making changes on IoT devices, software updates can be pushed on to the fog device(s). 3) Fog computing will bring all the advantages of edge-computing, such as the agility, scalability, decentralization, etc.

As cloud being a centralized resource out of users control, it represents every possible opportunity to violate privacy. Unfortunately, privacy has become a luxury today, a situation that will be exacerbated in the IoT (Zhang et al., 2015). Hence, a remedy is necessary to enhance the privacy needs of the users in these services and fog computing is a strong candidate to provide this.

Figure 1. Fog computing proposed as a gateway in between cloud computing and IoT

Cloud Computing   Fog Computing   Internet of Things

Fog computing actually is a tool for cloud-based services (CBS) that can be thought of as an interface in between the real end-devices and the rest of the CBS. CBS offers three service models, namely Infrastructure as a Service (IaaS), Platform as a Service (PaaS) and Software as a Service (SaaS) (Butun, Kantarci & Erol-Kantarci, 2015). We are projecting that fog computing paradigm will act as an interface for these CBS service models so that intended services can be used by the front-end users seamlessly and promptly.

The *Security Plane* for CBS proposed by Butun *et al. (2015)* was intended to be used for the front-end IoT devices and to be an interface to the cloud. After the proposal of fog computing, this *Security Plane* kind of solution is highly implementable. Therefore, we think of fog computing to provide extra services such as security to the edge of the cloud for the CBS. For example, the usage of fog computing would bring benefits to the Intrusion Detection Systems (IDS) that are devised for IoT. Hence early detection is important to stop ill effects of intrusions, fog computing would bring early detection opportunities to IDS algorithms working on IoT.

Fog computing brings three immediate advantages over cloud computing: 1) Enhanced service quality to mobile users. 2) Enhanced efficiency to the network. 3) Enhanced location awareness. Among these benefits, the major benefit of fog computing over the cloud is that the support for location awareness which might be very useful for the applications that are employing location based services (LBS) (Luan et al., 2015).

BACKGROUND

Large-scale IoT deployments created situations which cloud computing could not handle efficiently and effectively. For instance, applications which require low latency while processing the data on the edge of the network. In real life, a massive amount of data is being collected by IoT from many different sensors in various environments such as factory production lines, vehicles, machines, elevators etc. or individual purposes such as smart home systems, hobby related sensors, etc. These sensing devices have different characteristics and features. They are connected to each other via hardwire or WiFi. Large-scale device deployments in heterogeneous environments bring management issues. Hence, intelligent communications approaches are needed in which efficiency and robustness are prioritized.

Using a cloud network to stream data and analyze data has its limitations such as bandwidth consumption and communication costs. If the user data are sensitive, securing the data is another important issue. The data are important for auditing purpose or controlling the assets to improve efficiency or preventing disasters etc. The data analysis could be done on site by running the software at local stations. The cloud would be used as storing the analysis result for historical and audit purposes. The data aggregation will reduce the bandwidth and also bandwidth related cost.

Figure 2 presents various possible application fields of fog computing: Smart Office concept can be an example of the generic relation of IoT devices and fog computing.

Smart Factory is an example of industrial IoT (IIoT) and fog computing application. There could be many IoT devices, sensors (temperature, pressure etc.), electric actuators or other control devices could be involved. Smart Home concept is emerging with IoT devices and home appliances such as TV, washing machine, dryer, refrigerator etc. as they are getting smarter and intelligent. In Smart Traffic example, data collection on site and immediately analyzing and processing data on the edge may help in fast decision making locally, instead of sending data to a central location. For instance, in case of an emergency, the traffic lights can be controlled

Figure 2. An illustration of four different possible fog computing applications with IoT: Smart office, smart factory, smart home and smart traffic

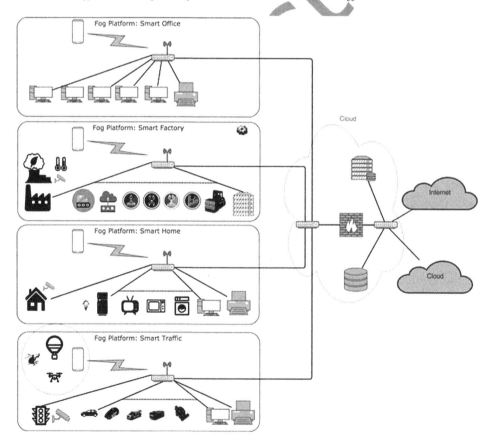

to open a way for emergency vehicles such as fire trucks and ambulances based on local IoT devices. In these four different scenarios, the common idea is that the devices generate a massive amount of data and may need to collaborate with each other and to take critical decisions reducing the delay. Hence, an agile response is important and the philosophy of fog computing may help to overcome bandwidth and latency related problems in this manner.

Because of introducing agile response nearby the edge components, we are expecting fast implementation and business growth of fog computing for future IoT applications such as smart-traffic and smart-factories. Thereby, the integration will not remain in just IoT but expand to industrial IoT (IIoT) and further other areas. This will impose its own challenges to IIoT (Zhang et al., 2015), as well as bringing benefits.

IoT and fog computing can be helpful in designing "smart" things such as smart home, smart traffic lights, smart cities, etc. For instance, the sensors in a smart traffic system can detect accidents or sense the road conditions due to weather or some other factors and inform the drivers. A traffic jam can be regulated by a smart traffic system. In recent years, due to the usage of IoT and other sensors, the data generated by end-devices increased massively. The question is where/when/how should these data be analyzed?. In cloud-centric design, IoT devices generate data and send them to the cloud (operates as a central server) for storage and analyses. However, in fog computing, the data is analyzed on the edge stations and just necessary results are being sent to the cloud.

Fog computing concept is recently introduced by CISCO [8], which is a new vision that enables IoT devices to run on the edge of the network. According to Bonomi *et al. (2012)* "Fog Computing" is not an alternative for "Cloud Computing". Fog extends the cloud computing and complements the cloud computing with the concept of smart devices which can work on the edge of the network. According to CISCOs vision, fog computing has following characteristics: 1- Low latency, 2- Location awareness, 3- Geographical distribution, 4- Mobility, 5- Very large number of nodes, 6- A predominant role of wireless access, 7- Streaming and real-time applications, 8- Heterogeneity (Cisco White Paper, 2015).

Table 1 presents fog computing and cloud computing concepts in a comparative way (Stallings & Brown, 2018). As can be seen, fog computing presents more agile and rapid response when compared to cloud computing, henceforth represents a strong candidate as a technological solution for future IoT and IIoT based implementations. Fog computing would be a preferable approach with various IoT designs and applications such as Smart Home, Smart Traffic (Transportation and Connected vehicles etc.), Smart Grid, Industrial Automation and integration with IIoT, Smart Health-care Systems, etc.

The benefits of fog computing for IoT (and IIoT) can be summarized as follows:

Table 1. Comparison of cloud and fog computing concepts

Feature	Cloud Computing	Fog Computing
Access	Wired or wireless	Wireless
Access to the service	Through server	At the edge device
Availability	Mostly available	Mostly volatile
Content distributed to	Edge device	Anywhere
Content generator	Man made	Sensor made
Content generation at	Central server	Edge device
Control	Centralized	Distributed
Latency	High	Minor
Location of resources (i.e. processing and storage)	Center	Edge
Mobility	Not supported	Supported
Number of users	Millions	Billions
Virtual infrastructure location	Enterprise server	User devices

- **Reducing Cost:** The data will be processed on edge rather than cloud
- **Reducing the Delay:** Critical applications require low latency to interpret the data and to take a decision. The cloud computing is not suitable to serve this task.
- **Agile Response:** Real-time applications may benefit from fog computing concept to gain speed during analysis or decision-making phase.
- **Increased Security:** With fog computing, service providers can filter out sensitive personally identifiable information (PII) and process it locally, sending the non- sensitive information to the cloud for further processing (Microsoft IoT, 2017).

FOG COMPUTING USAGE IN IOT

In this section, we introduced a subset of possible attack scenarios from real-life and discussed possible related mitigation methods.

Coin, bill and card-based systems suffer from multiple attack vectors. Asking the following question "How to hack a vending machine?" on Google returns thousands and thousands of results. Whether the hacks work or not does not really mean anything, the information of possible attack vectors poses a great threat to existing vending machine domain since one attack vector may work with an old (vulnerable) model. In early 80-90s, many coin-operated machines including but not limited to vending machines, arcade machines, public phones etc. suffered from simple Coin-on-a-String trick (Microsoft IoT, 2017). Later, this problem is mitigated with the one-way ratchet. Coin or card systems can be bypassed by attacker (YouTube, n.d.), the machine can be tampered (YouTube, n.d.). Paper bills tampered with plastic tape or other materials to get them back from machine after the credit is earned or attacker tries to machine spit the bill back after it is credited.

Even the vending machines in one of the most secured places on the world can be hacked, such as the ones in Central Intelligence Agency (CIA) facilities. According to BuzzFeed News, a group of CIA contractors exploited vulnerability in the vending machines electronic payment systems to buy snacks at no cost (Leopold & Mack, 2017). The total loss is around $3,314, but the most shocking fact is even vending machines in CIA are vulnerable and the unexpected can happen. Apparently, attackers disconnected the FreedomPay network cable connected to vending machines to exploit an "Availability" issue which resulted in the machine permitting purchases made by unfunded FreedomPay cards. Attackers are later on identified by agency's surveillance cameras. The extreme example above from real-life has shown us that we may more way to go in securing vending machines kind of payment systems. Luckily, now fog computing IoT technology enables us to implement more secure and agile payment systems as follows:

Smart Laundromats

In the real life, there have been many cases of Laundromat system hacking reported (Reddit, n.d.). Accordingly, it can be stated that none of the Laundromat systems (whether token based, magnetic card based, or even smart card based) that are being used today is secure. One of the main reasons is that the machine usage is not controlled via the server but at the machines. When a machine is hacked, or a token (card) is hacked, there is no mechanism to check the validity (whether it is authentic or not) of the transaction (Rayani, Bhushan & Thakare, 2018). Therefore, we project real-time (or close to real-time) usage of authentication mechanism that is governed by a central server (Authentication Management) and served to the edge devices (Laundromats) with the adoption of fog computing.

Smart Vending Machines

As an application of fog supported-IoT to vending machines, a vending machine can report missing items to the vendor so that they can be shipped on time. Besides, auto status check report can be generated and can be sent to the vendor for maintenance purposes. Smart vending machines mitigate the security problems but much more can be achieved from a "smart" machine. For instance, detailed sales reports (Poluru et al., 2019) can be generated for the vendor. A particular product can be tracked throughout the year, and the vendor can get detailed insight about the sales of a product or user buying habits like which product sales are best, when, where, etc. Product-A sales are best in February, user-1 buys product-B on Monday morning but buys product-C on Tuesday evening, etc.

Smart Chip Card Systems

Smart Chip Card Systems are relatively secured than coin or paper bill-based systems. The threat model for these systems is unencrypted or not well-encrypted cards. With a card reader/writer, the value in the card can be easily updated if the necessary preemptive steps are not taken. Another attack vector would be, an attacker may clone the card and get unlimited credit if there is not a mechanism to do validation (checking transaction with a server etc.) If IoT is embedded with the device in the production phase, it is unlikely that it will be physically tampered by an attacker easily (assuming human security details are overseeing the machine). A possible solution is designing a fog computing-based system (Bhushan & Reddy, 2018) which runs a micro-service to validate the transactions. Smart Chip Card can be an identifier for a legal user, once it is used in a device, the micro service on fog computing system validates the user and transaction or escalates the situation and asks mobile application based authentication. For instance, if the card is used in a different location (same apartment complex but different building etc.) this can be reported as an instance. Another distinct advantage of using fog computing-based IoT is the reduction of possible operational cost.

SECURITY ISSUES OF FOG COMPUTING IN IOT

According to the scientific projections, fog computing is expected to be one of the main backbone structure of IoT in the near future. Inevitably, there will be implications of this integration. In ideal conditions, extra introduced components (Bhushan & Reddy, 2016) are desired to bring no further burden on the overall operation of the existing system. However, this is not the fact in real life scenarios. Sometimes they bring an extra load (e.g. processing and memory storage), and sometimes (preferably) decrease existing load. The same is valid for security features.

There are six features (most important ones being CIA, i.e. confidentiality, integrity and availability) that we considered in the case of a failure (capture) in defending the fog computing gateway (FCG):

1. **Access Control:** FCG devices provide a gateway between IoT network and cloud. However, the functioning is like providing field data from the IoT to cloud and command messages from the cloud to IoT. There is no way of accessing databases of the cloud from FCG devices, on the other hand, it is possible to command and conquer all IoT devices connected to a rouge FCG device.

2. **Authentication:** Depending on the authentication algorithm design, if several layered authentication methodology (one at FCG, one at the cloud, etc.) is used then this might be a very secure solution (Bhushan & Pradeep, 2016). Any compromise would only affect limited number of IoT devices. Otherwise, if all authentication operation is left to the FCG devices, this might create problems when the FCG devices get compromised.

3. **Availability:** Depending on the critical position of the FCG, we expect a significant impact on the availability of the IoT resources if the communications are blocked. However, this will not affect the cloud side marginally.

4. **Confidentiality:** Confidentiality of the data at FCG has a moderate impact on IoT network, whilst has a minor impact on the cloud (all the devices connected to FCG gets affected, however, the rest of the IoT network and the cloud remains safe operation).

5. **Integrity:** Depending on the communications scheme, we expect minor (if end-to-end encryption is not employed) to none (with encryption) effect of FCG on the integrity of the messages.

6. **Privacy:** As in any service, privacy of the users in IoT is critical and any leakage through FCG devices might have serious consequences. This will affect all users that are using the IoT though that hacked FCG device. However, the rest of the data (resulting from other FCGs) at the cloud will still be secure and private.

CONCLUSION

This paper discusses several security and privacy issues in the context of fog computing, which is a new computing paradigm to provide elastic resources at the edge of network to nearby devices. Throughout this article, authors have discussed the implications of using fog computing as backbone architecture for IoT. According to findings, authors have stated that usage of fog computing for cloud-based IoT systems might have several benefits; in terms of cost, QoS and more importantly, security.

REFERENCES

Atlam, H. F., Alenezi, A., Hussein, R. K., & Wills, G. B. (2018). Validation of an Adaptive Risk-Based Access Control Model for the Internet of Things. *Int. J. Comput. Netw. Inf. Secur.*, *10*, 26–35.

Atlam, H. F., Alenezi, A., Walters, R. J., & Wills, G. B. (2017). An Overview of Risk Estimation Techniques in Risk-based Access Control for the Internet of Things. *Proceedings of the 2nd International Conference on Internet of Things, Big Data and Security (IoTBDS 2017)*, 254–260. 10.5220/0006292602540260

Bhushan, S. B., & Pradeep, R. C. (2016). A Network QoS Aware Service Ranking Using Hybrid AHP-PROMETHEE Method in Multi-Cloud Domain. *International Journal of Engineering Research in Africa*, *24*, 153–164. doi:10.4028/www.scientific.net/JERA.24.153

Bhushan, S. B., & Reddy, P. (2016). A four-level linear discriminant analysis based service selection in the cloud environment. *International Journal of Technology*, *5*, 859–870. doi:10.14716/ijtech.v7i5.3546

Bhushan, S. B., & Reddy, P. C. (2018). A hybrid meta-heuristic approach for QoS-aware cloud service composition. *International Journal of Web Services Research*, *15*(2), 1–20. doi:10.4018/IJWSR.2018040101

Bonomi, F., Milito, R., Zhu, J., & Addepalli, S. (2012). Fog computing and its role in the internet of things. In *Proceedings of the First Edition of the MCC Workshop on Mobile Cloud Computing*. ACM. Available: http://doi.acm.org/10.1145/2342509.2342513

Butun, I., Kantarci, B., & Erol-Kantarci, M. (2015). Anomaly detection and privacy preservation in cloud-centric internet of things. In *Communication Workshop (ICCW), 2015 IEEE International Conference on*. IEEE. 10.1109/ICCW.2015.7247572

Cisco. (2015). *Fog computing and the internet of things: Extend the cloud to where the things are.* Cisco White Paper.

Coin base laundromat hack. (n.d.). Available: https://www.youtube.com/watch?v=YS7rguwrauo

Friedman, V. (2018). *On the edge: Solving the challenges of edge computing in the era of iot.* Available: https://data-economy.com/on-the-edge-solving-the-challenges-of-edge-computing-in-the-era-of-iot/

Giang, N., Kim, S., Kim, D., Jung, M., & Kastner, W. (2014). Extending the EPCIS with Building Automation Systems: A New Information System for the Internet of Things. *Proceedings of the 2014 Eighth International Conference on Innovative Mobile and Internet Services in Ubiquitous Computing*, 364–369. 10.1109/IMIS.2014.50

2015 . Hack my laundry card? (n.d.). Available: https://www.reddit.com/r/hacking/\comments/2pjy5x/hack my laundry card

Laundromat hack with lock pick. (n.d.). Available: https://www. youtube.com/watch?v=YsuLzCfNqYo

Leopold & Mack. (2017). *Buzzfeed: A bunch of cia contractors got fired for stealing snacks from vending machines.* Available: https://www.buzzfeed.com/jasonleopold/cia-vending-thefts

Luan, T. H., Gao, L., Li, Z., Xiang, Y., & Sun, L. (2015). *Fog computing: Focusing on mobile users at the edge.* Available: http://arxiv.org/abs/1502.01815

Microsoft IoT. (2017). *Five ways edge computing will transform business.* Available: https://blogs.microsoft.com/iot/2017/09/ 19/five-ways-edge-computing-will-transform-business/

Poluru, R. K., Bhushan, B., Muzamil, B. S., Rayani, P. K., & Reddy, P. K. (2019). Applications of Domain-Specific Predictive Analytics Applied to Big Data. In *Sentiment Analysis and Knowledge Discovery in Contemporary Business* (pp. 289–306). IGI Global. doi:10.4018/978-1-5225-4999-4.ch016

Rayani, P. K., Bhushan, B., & Thakare, V. R. (2018). Multi-Layer Token Based Authentication Through Honey Password in Fog Computing. *International Journal of Fog Computing, 1*(1), 50–62. doi:10.4018/IJFC.2018010104

Stallings, W. & Brown, L. (2018). *Computer security: principles and practice.* Pearson Education.

Zhang, B., Mor, N., Kolb, J., Chan, D. S., Lutz, K., Allman, E., ... Kubiatowicz, J. (2015). *The cloud is not enough: Saving iot from the cloud.* HotStorage.

Chapter 4
Analysis of Identity-Based Cryptography in Internet of Things (IoT)

Aravind Karrothu
Vellore Institute of Technology, India

Jasmine Norman
Vellore Institute of Technology, India

ABSTRACT

Fog networking supports the internet of things (IoT) concept, in which most of the devices used by humans on a daily basis will be connected to each other. Security issues in fog architecture are still a major research area as the number of security threats increases every day. Identity-based encryption (IBE) has a wide range of new cryptographic schemes and protocols that are particularly found to be suitable for lightweight architecture such as IoT and wireless sensor networks. This chapter focuses on these schemes and protocols in the background of wireless sensor networks. Also, this chapter analyses identity-based encryption schemes and the various attacks they are prone to.

INTRODUCTION

Recent days, many networking systems are deployed for accessing other real time devices/gadgets to communicate with each other, which is considered as Internet of Things (IoT). This is the biggest step for internet but, at the same time the security concerns need to be addressed for various applications such as smart activities like

DOI: 10.4018/978-1-7998-0194-8.ch004

smart house, transportation, industrial and other smart devices. IoT devices deployed at typical locations are susceptible to attacks like device conciliation and false data modification. At the same time, IoT has to maintain a light-weight security mechanism and thus it becomes a prominent research area for the security researchers.

The IoT architecture is shown in Figure 1 and it is treated as 3-tier construction with every sensor node communicate with each other and transmits the data to a recognized gateway, every gateway again acts as a node and transmits the data to root level node called server. Server handles the data in terms of maintaining and processing with data centres. In 2016, S. Sankaran proposed a framework (Sankaran, 2016) for IoT using IBC and developed the functionality of IoT in a hierarchal manner and it shown in Figure 2. In this figure, every individual node appeared as a leaf node and can access with upper layer using their own IDs, and every node can communicate with other nodes too. Later the data transmits to gateway with the help of same IDs and parallelly root level node can access the data from 'n' gateway nodes and allocated IDs and communication is done with IDs in between root level node and leaf nodes. In this manner IBC scenario can apply in IoT for providing security. Data centres maintained by server handles data accessing from higher level to lower level, as the server act as third party. Third party also to be maintained in trustworthy manner else there is a chance for vulnerable attacks.

Lightweight security is classified into three categories, symmetric key based, public key cryptography (PKC) and hybrid key cryptography. Malan et al., confirmed that PKC is more applicable for smart world for device authentication in IoT (Malan, Welsh & Smith, 2004). Identity based Cryptography (IBC) is broadly used for many application fields and IoT has one of the parts on this consideration. In any system, IoT devices/entities can allow with proper authenticate accessibility (IDs) and communicate each and also provide secure communication with their identities to make public keys for encryption of the messages, so-called IBC is more reliable

Figure 1. Illustration of Internet of Things

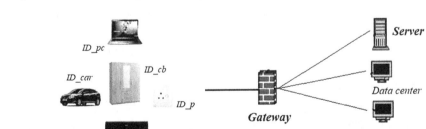

Figure 2. Hierarchal architecture of IoT

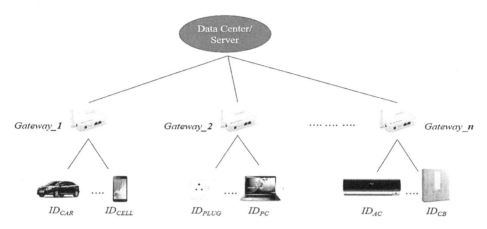

for IoT environment and briefly explained in earlier proposals (Markmann, Schmidt & Wahlisch, 2015; Hengartner & Steenkiste, 2005; Oliveira et al., 2008).

Security answers for IoT depended on symmetric encryption calculations like SkipJack or RC5 for validation and secrecy, because of their asset confinements. These hubs can't bear to utilize overwhelming weight methods of PKC, such as RSA or any other algorithms. The exploration in cryptography for remote sensor systems examined more successful methods of PKC using Elliptic Curves and Weil Pairings. Elliptic Curve Cryptography (ECC), is a PKC that has promising answers for WSNs since ECC devours fundamentally less assets than the vast majority of the PKCs, for a given security level. To utilize ECC effectively in WSNs, it is fundamental to verify open keys, generally the system will be inclined to man-in-the-centre assaults. Open key verification is normally done by Public Key Infrastructure (PKI), which issues endorsement and obliges clients to gather and amass, confirm and trade them. This outcome in high overheads of capacity, calculation and correspondence expenses, as it is very little reasonable for WSNs. In spite of the fact that RSA is broadly utilized, the major separating issues with IBC were appeared in Table 1. IBC is a technique for distinguishing the clients remarkably with their personalities (e.g. IP or email addresses) and can scramble with their ids the data of clients and trade the keys.

By a known information of a user such as IP address, phone number, node id etc. it is possible to generate a public key. A private key generator is used to generate the private keys which acts as a trusted third party. Firstly, the PKG announces a master public key, and maintains a master private key and then a public key is generated by merging both the master public key and user's identities. The user associated with the PKG, to generate the private key with the help of master private key which is helpful for decryption and it was clearly represented in Figure 3.

Table 1. Differentiate between two major cryptosystems

Parameters	RSA	IBC
Based on	Prime numbers	Elliptic curves
Public Key	getting from two large prime numbers (available for all)	any string of bits to be used as a public key
Private key	getting from two large prime numbers (securely maintained)	Generated by third party/private key generator (PKG)
Encryption	$M^e \bmod n = C$	$P + m \in M + identity = C$
Decryption	$C^d \bmod n = M$	Accepts d, P and C returns M
PKG – Trust	Partially trusted	Fully trusted
PKG - Online/Offline	Offline PKG	Online PKG
End to end encryption	Strong end-to-end (only receiver can decrypt)	Weaker end-to-end encryption (PKG can decrypt)
Key generation	Random key generation	Generated from user's id and generated from PKG
Key revocation	Revocation via CRLs, OCSP	Revocation via short-lived keys (no database required)
Authentication	By centralised authentication manage	Central service required but no need to be online
Need for certificate	Maintained by Certificate authority (CA)	Not needed
Applications	In public key encryption	Email
Suitable areas	Heavy devices	Light devices
Complexity	Less	More
Implementations	Many systems	Voltage Security, MIRACLE, etc.,
Security model	By key exchanging	Selective and adaptive
Attacks	If keys are easy then attacks are possible	If PKG untrustworthy then keys will leak to attackers
Major weakness	Key size	Key escrow
Usage Percentage	>80%	<10%
Lifetime	Long	Short
Time component	Not used	Used

In 1984, Adi Shamir proposed the first IBE system (Shamir, 1984) which is theoretically explained but failed to prove practically. Later Boneh and Franklin developed the first practical implementation of IBE system (Boneh & Franklin, 2003) called BF scheme based on Weil pairings with finite fields and elliptic curves. In the same year another author, Clifford Cocks proposed Cocks IBE system based on the hardness of the quadratic residues. In 2003, Ryuichi Sakai and Masao Kasahara

Figure 3. Identity based cryptosystem

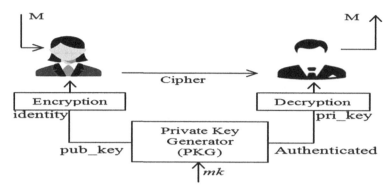

proposed an algorithm called Sakai - Kasahara key encryption algorithm (SAKKE) (Chen et al., 2006). It is also based on pairings with elliptic curves and finite fields, based on Bilinear Diffie-Hellman (BDH) problem. The above algorithms are the initial step for developing different IBE schemes for providing light weight security in IoT. Any proper and secure communication initiated with a million of smart and sensor devices and these IoT devices store their secure information in cloud centres through a proper channel called fog gateways and these gateways act as a bridge in between sensor devices and cloud storages. This complete process explained by different authors with different approaches in Bhushan and Reddy (2016), Poluru et al. (2019), and Bhushan and Reddy (2018). Mainly this article focuses on how an identity-based cryptography works in IoT environment and given a basic idea of IBC with the taxonomy and it shown in Figure 4. The rest of the paper is structured as follows. Firstly, the paper focuses on a brief idea about taxonomy of IBC and summarizes the classification of different forms with their justification in section 2 to 4 and Section 5 gives the future directions and conclusion.

KEY AGREEMENT (KA)

ID-based key agreement protocols become popular due to its vast advantages. The benefits of ID-based key agreement over other method, is that these systems works well without PKI. It is the distribution of authentication techniques with the help of parameters. Thus, it is easy to implement these protocols in secured organizations like government administrations and commercial units, and most of their security is compromised. In the year 2000, tripartite key agreement protocol was presented by Joux (Hou et al., 2010). This protocol is prone to man-in-the-middle attack. It was also important for initiating the development of pairing based cryptography.

Figure 4. Taxonomy of identity based cryptography

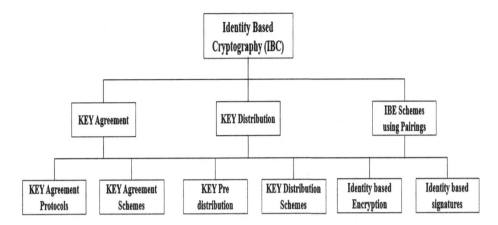

KEY Agreement Protocols

Smart's Protocol

The parties X and Y authenticate with each other and establish a shared secret key as described in Smart ID - based Agreement Key (AK) protocol (Choie, Jeong & Jiang, 2005). Firstly, X picks $x \in_r S^*_l$ computes $B_X = xM$ and sends B_X to Y. Also Y is computed as $B_Y = yM$, for random y and sends B_Y to X, after receiving messages from each other side, X computes the shared secret key (K) by

$$K_X = e(xN_Y, M_{KGC}) \rightarrow e(A_X, B_Y), \ K = kdf(k_X),$$

and Y computes K by

$$K_Y = e(yN_X, M_{KGC}) \rightarrow e(A_Y, B_X), \ K = kdf(k_Y),$$

Where $kdf: G_{p2} \rightarrow \{0, 1\}^*$ is a key derivation function. This protocol does not provide the forward secrecy because

$$k_X = e(A_X, B_Y) \rightarrow e(A_Y, B_X) = k_Y.$$

This protocol was prone to man-in-the- middle attack and the keys where compromised by impersonation and also does not provide forward secrecy.

Chen - Kudla (CK) Protocol

Chen - Kudla proposed a two-pass AK protocol (Chen & Kudla, 2003), where two users X and Y interchange $B_X = xN_X$ and $B_Y = yN_Y$. Then they calculate

$$K_X = e(A_X, B_Y + xN_Y) = e(B_X + yN_X, A_Y) = k_Y.$$

This protocol allows implicit authentication and perfect forward secrecy (Choie, Jeong & Jiang, 2004). But Key Generation Center's (KGC) forward secrecy is another problem in identity-based AK protocol, i.e., if at any stage KGC's secret is compromised, then the previously established session keys should not be compromised. The authors modified the two-pass protocol to provide KGC forward secrecy which prevents the agreement of session keys from KGC. Let X and Y exchange

$$U_X = xN_X, V_X = xM \text{ and } U_Y = yN_Y, V_X = yY.$$

After receiving messages from other side, they compute K by

$$K_X = e(A_X, U_Y + xN_Y), K = kdf(k_X, xV_Y), \text{ and } K_Y = e(U_X + yN_X, A_Y) K = kdf(k_Y, yV_X),$$

Where *kdf*: $G_{p2} \times G_{p1} \rightarrow \{0, 1\}^*$ is a key derivation function.

Ryu, Yoon, and Yoo's Protocol

In Ryu, Yoon, and Yoo's protocol for key agreement has the following steps:

1. X chooses $x \in S^*_m$ randomly, calculates $B_X = xM$, and sends B_X to Y.
2. Y chooses $y \in S^*_m$ randomly, calculates $B_Y = yM$, and sends B_Y to X.
3. X calculates the session key $K_{XY} = H(X, Y, xB_Y, e(A_X, N_Y))$ and Y calculates $K_{YX} = H(X, Y, yB_X, e(N_X, A_Y))$.
4. If both X and Y go with the protocol they will end up with the identical session key $K_{XY} = K_{YX} = H(X, Y, xyM, e(N_X, N_Y)^a)$.

This protocol is vulnerable to key reveal and key is compromised by impersonation and reflection attacks (Islam & Biswas, 2012) which can be prevented if some symmetric information to replace $e(N_X, N_Y)^a$ is used. This will yield a protocol with high security. But this protocol is unable to prevent man-in-the- middle attack.

XIE'S Protocol

This protocol is based on the Private Key Extraction II algorithm. Let $H_1(ID_x) = x$ and $H_1(ID_y) = y$, where X and Y interchanges the temporary available keys X_{KX} and Y_{KX}. Then, it calculates

$$K_X = e(Y_{KX}, d_X)^{u+1}e(M, M)^u;$$

B calculates

$$K_Y = e(X_{KX}, d_Y)^{v+1}e(M, M)^v$$

and the generated session key is

$$K = K_X = K_Y = e(M, M)^{uv+u+v}.$$

This protocol is vulnerable to impersonation attack, which means an attacker, can impersonate X to Y at any cost. For example, an attacker *D* desires to impersonate X to Y. *D(X)* represents *D* conceals as X. First, *D(X)* sends $X_{KX} = -(yM+aM)$ to Y impersonating X, at the delivery of the message, Y sends $Y_{KX} = v(xM+aM)$ and computes the session key.

$$K_Y = e(-(yM+aM), d_Y)^{v+1}e(M, M)^v = e(M, M)^{-v-1} \cdot e(M, M)^v = e(M, M)^{-1}$$

By bi-linearity of e, the value $e(M, M)^v$ vanishes in the generated session key. Consequently, D is also capable to calculate $K_Y=e(M, M)^{-1}$ from recognized value. As the result, D succeeds to impersonate X to Y along with detailed information of the session key K_Y. From the attack, it is evident that the protocol is sensitive against man-in-the-middle attacks and key is compromised by impersonation (Islam & Biswas, 2012; Holbl, Welzer & Brumen, 2012).

Choie - Jeong Lee Protocol

This protocol based on the Private Key Extract I algorithm, where X sends (U_x, V_x) to Y and Y verifies $e(V_x, M) = e(N_x, U_x)$. If the equation satisfies, Y replies with (U_y, V_y) to X and calculates $K_y = yU_x$. After being delivered, X verifies $e(V_y, M) = e(N_y, U_y)$. If the equation satisfies, X calculates $K_x = xU_y$. The generated session key is

$$K = kdf(K_X, N_X, N_Y) = kdf(K_Y, N_X, N_Y) = kdf(xyaM, N_X, N_Y),$$

where *kdf* is a key derivation function. In this protocol, anyone can come up with a valid pair (U_X, V_X) satisfying $e(V_X, M) = e(N_X, U_X)$ as follows. An attacker uncertainly picks x and then calculates $U_X = xM$ and $V_X = xN_X$. Then the pair is susceptible to the verification equation

$$e(V_X, M) = e(N_X, U_X).e(V_X, M) = e(xN_X, M) = e(N_X, xM) = e(N_X, U_X)$$

At that point, an assailant can produce every client's mark on the transitory open key without the learning of relating long haul private key. What's more, this assault opposes the assailant to increase any learning of the concurred session key; so the mark plot changed in accordance with cryptographic conventions ought to be secure (Kishore & Rao, 2012).

Shim's Protocol

In Shim's protocol, the key agreement has the following the steps and it proposed by Yuan and Li (2005).

1. X picks $x \in S_m^*$ randomly, and calculates $B_X = xM$, and sends B_X to Y.
2. Y picks $y \in S_m^*$ randomly, and calculates $B_Y = yM$, and sends B_Y to X.
3. X calculates $K_{XY} = e(xM_{pub} + A_X, B_Y + N_Y)$, and it considered as a shared security key
4. Correspondingly, Y calculates the shared security $K_{XY} = e(B_X + N_X, yM_{pub} + A_Y)$
5. 5. If X and Y, both using the same rules, at that time the both estimate the similar shared secret and the session key is

$$K_{XY} = K_{YX} = e(M, M)^{xys} \, e(M, N_Y)^{xa} \, e(N_X, M)^{ya} \, e(N_X, N_Y)^a, \text{ finally } H(X, Y, K_{XY})$$

Shim's protocol is prone to man-in-the-middle attack and it follows (Islam & Biswas, 2012; Holbl, Welzer & Brumen, 2012; Yuan & Li, 2005).

1. One intruder interrupts B_X from X. He sends $B'_X = x'M - N_X$ to Y, where x' is added by the intruder.
2. And also invader interrupts B_Y from Y. He sends $B'_Y = y'M - N_Y$ to X, where y' is also chosen by invader.
3. Then the attacker shares the secret and attacks shim's protocol.

Mccullagh – Barreto's Protocol

McCullagh and Barreto developed an ID based Authenticated protocol [10]. Initially the Key Generation Center (KGC) allotted the private keys to both users X and Y. ID_X and ID_Y is two identities of the two users X and Y respectively. They considered $x = H(ID_X)$ and $y = H(ID_Y)$. X had one public key M_X is $(x + a)M$, and it can be referred as $xM + aM$. KGC calculates X's private key as $A_X = (x + a)^{-1}M$ and it sends to X through a proper and secure channel. The similar process is done to Y also the public key and the private key of Y, are $M_Y = (y + a)M$, and $A_Y = (y + a)^{-1}M$ correspondingly. The shared security is $S_{XY} = e(M, M)^{rXrY}$.

This protocol was vulnerable to key compromise impersonation attack and key replicating attack (Islam & Biswas, 2012; Holbl, Welzer & Brumen, 2012).

For example a foe F send $r_Y(y + a)M$ to X and acquire the shared secret key by computing

$$S_{XY} = e(y + a)M, (x + a)^{-1} M)^{rY}.$$

Scott's Protocol

This protocol has a key exchange with password authentications for the private key where the trusted authority have to choose a master secret α and allocates to the private keys $g^{\alpha}_{ID X}$ and $g^{\alpha}_{ID Y}$ to X and Y correspondingly. X may use x to store its private key as: $g^{\alpha-x}_{ID X}$. The protocol fails to provide the password protection. During the key agreement selection, X selects $\alpha \in_R S^*_n$ and sends $e(g_{ID X}, g_{ID Y})^{\alpha u}$ to Y. Then, Y selects $v \in_R S^*_n$ and sends $e(g_{ID X}, g_{ID Y})^{\alpha v}$ to X. the shared secret key is $e(g_{ID X}, g_{ID Y})^{\alpha uv}$.

This protocol was insecure as it is prone to man-in-the-middle attack (Islam & Biswas, 2012). For example, an invader may select a random number c and exchanges the message from X to Y to $e(g_{ID X}, g_{ID Y})^{\alpha uc}$ and vice versa.

Key Agreement Schemes

The Key agreement and the encryption schemes are the appropriate cryptography for WSNs as it has some restrictions like storage resources, power consumption and computation ability (Kishore & Rao, 2012; Yang et al., 2006). Before IBE technique, some methods like traditional public key method and symmetric key method are in use. Identity-based key agreement scheme is based on ECC type algorithm.

Trusted - Server System

This scheme provides an agreement between the nodes by using a server and it must be trustworthy (Yang et al., 2006). The sensor networks do not have proper resourceful requirements like limited power and low computing capabilities for that reason this method do not fit for WSN and also the agreement between the nodes is not trustworthy (E.g. Kerberos). It constructs using the symmetric key cryptography and requires a trusted third party.

Public Key Scheme

This (self-enforcing) scheme is based on the symmetric cryptography, for example available key certificates are used for the key agreement. The partial computation and energy properties of sensor nodes, doesn't appropriate to use it for public key algorithms (e.g. Diffie-Hellman key agreement/RSA) (Hou et al., 2010).

KEY DISTRIBUTION SCHEMES

Key distribution scheme is applied in allocating a session key for multicast communications like hypermedia, compensated TV, and different software on the exposed network (Park et al., 2010). A few of the key distribution schemes which are based on ID based cryptography are discussed later sub section.

KEY Pre-Distribution Scheme (KPS)

In this scheme, the user's IDs are hashed along with secret key information for computing keys that has been shared with all the users before arranging by a trusted entity, and also the maximum part of the sensor network is developed without any planning, that's why users do not have minimum knowledge about neighbours. So, KPS is developed with different trivial schemes and various techniques. Firstly, the memory cost is less because all the nodes in the network are shared by the same secret master key, so it is not secure. Next, a pairwise secret key is shared with every pair of users. Thus, this scheme would give a finest flexibility to compromise nodes, and every user can store *n-1* keys, where *n* is the total no. of users participated in the sensor network, for this reason the memory cost would be too expensive.

Few schemes are proposed to reduce the memory storage for large networks. Blom's scheme, which is combined with a security factor *k* where each user's memory storage must be *k+1* and this storage requirement is optimum. This scheme can provide security against adversaries and has been proved mathematically with a list of assumptions. In 2002, Eschenauer and Gligor proposed a randomized approach for the key pre-distribution for sensor networks. Every node is allocated with k random keys from the pool of secret keys in the network (Yagan, 2012). In this scheme, an attacker randomly adds a number of nodes in the network to remove keys from the existing nodes to their nodes. In this situation, the links which are involving in this procedure are directly or indirectly broken.

In 2004, the Deterministic key pre-distribution system was developed by Wei and Wu, where keys are distributed to nodes in a deterministic manner. Firstly, it selects a system in the network and creates blocks where each block is allotted to every node; these blocks are the identifiers of the keys and particular nodes. This scheme has several advantages (Bechkit et al., 2013):

- Simple set-up
- No need to verify expected properties of the WSN
- Simple common-key detection and path-key formation

In 2005, Lee and Stinson proposed a scheme using transversal designs to construct KPS. These designs are equivalent to orthogonal arrays, and it is related to statistical design of experiments. In this scheme, every pair of nodes shared a pairwise keys are calculated with the combination of public information and secret information. In Bechkit et al. (2013), security can be established with the random oracle model, which delivers a mathematical model of a perfect hash function. The storage requirement of this scheme is reduced by almost half of the trivial scheme.

KEY Distribution Schemes

Chikazawa-Inoue Scheme

Inoue and Chikazawa in 1990 proposed a non-interactive identity based key distribution scheme. This scheme was defenceless from Simbo and Kawamura (SK) attack using a Euclidean algorithm, where the secure data of the main-station can be derived by the collusion of two sub-stations. Also this scheme was secure from man-in-the-middle attack, node capture and long-term key reveal attacks.

Chikazawa-Yamagishi Scheme

This proposal explained by Chikazawa and Yamagishi and it was upgrading of Chikazawa - Inoue scheme (Jung, 2004). It can provide security from SK attack by randomly introduced a few innovative variables. But this method takes additional time for the packets transmission than earlier scheme. These authors also failed to protect from session state reveal attack, long term key-reveal attack and man-in-the-middle attack.

Tseng-Jan Scheme

This is (Chang, Hwang & Yang, 2004) the enhancement of earlier scheme (Jung, 2004), the upgraded method has given improved to prove the better results and needs littler transmission of the packets than the old method. This scheme explained in three phases.

- In first phase (System set-up), selects p and q which are large prime numbers and produces g by $q/(p-1)$, and allocates a secret key $x_i \in Z_q^*$ to the particular user through a secret medium and announces the related public key $y_i = g^{xi}$ mod p
- In Second phase (key distribution), all the users participates in a group where one user is appointed as a group head and executes the given stages for allocating the key shared by the users
  - Selects an integer randomly r $\in Z_q^*$ and T is the time-sequence getting from the system
  - Calculate

$R = g^r \bmod p$ and $S = r + H(T\|R)x_c \bmod q,$

where H is one-way hash function and $\|$ is concatenation

- Compute the secret key for an individual user from that group as $k_i = y_i^r \bmod p$
- Select a key randomly, K $\in Z_q^*$ then construct a polynomial of degree n as

$P(x) = \prod_{i=1}^{n} (x - k_i) + k \bmod p = x^n + c_{n-1}x^{n-1} + \ldots + c_0 \bmod p.$

- The group head broadcasts $\{R, S, T, c_{n-1}, c_{n-2}, \ldots, c_0\}$
  - The third phase (key retrieval), every user receives $\{R, S, T, c_{n-1}, c_{n-2}, \ldots, c_0\}$ which involves the following steps.
  - Verify the equation and the T value $g^S = R y_c^{H(T\|R)} \bmod p$
  - Calculate the secret key key which is mutual with each user as $k_i = R^{xi} \bmod p$
  - Recover K, by computing

$$P(k_i) = (k_i)^n + c_{n-1}(k_i)^{n-1} + \ldots\ldots + c_1 k_i + c_0 \bmod p = K \bmod p$$

This scheme is defenceless from man-in-the-middle attack, triangle attack and long-term key reveal attacks.

Jeong-Know-Lee Scheme

This scheme was proposed by Jeong, know and Lee, and it can be used to secure against session state reveal attacks and long-term key reveal attacks. But this scheme suffers from scalability, Abuse and Inefficiency (Park, Yi & Lee, 2010).

- **No Scalability:** Only suitable for present users in the network and if any user added, then this scheme cannot provide a proper registration. For that reason, it is not suitable for a dynamic user group.
- **Abuse:** This scheme applies additional algorithms, MAC and symmetric encryption scheme to provide security from the session state reveal attacks and long-term key reveal attacks.
- **Inefficiency:** This scheme deals with complex calculations to secure against session state reveal attacks and long-term key-reveal-attacks

IBE SCHEMES USING WEIL PAIRINGS

IBE Signature Schemes

In wireless sensor networks, the important task is the transmission of data in between the nodes. Because every sensor network has a large number of small sensor nodes with one or more locations and these BSs acts as an interface between both user and other nodes. WSNs have used in many applications like in military for tracking the particular target, and many more (Li, Zhong & Takagi, 2012). So, Security is very important in this communication phase and many systems such as Multi-Layer Token Based Authentication Through Honey Password and other authors try to provide an authenticated entry in fog computing (Rayani, Bhusham & Thakare, 2018). In earlier time digital signature was used for solving the problems to provide authentication and confidentiality. In recent time IBC has been used to sensor devices.

Clustering is a best technique to improve the performance of the system in WSN. In the existing systems, they used two secure and efficient data transmission (SET) protocols (Lu, Li & Guizani, 2014) for clustered wireless sensor network (CWSN), named SET-IBS by using the Identity Based digital Signature scheme (IBS) and

Table 2. Various security schemes and protocols for identity-based cryptography

Method	Type of Scheme / Protocol	MIM	NC	KCI	KRA	SSRA	KCA	SFA
KEY Agreement Protocols	Smart's Protocol	yes	-	-	-	-	yes	-
	Chen – Kudla (CK) Protocol	-	-	-	yes	-	yes	-
	Ryu, Yoon and Yoo's Protocol	-	-	yes	yes	-	-	-
	Xie's Protocol	yes	-	yes	-	-	-	-
	Choie - Jeong Lee Protocol	-	-	-	-	-	-	yes
	Shim's Protocol	yes	-	yes	-	-	yes	-
	McCullagh – Barreto's Protocol	-	-	yes	yes	-	-	-
	Scott's Protocol	yes	-	-	-	-	-	-
KEY Distribution Schemes	Chikazawa-Inoue Scheme	yes	yes	-	yes	-	-	-
	Chikazawa-Yamagishi Scheme	yes	-	-	yes	Yes	-	-
	Tseng-Jan Scheme	yes	-	-	yes	-	-	-

MIM–Man-In-the-Middle attack; NC–Node capture attack; KCI–Key compromise Impersonation; KRA–Key reveals attack (long-term); SSRA –Session state reveals attack; KCA– Imperfect-key Control attack; SFA– Signature Forgery attack;

SET-IBOOS by using Identity Based Online/Offline digital Signature scheme (IBOOS). With the use of these protocols, it is easy to provide an authenticated data in sensor networks.

SET-IBS Scheme

A sheltered data transmission in SET-IBS depends on IBC, in which every user needed their information identity and public keys. Then, the users can acquire the conforming private keys without any assisted data communication, which is effective in transmission and energy can be saved.

The functions of SET-IBS is divided by rounds (Anbarasi & Gunasekaran, 2014). Every round comprises of a set-up segment for assembling the clusters from clustering head (CH), and a steady-state segment for communicating the information from sensor nodes to the base station (BS). In each round the timeline is separated into sequential time slots/frames by the Time Division Multiple Access (TDMA) control as shown in Figure 5.

Online/Offline Signature (OOS) Scheme

Online/Offline Signature scheme was explained in this section which is used for message authentication. Offline part was implemented first for the message to be authenticated, to convert as accessible. This stage requires a greater number of calculations for generating signature and gets the final outcome in fractional way. After getting the resultant data, the online part begins. In this stage, we get the partial signature from the offline stage and implemented using the specific negligible rapid

Figure 5. Operation of secure data transmission

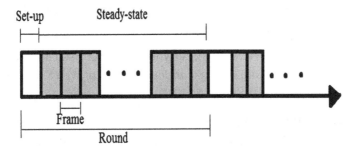

calculations to attain the concluding signature. The online stage is supposed to be very fast, when compared to offline stage which can be achieved by other capable devices. In OOS, the IBOOS (Identity based OOS) which is the identity-based version, and those messages signed with a user's private key is confirmed with user's identity is generated by PKG. These protocols provide best performance when compared to earlier secure protocols for cluster wireless sensor networks CWSNs.

CONCLUSION

The security in IoT is highly critical as they find new applications. The existing solutions of other networks cannot be applied to IoT due to resource constraints. IBC is promising solution, as it is a lightweight cryptography technique which reduces the burden on the nodes. A thorough analysis of the same has been made in this chapter with respect to IoT. The various protocols and the attacks that they are prone to also are presented. Our future work is to propose a cost effective pairing based solution for IoT.

REFERENCES

Anbarasi, S. R., & Gunasekaran, S. (2014, October). The Feasibility of SETOIBS and SRT-IBOOS protocols in Cluster-based wireless sensor networks. *International Journal of Innovative Research in Computer and Communication Engineering, 2*(10).

Bechkit, W., Challal, Y., Bouabdallah, A., & Tarokh, V. (2013, February). A Highly Scalable Key Pre-distribution Scheme for wireless sensor networks. *IEEE Transactions on Wireless Communications, 12*(2), 948–959. doi:10.1109/TWC.2012.010413.120732

Bhushan, S. B., & Reddy, P. (2016). A four-level linear discriminant analysis-based service selection in the cloud environment. *International Journal of Technology, 5,* 859–870. doi:10.14716/ijtech.v7i5.3546

Bhushan, S. B., & Reddy, P. C. (2018). A hybrid meta-heuristic approach for QoS-aware cloud service composition. *International Journal of Web Services Research, 15*(2), 1–20. doi:10.4018/IJWSR.2018040101

Boneh & Franklin. (2003). Identity-Based Encryption from the weil pairing. *Society for Industrial and Applied Mathematics (SIAM). Journal of Computers, 32*(3), 586–615.

Boujelben, M., Youssef, H., Mzid, R., & Abid, M. (2011, April). IKM – An identity-based key management scheme for heterogeneous sensor networks. *Journal of Communication, 6*(2).

Chang. (2004). Cryptanalysis of the Tseng-Jan anonymous conference key distribution system without using a one-way hash function. *Information and Security. International Journal (Toronto, Ont.), 15*(1), 110–114.

Chatterjee, K. (2012). *An Improved ID-Based Key Management Scheme in Wireless Sensor Network* (Vol. 7332). Springer.

Chen, Cheng, Malone-Lee, & Smart. (2006). Efficient ID-KEM based on the Sakai-Kasahara key construction. *IEEE Proceedings Information Security, 153*(1).

Chen & Kudla. (2003). *Identity-based Authenticated Key agreement protocols from pairings*. Academic Press.

Choie. (2005). Efficient identity-based authenticated key agreement protocol from pairings. In Applied Mathematics and Computation (vol. 162, pp. 179–188). Elsevier.

Hafizul Islam, S. K., & Biswas, G. P. (2012). An improved pairing-free identity-based authenticated key agreement protocol based on ECC. *Procedia Engineering, 30,* 499–507. doi:10.1016/j.proeng.2012.01.890

Hengartner, U., & Steenkiste, P. (2005). Exploiting hierarchical identity-based encryption for access control to pervasive computing information. *First International Conference on Security and Privacy for Emerging Areas in Communications Networks (SECURECOMM'05)*, 384–396. 10.1109/SECURECOMM.2005.18

Holbl, Welzer, & Brumen. (2012). An improved two-party identity-based authenticated key agreement protocol using pairings. *Journal of Computer and System Sciences, 78,* 142-150.

Holbl, M. (2010). *Two proposed identity-based three-party authenticated key agreement protocols from pairings. Computer and Security, 29,* 244–252.

Hou, M., Xu, Q., Shanqimg, G., & Jiang, H. (2010, July). Cryptanalysis on Identity-based Authenticated Key agreement protocols from Pairings. *Journal of Networks, 5*(7). doi:10.4304/jnw.5.7.855-862

Jung, B. E. (2004, February). On the forward secrecy of Chikazawa-Yamagishi ID based key Sharing Scheme. *IEEE Communications Letters, 8*(2), 114–115. doi:10.1109/LCOMM.2004.823407

Kishore. (2012). Improved ID Based Key Agreement Protocol Using Timestamp. *International Journal of Computer Science and Information Technology, 3*(5), 5200–5205.

Li, F., Zhong, D., & Takagi, T. (2012, December). Di Zhong and Tsuyoshi Takagi, "Practical Identity-based Signature for wireless sensor networks. *IEEE Wireless Communications Letters, 1*(6), 637–640. doi:10.1109/WCL.2012.091312.120488

Lu, H., Li, J., & Guizani, M. (2014, March). Secure and efficient data transmission for Cluster based wireless sensor networks. *IEEE Transactions on Parallel and Distributed Systems, 25*(3), 750–761. doi:10.1109/TPDS.2013.43

Malan, D. J., Welsh, M., & Smith, M. D. (2004). A public-key infrastructure for key distribution in tinyos based on elliptic curve cryptography. *Sensor and Ad Hoc Communications and Networks, 2004. IEEE SECON 2004. 2004 First Annual IEEE Communications Society Conference on,* 71–80. 10.1109/SAHCN.2004.1381904

Markmann, T., Schmidt, T. C., & Wahlisch, M. (2015). Federated end-to-end ¨ authentication for the constrained internet of things using ibc and ecc. *Proceedings of the 2015 ACM Conference on Special Interest Group on Data Communication,* 603–604. 10.1145/2785956.2790021

Oliveira, L. B., Scott, M., Lopez, J., & Dahab, R. (2008). Tinypbc: Pairings for authenticated identity-based non-interactive key distribution in sensor networks. *Networked Sensing Systems, 2008. INSS 2008. 5th International Conference on,* 173–180. 10.1109/INSS.2008.4610921

Park, Wan, Yi, & Lee. (2010). Simple ID-based Key Distribution Scheme. *IEEE, fifth International Conference on Internet and Web applications and Service.* 10.1109/ICIW.2010.61

Poluru, R. K., Bhushan, B., Muzamil, B. S., Rayani, P. K., & Reddy, P. K. (2019). Applications of Domain-Specific Predictive Analytics Applied to Big Data. In *Sentiment Analysis and Knowledge Discovery in Contemporary Business* (pp. 289–306). IGI Global. doi:10.4018/978-1-5225-4999-4.ch016

Qin, Z., Zhang, X., Feng, K., Zhang, Q., & Huang, J. (2014). An Efficient Identity-based Key Management scheme for wireless sensor networks using the Bloom Filter. *Sensors (Basel)*, *14*(10), 17937–17951. doi:10.3390141017937 PMID:25264955

Rayani, P. K., Bhushan, B., & Thakare, V. R. (2018). Multi-Layer Token Based Authentication Through Honey Password in Fog Computing. *International Journal of Fog Computing*, *1*(1), 50–62. doi:10.4018/IJFC.2018010104

Sankaran, S. (2016). Lightweight security framework for IoTs using identity-based cryptography. *2016 International Conference on Advances in Computing, Communications and Informatics (ICACCI)*, 880-886. 10.1109/ICACCI.2016.7732156

Shamir. (1984). Identity-based cryptosystems and signature schemes. *Advances in Cryptology, 196*, 47-53.

Yagan, O. (2012, June). Performance of the Eschenauer-Gligor key distribution scheme under an ON/OFF Channel. *IEEE Transactions on Information Theory*, *58*(6), 3821–3835. doi:10.1109/TIT.2012.2189353

Yang, Rong, Veigner, Wang, & Cheng. (2006). Identity Based Key Agreement and Encryption for Wireless Sensor Networks. *International Journal of Computer Science and Network Security, 6*(5B).

Yuan & Li. (2005). *A new efficient ID based Authenticated Key Agreement protocol*. Academic Press.

Chapter 5
Cloud Security Architecture Based on Fully Homomorphic Encryption

Vaishali Ravindra Thakare
https://orcid.org/0000-0002-5148-5672
Vellore Institute of Technology, India

K. John Singh
Vellore Institute of Technology, India

ABSTRACT

Cloud computing is a new environment in computer-oriented services. The high costs of network platforms, development in client requirements, data volumes and weight on response time pushed companies to migrate to cloud computing, providing on-demand web facilitated IT services. Cloud storage empowers users to remotely store their information and delight in the on-demand high quality cloud applications without the affliction of local hardware management and programming administration. In order to solve the problem of data security in cloud computing system, by introducing fully homomorphism encryption algorithm in the cloud computing data security, another sort of information security solution to the insecurity of the cloud computing is proposed, and the scenarios of this application is hereafter constructed. This new security arrangement is completely fit for the processing and retrieval of the encrypted data, successfully prompting the wide relevant prospect, the security of data transmission, and the stockpiling of the cloud computing.

DOI: 10.4018/978-1-7998-0194-8.ch005

INTRODUCTION

Enterprises are the quick approaching new advanced time in which we store our information and perform our extravagant computation remotely. With the use of cloud there are numerous points of interest in expenses and usefulness, but the issue with the cloud is secret data may not be secure (Bhushan & Reddy, 2016; Bhushan & Pradeep, 2016). Today, enterprises are looking towards cloud computing environment to expand their on-premise infrastructure, but most cannot afford the cost of the danger of trading off the security of their applications and information. Recent advances in Fully homomorphic encryption (FHE) allows us to perform arbitrarily complex dynamically picked computations on encrypted data, despite not having the secret decryption key. Processing encrypted data homomorphically requires greater number of computations than processing the data unencrypted.

Scientifically talked is a homomorphic cryptosystem, a cryptosystem whose encryption function is a homomorphism and thus preserves group operation performed on cipher texts. The two group operations are the arithmetic addition and multiplication (Bhushan & Reddy, 2018, 2016). A homomorphic encryption scheme is said to be additive if the followings holds:

$$E(x+y) = E(x) + E(y)$$

What's more it is said to be multiplicative if

$$E(x, y) = E(x) * E(y)$$

Where E characterizes an encryption function.

The cryptosystem that support either of the two operations are said to be partially homomorphic encryption system, and the once that supports both the additions and multiplications of cipher texts is called as fully homomorphic encryption (FHE).

Cloud Computing and Fully Homomorphic Encryption

The progression of FHE has empowered the cloud service providers a better approach to ensure confidentiality and privacy of user data. a solution to the old open issue of developing a fully homomorphic encryption scheme. This idea, formerly called a privacy homomorphism, was presented by Rivest, Adelman and Dertouzous (Rivest, Adleman & Dertouzos, 1978; Poluru et al., 2019) shortly after the invention of RSA by Rivest, Shamir and Adleman.

To provide the better security we are going to extend the security solution for cloud computing with the help of fully homomorphic encryption cryptosystem.

Principle Fully Homomorphic Encryption

Craig Gentry develop homomorphism encryption plan including 4 techniques. They are the key generation, encryption, decryption algorithm and additional Evaluation algorithm. Fully homomorphic encryption incorporates two fundamental homomorphism types. They are the multiply homomorphic encryption algorithm and additively homomorphic encryption algorithm. The multiplication and addition with Homomorphic properties. Homomorphic encryption algorithm underpins just addition homomorphism and multiplication homomorphism before 2009. Fully homomorphic encryption is to discover an encryption algorithm, which can be any number of addition algorithm and multiplication algorithm in the encoded information. For just, this paper utilizes a symmetrical completely encryption homomorphic algorithm proposed by Craig Gentry (Gentry & Halevi, 2010; Rayani, Bhushan & Thalare, 2018)

Encryption Algorithm

The encryption parameters p, q and r, where p is a positive odd number, q is a large positive integer, p and q determined in the key generation phase, p is an encryption key, and r is a random number encrypted when selected.

For the text m, calculation

$$c = m + 2r + pq$$

Then you can get the cipher text.

Decipherment Algorithm

To plaintext

$$m = \left(c \bmod p\right) \bmod 2$$

Because the $p * q$ is much less than $2r + m$, then

$$\left(c \bmod p\right) \bmod 2 = \left(2r + m\right) \bmod 2 = m$$

Homomorphism Verification

The Homomorphism Additive Property Verification

Suppose there are two groups of the plaintext m1 and m2. To scramble them turn into the cipher text.

$$c1 = m1 + 2r1 + pq1$$

$$c2 = m2 + 2r2 + pq2$$

To plaintext

$$m3 = m1 + m2$$

Due to

$$c3 = c1 + c2 = \left(m1 + m2\right) + 2\left(r1 + r2\right) + p\left(q1 + q2\right)$$

As long as the

$$\left(m1 + m2\right) + 2\left(r1 + r2\right)$$

is much less than P, then

$$c3 = \left(c1 + c2\right) \bmod p = \left(m2 + m1\right) + 2\left(r1 + r2\right)$$

This algorithm fulfills the additive homomorphic conditions

The Homomorphic Multiplicative Property Verification

To plaintext

$$m4 = m1 * m2$$

Due to

$$c4 = c1 * c2 = \left(m1 + 2r1 + pq1\right) * \left(m2 + 2r2 + pq2\right)$$
$$= m1m2 + 2(2r1r2 + r1m2 + r2m1 + p\left[pq1q2 + q2\left(m1 + 2r1\right) + q1\left(m2 + 2r2\right)\right]$$

As long as the

$$m1m2 + 2\left(2r1r2 + r1m2 + r2m1\right)$$

is much less than P, then

$$c4 = \left(c1 * c2\right) \bmod p = m1m2 + 2\left(2r1r2 + r1m2 + r2m1\right)$$

This algorithm fulfills the multiplicative homomorphic conditions

APPLICATION SCENE AND SECURITY ARCHITECTURE (Li et al., 2012)

Privacy Protection

User is storing their data in cloud, by means of security it is stored in encrypted form and while transmitting the data cloud service provider and user ensures that plaintext information can not be found to others. That implies both will ensure the safe storage and transmission of data.

Data Processing

Fully homomorphic encryption component empowers clients or the trusted third-party process cipher text data straightforwardly, rather than the original data. Users can acquire number of arithmetic results to decrypt to get good information. for example, in medical data system, electronic medical records are in the form of cipher text and are stored over the cloud server.

Figure 1.

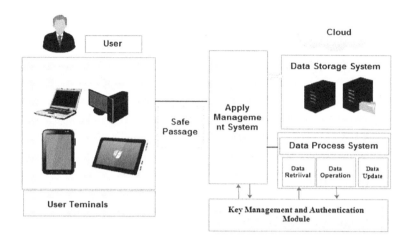

Retrieval of Cipher Text

Fully homomorphic encryption technology based on retrieval of cipher text method, FHE not only ensures the privacy and efficiency of retrieval but also the retrieval data can be added and multiply without changing the plaintext.

CONCLUSION

Security is the most widely recognized issue for Cloud Computing. While storing, transmitting and retrieving the data from cloud server security infrastructure is needed. Encryption is the common technology to ensure the data security of cloud computing. To provide safeguard to web and cloud services Gentry proposed Fully Homomorphic Encryption (FHE) scheme from his previous encryption model i.e., somewhat homomorphic encryption scheme.

Taking into account the cloud security issues this paper presented the idea of fully homomorphic encryption scheme and proposed a security architecture which ensures the security of transmitting and storage of data over the cloud server

REFERENCES

Bhushan, S. B., & Pradeep, R. C. (2016). A Network QoS Aware Service Ranking Using Hybrid AHP-PROMETHEE Method in Multi-Cloud Domain. International Journal of Engineering Research in Africa, 24, 153-164. doi:10.4028/www.scientific. net/JERA.24.153

Bhushan, S. B., & Reddy, P. (2016). A four-level linear discriminant analysis-based service selection in the cloud environment. *International Journal of Technology, 5*, 859–870. doi:10.14716/ijtech.v7i5.3546

Bhushan, S. B., & Reddy, P. C. (2018). A hybrid meta-heuristic approach for QoS-aware cloud service composition. *International Journal of Web Services Research, 15*(2), 1–20. doi:10.4018/IJWSR.2018040101

Gentry, C., & Halevi, S. (2010). *Implementing Gentry's fully-homomorphic encryption scheme*. Preliminary version. Retrieved from https://researcher.ibm

Li, J., Song, D., Chen, S., & Lu, X. (2012). A simple fully homomorphic encryption scheme available in cloud computing. *IEEE 2nd International Conference*, 214-217. 10.1109/CCIS.2012.6664399

Poluru, R. K., Bhushan, B., Muzamil, B. S., Rayani, P. K., & Reddy, P. K. (2019). Applications of Domain-Specific Predictive Analytics Applied to Big Data. In *Sentiment Analysis and Knowledge Discovery in Contemporary Business* (pp. 289–306). IGI Global. doi:10.4018/978-1-5225-4999-4.ch016

Rayani, P. K., Bhushan, B., & Thakare, V. R. (2018). Multi-Layer Token Based Authentication Through Honey Password in Fog Computing. *International Journal of Fog Computing, 1*(1), 50–62. doi:10.4018/IJFC.2018010104

Rivest, R., Adleman, L., & Dertouzos, M. (1978). *On data banks and privacy homomorphisms. Academic Press.*

van Dijk, M., Gentry, C., Halevi, S., & Vaikuntanathan, V. (2010). Fully homomorphic encryption over the integers. In H. Gilbert (Ed.), EUROCRYPT. LNCS (Vol. 6110, pp. 24–43). Springer. http://epubs.siam.org/doi/abs/10.1137/120868669

Wikipedia. (n.d.). *Cloud computing* [EB/OL]. Retrieved from http://en.wikipedia. org/wiki/Cloud_Computing

Zhao, F., Li, C., & Chun, F. L. (2014). A cloud computing security solution based on fully homomorphic encryption. *IEEE 16th International Conference*, 485-488.

Chapter 6
Object Detection in Fog Computing Using Machine Learning Algorithms

Peyakunta Bhargavi
Sri Padmavati Mahila Visvavidyalayam, India

Singaraju Jyothi
Sri Padmavati Mahila Visvavidyalayam, India

ABSTRACT

The moment we live in today demands the convergence of the cloud computing, fog computing, machine learning, and IoT to explore new technological solutions. Fog computing is an emerging architecture intended for alleviating the network burdens at the cloud and the core network by moving resource-intensive functionalities such as computation, communication, storage, and analytics closer to the end users. Machine learning is a subfield of computer science and is a type of artificial intelligence (AI) that provides machines with the ability to learn without explicit programming. IoT has the ability to make decisions and take actions autonomously based on algorithmic sensing to acquire sensor data. These embedded capabilities will range across the entire spectrum of algorithmic approaches that is associated with machine learning. Here the authors explore how machine learning methods have been used to deploy the object detection, text detection in an image, and incorporated for better fulfillment of requirements in fog computing.

DOI: 10.4018/978-1-7998-0194-8.ch006

INTRODUCTION

Fog computing conjointly called fogging could be a distributed computing infrastructure during which some application services are handling at the network edge in a elegant device. Fog computing is a paradigm which monitors the data and helps in detecting an unauthorized access. According to Cisco, the spacious geological involve the Fog computing, and it is well suitable for real time analytics and big data. Fog computing involve an intense geographical allocation of network and provide a trait of site access. With this any unauthorized activity within the cloud network will be detected. To get the advantage of this method a user ought to get registered with the fog. Once the user is prepared to filling up the sign up form he can get the message or email that he's able to take the services from fog computing. A learn by IDC estimates that by 2020, 10 percent of the world's information will be formed by edge devices. This will additional drive the necessity for a lot of economical fog computing solutions that give low latency and holistic intelligence at the same time.

Machine learning could be a branch of artificial intelligence that aims at enabling machines to perform their jobs skillfully by exploitation intelligent software system. Machine Learning is a natural outgrowth of the intersection of Computer Science and Statistics. The statistical learning methods constitute the backbone of intelligent software that is used to develop machine intelligence. Because machine learning algorithms need information to find out, the discipline must have connection with the discipline of database. Similarly, there are familiar terms such as Knowledge Discovery from Data (KDD), data mining, and pattern recognition. Machine learning algorithms are helpful in bridging this gap of understanding. The goal of learning is to construct a model that takes the input and produces the specified result. The models are often thought-about as an approximation of the method we would like machines to mimic. In such a scenario, it's doable that we have a tendency to acquire errors for a few input, however most of the time, the model provides correct answers. Hence, a new calculation of performance (moreover recital of metrics of speed and memory usage) of a machine learning algorithm will be the correctness of result.

FOG COMPUTING

Fog computing is that the thought of a network stuff that stretches from the outer edges of wherever information is made to wherever it'll eventually be hold on, whether or not that is in the cloud or in a customer's data center.

Fog is another layer of a distributed network location and is closely related to cloud computing and also the internet of things (IoT). Public infrastructure as a service (IaaS) cloud vendors will be thought of as a high-level, global endpoint for data; the edge of the network is where data from IoT devices is created.

Fog computing is that the plan of a distributed network that connects these two environments. "Fog provides the primitive link for what information must be pushed to the cloud, and what can be analyzed locally, at the edge," explains Mung Chiang, dean of Purdue University's College of Engineering and one in all the nation's prime researchers on fog and edge computing.

Fog computing will be perceived each in hefty cloud systems and big data structures, making reference to the growing difficulties in accessing information objectively. This leads to an absence of quality of the obtained content. The things of fog computing on cloud computing and big data system might vary. However, a common aspect is a limitation in accurate content distribution, an issue that has been tackled with the creation of metrics that attempt to improve accuracy.

To extend cloud computing and bring high performance computing capability to the edge of an enterprise's network, fog computing was introduced by Cisco (Bonomi et al., 2017). Fog computing, also known as edge computing or fogging, is a computing model that provides high performance computing resources, data storage, and networking services between edge devices (e.g., wireless router and wide area network access device) and cloud computing data centers (Bonomi et al., 2014; Aazam & Huh, 2014; Yi, Li & Li, 2017). In cloud computing, the massive amounts of data have to be transmitted to data centers on the cloud, yielding significant performance overhead. As opposed to cloud computing, computationally intensive workloads such as training large datasets and visualizing data analytics are conducted in fog computing at locations where large volumes of data are collected and stored instead of centralized cloud storage. One of the key benefits of fog com-putting is that it enables users to avoid transferring numerous data between edge devices and cloud computing data centers by moving computing nodes closer to local physical objects or devices and executing applications directly on big data. Because fog computing is in close proximity to the source of raw data, fog computing is able to considerably reduce latency.

Benefits of Fog Computing

Fundamentally, the event of fog computing frameworks provides organizations, additional decisions for process data where it's most acceptable to act thus. For some applications, information might process as quickly as potential – as an example, during a producing use case wherever connected machines got to be ready to respond to an incident as soon as possible.

Extending the cloud never to the items that generate and act on data profit the business within the following ways:

Figure 1. Architechture of fog computing
(Source from google)

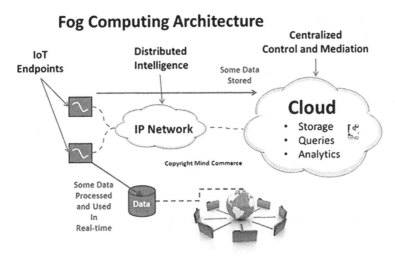

- **Bigger Business Agility**: With the proper tools, developers will quickly develop fog applications and deploy them wherever required. Machine manufacturers can offer MaaS to their customers. Fog applications program the machine to control within the means every client desires.
- **Higher Security**: Defined your fog nodes exploitation a similar policy, controls, and procedures you utilize in alternative elements of your IT environment. Use the same physical security and cyber security solutions.
- **Deeper Insights, With Privacy Control**: Analyze sensitive information domestically rather than causation it to the cloud for analysis. Your IT team will monitor and manage the devices that collect, analyze, and store information.
- **Lower Operating Expense**: Conserve network bandwidth process designed information domestically rather than causation it to the cloud for analysis

Fog computing will produce low-latency network connections between devices and analytics endpoints. This architecture in turn reduces the amount of bandwidth needed compared to if that data had to be sent all the way back to a data centre or cloud for processing. It can even be employed in situations wherever there's no bandwidth association to send information, therefore it should be processed getting ready to wherever it's created. As one more profit, users can place security features in a fog network, from segmented network traffic to virtual firewalls to protect it.

Working of Fog Computing

The devices wherever the info is generated and even collected don't have the type of computation power or the storage resources so as to perform all types of advanced analytical calculations nor machine learning tasks. As a result, fogging comes to participate since it plant on the edge and is capable to bring the cloud nearer in logic. Cloud servers have all of the necessary ability to do this stuff and they are normally excessively far away to actually aid in a appropriate approach. Because fogging works to attach the endpoints nearer, it's capable of bring regarding enormous results. In a fog setting, all of the processing generally takes place within a specific smart device or particular gateway. As a consequence, all of the data needs of what is being sent to the cloud are effectively reduced.

Fog Computing and Internet of Things

Because cloud computing is not viable for IoT devices, it is necessary to utilize fog computing instead. This as a result provides superior overall distribution capabilities and addresses the requirements of IoT much better in the finish. It is accomplished of managing the size of information that these kind of devices end up generate which make it the idyllic style of compute to hold them. Because fogging can successfully lessen the quantity of bandwidth that is necessary and since it has the potential to lessen the required back and forth contact with the cloud and the variety of sensors, it is going to assist string the whole thing jointly lacking falling the overall presentation of the process or devices.

Applications of Fog Computing

Fog computing is that the adorning stages of being extended in formal deployments, however there are a mixture of use cases that are known as potential ideal scenario for fog computing.

- **Connected Car:** Autonomous vehicle is that the new trend going down on the road. Software that is used to add automatic steering, enabling literal "hands free" operations of the vehicle. Starting out with testing and release self-parking operations that do not need oblige a person behind the wheel. Fog computing are going to be the most effective choice for all internet connected vehicles why as a result of fog computing provides real time interaction. Cars, access purpose and traffic lights are able to move with one another and then it makes safe for all. At some purpose in time, the connected car will start saving lives by reducing automobile accidents.

- **Smart Cities and Smart Grids:** Like associated cars, utility systems are gradually more using real-time information to extra powerfully run systems. Sometimes this information is in remote areas, so processing close to where it's created is essential. Other times the information must be aggregate from an outsized variety of sensors. Fog computing architectures may well be devised to resolve each of those problems.

- **Real-Time Analytics:** A bunch of use cases incorporate period analytics. From construct systems that want to be clever to retort to events as they occur, to financial institution that utilize real-time information to notify trading decision or check for con. Fog computing deployments can help facilitate the transfer of data between where its created and a variety of places where it needs to go.

- **Self Maintaining Train:** Another request of fog computing is self maintaining trains. A train ball-bearing watching detector can sense the changes within the temperature level and any disorder can mechanically alert the train operator and create maintenance in keeping with. Thus we can avoid major disasters.

- **Wireless Sensor and Actuator Networks (WSAN):** The actual Wireless Sensor Nodes (WSNs), were designed to extend battery life by operating at predominantly low power. Actuators serves as Fog devices which control the measurement process itself, the consistency and the oscillatory behaviours by creating a closed-loop system. For example, in the lifesaving air vent sensors on vent monitor air environment flowing in and out of mine and mechanically change air-flow if situation suit risky to miners. Most of those WSNs entail less bandwidth, less energy, very low processing power, functioning as a sink in a unidirectional manner.

- **Smart Building Control:** In localised sensible building manage wireless sensors are installed to assess temperature, humidity, or levels of diverse gaseous components in the building atmosphere. Thus, information can be exchanged among all sensors in the floor and the reading can be combined to form reliable measurements. Using distributed high cognitive process, the fog devices react to information. The system gears up to figure along to lower the temperature, input contemporary air and output wetness from the air or increase wetness. Sensors reply to the movements by shift on or off the lights. Observance of the outlook the fog computing is applied for elegant buildings which might maintain basic wants of preserving external and internal energy.

- **IoT and Cyber-Physical Systems (CPSs):** Fog computing has a major role in IoT and CPSs. IoT is a network that can interconnect ordinary physical objects with identified address using internet and telecommunication. The characteristic of CPSs is the combination of system's computational and physical elements. The association of CPSs and IoT will transform the world with computer-based control and communication systems, engineered systems and physical reality. The object is to integrate the concept and precision of software and networking with the vibrant and uncertain environment. With the growing cyber physical systems, we will be able to develop intelligent medical devices, smart buildings, agricultural and robotic systems.

- **Software Defined Networks (SDN):** SDN is an emergent computing and networking notion. SDN notion jointly with fog computing will choose the key topic in vehicular networks unequal connectivity, collision and high package loss rate.SDN chains vehicle to-vehicle with vehicle-to transportation communications and main control. It splits manage and communication layer, manage is finished by central server and server decides the communication path for nodes.

MACHINE LEARNING ALGORITHMS

The term 'machine learning' is often, incorrectly, interchanged with Artificial Intelligence, but machine learning is actually a subfield/type of AI. Machine learning is also often referred to as predictive analytics, or predictive modelling. At its most basic, machine learning uses programmed algorithms that receive and analyse input data to predict output values within an acceptable range. As new knowledge is fed to those algorithms, they learn and optimise their operations to enhance performance, developing 'intelligence' over time. There are four types of machine learning algorithms: supervised, semi-supervised, unsupervised and reinforcement.

Supervised Learning

In supervised learning, the machine is tutored by example. The operator provides the machine learning algorithm with a far-famed dataset that features desired inputs and outputs, and also the formula should realize a way to see a way to arrive at those inputs and outputs. While the operator knows the correct answers to the problem, the algorithm identifies patterns in data, learns from observations and makes predictions. The formula makes predictions and is corrected by the operator – and this method continues till the formula achieves a high level of accuracy/performance. Under the umbrella of supervised learning fall: Classification, Regression and Forecasting.

1. **Classification**: In classification tasks, the machine learning program must draw a conclusion from observed values and determine towhat category new observations belong. For example, once filtering emails as 'spam' or 'not

spam', the program must look at existing observational data and filter the emails accordingly.

2. **Regression**: In regression tasks, the machine learning program must estimate – and understand – the relationships among variables. Regression analysis focuses on one variable and a series of alternative dynamical variables – creating it notably helpful for prediction and forecasting.

3. **Forecasting**: Forecasting is the process of making predictions about the future based on the past and present data, and is commonly used to analyze trends.

Semi-Supervised Learning

Semi-supervised learning is analogous to supervised learning, but instead uses both labelled and unlabelled data. Labelled information is basically info that has purposeful tags so the formula will perceive the info, whilst unlabelled data lacks that information. By using this combination, machine learning algorithms can learn to label unlabelled data.

Unsupervised Learning

Here, the machine learning algorithm studies information to spot patterns. There is no answer key or human operator to supply instruction. Instead, the machine determines the correlations and relationships by analysing available data. In an unsupervised learning method, the machine learning algorithm is left to interpret large data sets and address that data accordingly. The formula tries to organise that information in how to explain its structure. This might mean grouping the data into clusters or arranging it in a way that looks more organised. As it assesses more data, its ability to make decisions on that data gradually improves and becomes more refined. Under the umbrella of unsupervised learning, fall:

1. **Clustering**: Clustering involves grouping sets of similar data (based on defined criteria). It's useful for segmenting data into several groups and performing analysis on each data set to find patterns.

2. **Dimension Reduction**: Dimension reduction reduces the number of variables being considered to find the exact information required.

Reinforcement Learning

Reinforcement learning focuses on regimented learning processes, where a machine learning algorithm is provided with a set of actions, parameters and end values. By process the system, the machine learning algorithm then tries to explore different options and possibilities, monitoring and evaluating each result to determine which one is optimal. Reinforcement learning teaches the machine trial and error. It learns from past experiences and begins to adapt its approach in response to things to realize the most effective attainable result.

Use of Machine Learning Algorithms

Choosing the right machine learning algorithm depends on several factors, including, but not limited to: data size, quality and diversity, as well as what answers businesses want to derive from that data. Additional concerns embrace accuracy, training time, parameters, data points and much more. Therefore, choosing the right algorithm is both a combination of business need, specification, experimentation and time available. Even the foremost full-fledged information scientists cannot tell you which ones algorithm program can perform the most effective before experimenting with others. We have, however, compiled a machine learning algorithm 'cheat sheet' which can assist you notice the foremost acceptable one for your specific challenges.

Common Popular Machine Learning Algorithms

Naive Bayes Classifier Algorithm (Supervised Learning: Classification)

The Naïve Bayes classifier is predicated on Bayes theorem and classifies each worth as sovereign of the other value. It permits us to forecast a class/category, base on a set of quality, using likelihood. Despite its ease, the classifiers does unexpectedly well and is often used owing to the fact it outperforms more sophisticated classification methods.

K Means Clustering Algorithm (Unsupervised Learning: Clustering)

The K Means Clustering algorithmic program could be a form of unsupervised learning, which is employed to reason unlabeled information, i.e. data without defined categories or groups. The algorithmic program works by finding teams at intervals the information, with the amount of teams drawn by the variable K. It then works iteratively to assign each data point to one of K groups based on the features provided.

Support Vector Machine Algorithm (Supervised Learning: Classification)

Support Vector Machine algorithms are unit of supervised learning models that analyze information used for classification and regression analysis. They primarily filter information into classes, which is achieved by providing a set of training examples, each set marked as belonging to one or the other of the two categories. The algorithm then works to build a model that assigns new values to one category or the other.

Linear Regression (Supervised Learning/Regression)

Linear regression is that the most elementary form of regression. Simple linear regression allows us to understand the relationships between two continuous variables.

Logistic Regression (Supervised Learning: Classification)

Logistic regression focuses on estimating the likelihood of an occasion occurring supported the previous information provided. It is accustomed cowl a binary dependent variable quantity, which is where only two values, 0 and 1, represent outcomes.

Artificial Neural Networks (Reinforcement Learning)

An artificial neural network (ANN) contains 'units' organized during a series of layers, each of which connects to layers on either side. ANNs are motivated by biological systems, such as the brain, and how they process information. ANNs are essentially a large number of inter connected processing elements, working in unison to solve specific problems.

ANNs also study by instance and through practice, and they are really helpful for modeling non-linear relations in high-dimensional information or where the association amongst the effort variables is tricky to recognize.

Decision Trees (Supervised Learning: Classification/Regression)

A decision tree is a flow-chart-like tree structure that uses a branching method to illustrate every possible outcome of a decision. Each node at intervals the tree represents a check on a particular variable – and every branch is that the outcome of that check.

Random Forests (Supervised Learning: Classification/Regression)

Random forests or 'random decision forests' is correlate ensemble learn technique, combining several algorithms to produce better result for classification, regression and other responsibilities. Each individual classifier is frail, but when mutual with others, can produce excellent results. The algorithmic program starts with a 'decision tree' (a tree-like graph or model of decisions) associated an input is entered at the highest. It then travels down the tree, with data being segmented into smaller and smaller sets, based on specific variables.

Nearest Neighbours (Supervised Learning)

The K-Nearest-Neighbour algorithm estimates however seemingly an information purpose is to be a member of one group or another. It essentially looks at the data points around a single data point to determine what group it is actually in. For example, if one aim is on a grid and therefore the formula is making an attempt to work out what group that information point is in (Group A or Group B, for example) it might look into the information points close to it to visualize what cluster the bulk of the points are in.

Clearly, there are a bunch of belongings to deem when it comes to choose the accurate machine learning algorithms for your business analytics. Conversely, you don't require to be a data scientist or skilled statistician to utilize these models for your trade. At SAS, our products and solutions utilize a comprehensive selection of machine learning algorithms, helping you to develop a process that can continuously deliver value from your data.

Machine Learning Algorithm in Fog Computing

In present days each human is allied to network using their pocket-sized mobile devices every time. The internet is interconnected with elastic communication network facilitate quality of human. The demand for human resources to understand the knowledge due to every present use of the networked static and mobile cameras has made many efforts in past decades. Normally the system depends on human operations to influence the process of capture video or image. Now a days there are many approaches for human operation to maintain the full concentration on the video for a longer time but it also not scalable as the number of cameras as sensors grows significantly. Mostly the human is aimed at the object detection and the task of irregular activity detection is taken by many types of machine learning algorithms (Sifre, 2014). The algorithm mechanically process to collect video frames in a cloud to detect, track and report any strange situation. The system is classified in three levels:

Level 1: Each object is identified through low-level feature extraction from video data or image

Level 2: The activities of each object are detected/renowned, quick alarm raise; and

Level 3: Doubtful activities profile build and past statistical analysis and also fine tuning during online training the decision-making algorithm.

In the above operation level 1 and level 2 by the edge devices in this detection and tracking tasks are done the results are outsourced to the fog layer for data analyzing and decision making and in the level 3 function is placed in fog computing level or even away on the cloud center allowed on edge processing power (Chen et al., 2016; Ribeiro, Lazzaretti & Lopes, 2017). In level 1 is mainly focus on the human object detection is essential as missing any objects in the frame will lead to undetected behavior. However human body can have different looks in different ambient lighting which has the harder for the kinds of models to achieve high detection accuracy.

In fog computing based object detection we load partial computation tasks from cloud to fog nodes. The operation includes different object detection in an image (ex: persons, cars, traffic signals etc), image preprocessing, feature extraction and clustering generation are deployed on fog nodes. The completed operations on fog are transferring only the identified objects to the cloud rather than original image.

The object detection consists of three main parts are as follows client, fog and cloud.

- **Client:** Client is liable for collecting images from the different spying camera and requesting the object service from fog nodes.
- **Fog Node:** Fog Nodes are situated at the edge of the network. This network edge device has the dedicated fog server. In practical client devices are directly access to the internet which can be used as fog node. Fog node is responsible for object detection, text detection and color clustering. The fog nodes are responsible for requests the resolution service to cloud. Finally, the object detector is transmitted to cloud for identity resolution.
- **Cloud:** Cloud is interred related with Fog Nodes, resolution server, information server. These are scheduled for resources and allocating computing tasks. It provides a standard object detection resolution service interfaces and fog nodes are accessed as connectivity in various IOT applications.

Edge Detection Method

There are different types of edge detection techniques. Each method detects the edges of an image. The Robert cross method performs simple and quick for computing. The input image may be grayscale and output will be the same. The next way is prewitt algorithm which is used to approximation the magnitude and orientation of an edge. The estimate needs to calculate different magnitudes in x and y directions the prewitt edge detection is simpler than sobel method (Cortes & Vapnik, 1995). This is a directional operator on the basis of odd size template. The algorithm consists the edge of the image is located at the place in which the brightness changes significantly, the neighborhood of the pixel gray value of pixels exceeds a set entry depending on the explicit steps for the edge. In this Laplacian of Gaussian smoothes and computes the Laplacian, this yields a double edge image. Locate edges then consists of verdict the zero crossings amid the double edges.

The edge detection of image has done to analyze the boundaries of object to work with the discontinuities in brightness as shown in below Figure 2.

SVM and CNN Method

The SVM is a supervised learning method for binary classification (Kingma & Ba, 2014) it objective is to find the optimal hyper plane f (w, x) = w. x+ b which is to separate the given class in to two data sets with features x $\in$ R$^{m.}$ SVM reads the parameters w by solving an optimization problem in Equation 1

$$\min \frac{1}{p} W^T W + C \sum_{I=1}^{P} MAX\left(0, 1 - y_i'\left(W^T X_i + b\right)\right) \tag{1}$$

Figure 2. (a) Normal image (b) Rainy traffic image (c) Traffic image (d) airport image (e) – (h) Images obtained after edge detection for input images (a)-(d)
(Sources from Google, STL Today, n.d.)

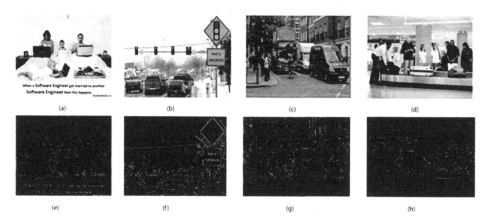

Where $W^T W$ is l1 norm, C means penalty parameter, y' is a main label, $W^T X_i + b$ is a predictor function. This can be interring connected to the CNN for the object identification in the image or video.

CNN is widely applied for the object classification and is challenging task for the CNN to fit in the network edge devices due to restrict constraints on resources. The time consuming and computing can be outsourced to the cloud and the network layer. The edge devices cannot afford the storage space for parameters and weight values of filters of the neural networks. In implementation CNN architecture depth wise separable convolution is used to reduce the computational cost of CNN without making much sacrificing the accuracy of the whole network which is specialized for human detection to reduce the unnecessary huge filter numbers in each layer this makes network implementation in edge (Chen et al., 2017).

The object detection is done with the image using SVM and CNN methods where object of each thing in the image is identified and mentioned with the type of the object as shown in Figure 3.

K-Means Algorithm

K-means clustering is a one of the unsupervised learning which is used for exploratory data analysis of labeled data the process of grouping a set of physical objects into classes of same objects is called clustering (Muthukrishnan & Radha, 2011; Rasmussen & Williams, 2006). A clustering is a collection of data objects that are same in the cluster and dissimilar to the objects in other clusters. It is useful method for the discovery of data distribution and pattern that under the k-means. The method

Figure 3. (a) Normal image (b) Rainy traffic image (c) Traffic image (d) Airport image (e) – (h) Images obtained after object detection for input images (a)-(d) (Sources from Google)

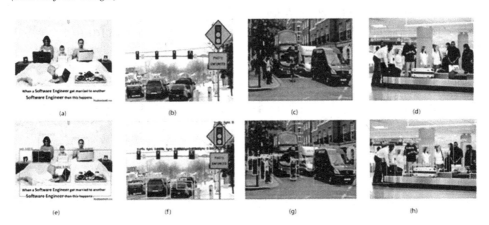

is simple and very easy to classify a given data set through a certain number of clusters which assumes the k-mean clusters. The idea is to derive k centers for each cluster the centers should be in sly way because different location causes different output. Next step is each point belonging to a given data set and associate to its nearer center. When there is no point then the step1 is completed and grouping is done. By these k centroids a loop is generated by this we may notice the K-centers change their locations step by step until no more changes takes place.

The cluster number specifies the maximum numbers of colours are used in the image as shown in the Figure 4.

Neural Network

A Neural Network usually involves a large number of process operation in parallel and arranged in tier. In this human visual system is one to effortlessly recognize a numbers or text in the image. The difficulty of visual pattern recognition becomes apparent to write or detect the text in an image. Neural network approach the program in a different way. These can be stated with Gaussian process and random forest regression.

- **Gaussian Processes (GP):** the outputs probabilistically by use of Gaussian distribution for approximating a set of functions (processes) in a high-dimensional space (Segal, 2004). The main argument for using GP is the fundamental assumption that the mapping of independent to dependent variables cannot be sufficiently captured by a single Gaussian process. GP also uses lazy learning, which delays generalization about training data until after a query has been made.

Figure 4. (a) Normal image (b) Rainy traffic image (c) Traffic image (d) Airport image (e) – (h) Images obtained after clustering for input images (a)-(d)
(Sources from Google)

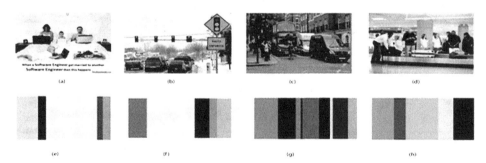

- **Random Forest Regression:** Random forests are a popular ensemble model belongs to the decision-tree class of ML algorithms. Random Forest Regression (RFR) works by fitting a number of decision trees, to various subsamples of the dataset that are then averaged to improve accuracy and reduce over-fitting in a popular process known as bagging.

The text can be recognized in any image using neural network along with Gaussian process and random forest regression, but it is difficult to identify the noisy (blur) text as shown in Figure 5.

CONCLUSION

This paper analyzed the machine learning algorithms in fog computing to detect objects, text in an image using different methods. Firstly, studied what is fog computing and how it vary with the cloud computing. Secondly, described about the different algorithms in machine learning algorithms and application of the machine learning algorithms. Finally, described how fog computing uses or take the images or videos for object detection. By using the images, founded edge detection with Gaussian model. And detected the objects using the methods SVM and CNN, founded the clustering in an image using K-means clustering algorithm, and also observed how to identify text in an image using neural network along with Gaussian and random forest regression. We can also detect face, identifying the person, and can analyze the live video and image through the machine learning algorithms.

Figure 5. (a) Normal image (b) Rainy traffic image (c) Traffic image (d) Airport image (e) – (h) Images obtained after text detection for input images (a)-(d) (*Sources from Google*)

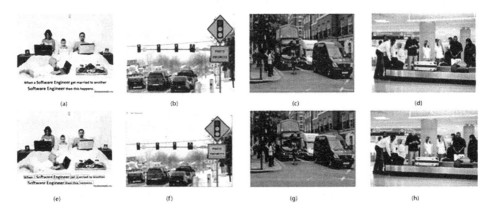

REFERENCES

Aazam, M., & Huh, E.-N. (2014). Fog computing and smart gateway based communication for cloud of things. *Proc. Future Internet of Things and Cloud (Fi Cloud).International Conference on*, 464–70.

Bonomi, F., Milito, R., Natarajan, P., & Zhu, J. (2014). *Fog computing: A platform for internet of things and analytics, Big Data and Internet of Things: A Roadmap for Smart Environments*. Springer.

Bonomi, F., Milito, R., Zhu, J., & Addepalli, S. (2017). Fog computing and its role in the internet of things. *Proc. Proceedings of the first edition of the MCCworkshop on Mobile cloud computing*.

Chen, N., Chen, Y., Blasch, E., Ling, H., You, Y., & Ye, X. (2017). Enabling smart urban surveillance at the edge. *2017 IEEE International Conference on Smart Cloud (Smart Cloud)*, 109–119. 10.1109/SmartCloud.2017.24

Chen, N., Chen, Y., Song, S., Huang, C.-T., & Ye, X. (2016). Smart urban surveillance using fog computing. *Edge Computing (SEC), IEEE/ACM Symposium on*, 95–96.

Christopher, M. (1995). *Bishop, Neural networks for pattern recognition*. Oxford University Press.

Cortes, C., & Vapnik, V. (1995). Support-vector Networks. *Machine Learning, 20*(3), 273–297. doi:10.1007/BF00994018

Kingma, D., & Ba, J. (2014). *Adam: A method for stochastic optimization*. Ar Xiv preprint ar Xiv: 1412.6980

Muthukrishnan & Radha. (2011). Edge Detection Techniques for Image Segmentation. *International Journal of Computer Science & Information Technology, 3*(6).

Rasmussen, C. E., & Williams, C. K. (2006). Gaussian processes for machine learning. MIT Press.

Ribeiro, M., Lazzaretti, A. E., & Lopes, H. S. (2017). A study of deep convolutional auto-encoders for anomaly detection in videos. *Pattern Recognition Letters*.

Segal, M. R. (2004). *Machine learning benchmarks and random forest regression*. Center for Bioinformatics & Molecular Biostatistics.

Sifre, L. (2014). *Rigid-motion scattering for image classification* (Ph.D. dissertation). PSU.

Waheetha & Fernandez. (2016). Fog Computing And Its Applications. *International Journal of Advanced Research in Basic Engineering Sciences and Technology, 2*(19), 56-62. Retrieved from https://www.networkworld.com/article/3243111/what-is-fog-computing-connecting-the-cloud-to-things.html

Yi, S., Li, C., & Li, Q. (2017). A survey of fog computing: concepts, applications and issues. *Proc. Proceedings of the 2015 Workshop on Mobile Big Data*, 37–42.

Chapter 7

Distributed Intelligence Platform to the Edge Computing

Xalphonse Inbaraj
PACE Institute of Technology and Sciences, India

ABSTRACT

With the explosion of information, devices, and interactions, cloud design on its own cannot handle the flow of data. While the cloud provides us access to compute, storage, and even connectivity that we can access easily and cost-effectively, these centralized resources can create delays and performance issues for devices and information that are far from a centralized public cloud or information center source. Internet of things-connected devices are a transparent use for edge computing architecture. In this chapter, the author discusses the main differences between edge, fog, and cloud computing; pros and cons; and various applications, namely, smart cars and traffic control in transportation scenario, visual and surveillance security, connected vehicle, and smart ID card.

INTRODUCTION

Cloud computing frees the enterprise and also the user from the specification of the many details. This blissfulness becomes a retardant for latency-sensitive applications, which need nodes within the neighborhood to satisfy their delay necessities. An rising wave of web deployments, most notably the web of Things (WoTs), requires mobility support and geo-distribution in addition to location awareness and low latency. We argue that a replacement platform is required to satisfy these requirements; a

DOI: 10.4018/978-1-7998-0194-8.ch007

platform we have a tendency to decision Fog Computing, or, briefly, Fog could be a cloud close to the ground (Bonomi, Milito & Natarajan, 2014). With the explosion of data, devices and interactions, cloud architecture on its own can't handle the influx of information. While the cloud gives us access to compute, storage and even connectivity that we can access easily and cost-effectively, these centralized resources can create delays and performance issues for devices and data that are far from a centralized public cloud or data center source.

Edge computing—also known as just "edge"—brings processing close to the data source, and it does not need to be sent to a remote cloud or other centralized systems for processing. By eliminating the distance and time it takes to send data to centralized sources, we can improve the speed and performance of data transport, as well as devices and applications on the edge.

Fog computing is a standard that defines how edge computing should work, and it facilitates the operation of compute, storage and networking services between end devices and cloud computing data centers. Additionally, many use fog as a jumping-off point for edge computing.

Therefore we can define some characteristics to define Fog Computing such that a) Low latency and location awareness; b) Wide-spread geographical distribution; c) Mobility; d) Very large number of nodes, e) Predominant role of wireless access, f) robust presence of streaming and real time applications, g) Heterogeneity.

Both fog computing and edge computing provide the same functionalities in terms of pushing both data and intelligence to analytic platforms that are situated either on, or close to where the data originated from, whether that's screens, speakers, motors, pumps or sensors.

Fog computing is projected to alter computing directly at the sting of the network, which might deliver new applications and services (Forman, 2003). For example, industrial edge routers are advertising processor speed, number of cores and built-in network storage. Those routers have the potential to become new servers and also its facilities the services at the edge of the network which are known as fog nodes. They can be resource-poor devices such as set-top boxes, access points, routers (Willis, Dasgupta & Banerjee, 2014), switches, base stations, and end devices, or resource-rich machines such as Cloudlet. Obviously, edge and fog computing architecture is all about Internet of Things (IoT)that deal with remote sensors or devices are typically where edge computing and fog computing architectures manifest in the real world. In this chapter, how Fog Computing was emerged and its various applications through its edge nods was discussed. For example, in the Fog Transportation System, the fog nodes perform some native analysis for native action, like alerting the vehicle concerning poor road conditions, triggering autonomous response to slow down, and perform some autonomous functions, although connections to higher layers are inaccessible and according to surveillance scenario, video analytics algorithms are often settled on fog nodes near to the cameras, and take advantage of the heterogeneous processor capability of fog, running parts of the video analytics algorithm on conventional processors or accelerators.

Both technologies can help organizations reduce their reliance on cloud-based platforms to analyze data, which often leads to latency issues, and instead be able to make data-driven decisions faster. The main difference between edge computing and fog computing comes down to where the processing of that data takes place.

Fully automated driving will be enabled in future by communication between vehicles and information based services increase road safety, improve more comfort. For the automotive industry, by providing advanced remote monitoring and diagnostics via over-the-air fleet management is becoming an urgent priority that will done by Low Power Wide Area (LPWA) connectivity and it can be done by allocating higher bandwidth that is best provided by technologies such as Wi-Fi and/or mobile broadband in shape of LTE and in Bitcoin, removing Electronic notecase after transaction was completed in order to ensure user anonymity and privacy protection (Tavel, 2007). Smart Id systems using Fog Computing providing e –attendance to various fields like schools, colleges and industry managements.

EMERGE OF EDGE AND FOG COMPUTING

Fog Computing is a highly virtualized platform that provides compute, storage, and networking services between end devices and traditional Cloud Computing Data Centers, typically, but not exclusively located at the edge of network. Compute, storage, and networking resources are the building blocks of Fog. "Edge of the Network", however, implies variety of characteristics that create the Fog a non-trivial extension of the Cloud.

The implementation of the edge layer can be classified into three types,

1.   Mobile Edge Computing (MEC)
2.   Fog Computing (FC)
3.   Cloudlet Computing (CC).

Fog Computing presents a computing layer leveraging devices like M2M gateways and wireless routers. These are called Fog Computing Nodes (FCNs) and are used to compute and store data from end devices locally before forwarding to the Cloud. On the other hand, MEC proposes deployment of intermediate nodes with storage and processing capabilities in the base stations of cellular networks thus offering Cloud Computing capabilities inside the Radio Area Network (RAN). The Cloudlets are based on dedicated devices with capacities similar to a data center but on a lower scale present in logical vicinity to the consumers allows end devices to offload Computing to the Cloudlet devices with resource provisioning similar to that of a data center.

Fog computing has its benefits thanks to its edge location, and thus is in a position to support applications (e.g. gaming, increased reality, real time video stream processing) with low latency necessities. This edge location can also provide rich network context information, such as local network condition, traffic statistics and client status information, which can be used by fog applications to offer context-aware optimization. One of the character of Fog is location-awareness; not only can the geo-distributed fog node infer its own location but also the fog node can track end user devices to support quality, which can be a game ever-changing issue for location-based services and applications. Furthermore, the interplays between fog and fog, fog and cloud become necessary since fog will simply gets native summary whereas the world coverage will solely be achieved at a higher layer that is shown in Figure.1.The omnipresence of sensible devices and fast development of normal virtualization and cloud technology create many fog node implementation offered. Obviously, edge and fog computing architecture is all about Internet of Things (IoT). Generally that will deal with remote sensors or devices are typically where edge computing and fog computing architectures manifest in the real world

MCC refers to associate infrastructure within which each the info storage and also the processing happen outside of the mobile devices (Das, Chakraborty & Roy-Chowdhury, 2014). MEC specialize in resource-rich fog servers like cloudlets running at the sting of mobile networks (Zhang, Zhu & Roy-Chowdhury, 2015). Fog computing distinguishes itself as a more generalized computing paradigm especially in the context of Internet of Things. The following definition will express about emerge of Fog and Edge computing

- **Fog computing** pushes intelligence down to the local area network (LAN) level of network architecture, processing data in a fog node or IoT gateway.
- **Edge computing** pushes the intelligence, processing power, and communication capabilities of an edge gateway or appliance directly into devices like PACs (programmable automation controllers).

ARCHITECTURE OF FOG COMPUTING

The fog extends the cloud to be nearer to the items that manufacture and act on IoT information (Figure 2). These devices, called fog nodes, can be deployed anywhere with a network connection: on a factory floor, on top of a power pole, alongside a

Figure 1. Fog computing that extends the services of cloud service to the edge of the network

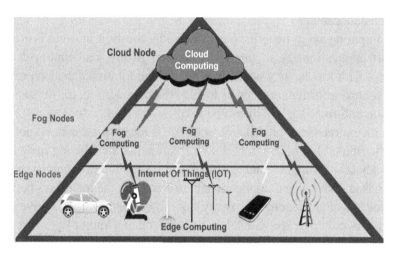

railway track, in a vehicle, or on an oil rig. Any device with computing, storage, and network connectivity can be a fog node. Examples embody industrial controllers, switches, routers, embedded servers, and video surveillance cameras. There is good reason: analyzing IoT data on the point of wherever it's collected minimizes latency. It offloads gigabytes of network traffic from the core network, and it keeps sensitive data inside the network. Analyzing IoT information on the point of wherever it's collected minimizes latency. It offloads the gigabytes of network traffic from the core network. And it keeps sensitive data inside the network.

The fog architecture is an intermediate layer between field applications (sensors, actuators, UI...) and the cloud. The principle of fog is to complement the cloud (centralized architecture) by a distributed set of autonomous micro systems, allowing the repatriation of intelligence at the edge of the network.

The fog node is designed based on architecture of fog .According to that, this is elaborated into two sections,

1. Architecture
2. Networking

The following procedure are used to describe the Fog Computing Service

1. The data is first partitioned into chunks.
2. The chunks are allocated to participating nodes.
3. The chunks are queued before transmission.

Figure 2. Architecture of fog computing

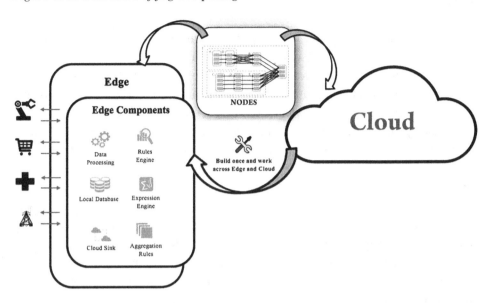

4. Based on the queue, the channels are allocated, which makes some chunks occupy the idle channels in the first batch and rest
5. of them wait for the next released channel.
6. After the distributed processing, the processed chunks are sorted by their finishing time.
7. Also using channel allocation, these chunks are returned to the host.
8. Finally, the chunks are reunited by the host.

NETWORKING ARCHITECTURE

Due to set at the sting of net, fog network is heterogeneous. The duty of fog network is to attach each element of the fog. However, managing such a network, maintaining property and providing services upon that, especially in the scenarios of the Internet of Things (IoT) at large scale, is not easy. Emerging techniques, like software-defined networking (SDN) and network perform virtualization (NFV), are proposed to create flexible and easy maintaining network environment. The employment of SDN and NFV will ease the implementation and management, increase network quantifiability and scale back prices, in many aspects of fog computing, such as resource allocation, VM migration, traffic monitoring, application-aware control and programmable interfaces.

SDN

SDN "When SDN conception is enforced with physically (not simply logically) centralized management, it resembles the fog computing ideas, with fog device acting as the centralized controller" (Stejmenovic, 2014). In the fog, every node ought to be able to act as a router for near nodes and resilient to node quality and churn, which suggests controller can even be put on the end nodes in fog network. The challenges of desegregation SDN into fog network is to accommodate dynamic conditions as quality and unreliable wireless link (Bhushan & Reddy, 2016).

NFV

NFV replaces the network functions with virtual machine instances. Since the key enabler of fog computing is virtualization and people VMs may be dynamically created, destroyed and offloaded, NFV will benefit fog computing in many aspects by virtualizing gateways, switches, load balancers, firewalls and intrusion detection devices and putting those instances on fog nodes.

Capacity

Capacity has 2 folds:

1. Network Information measure,
2. Storage Capability.

In order to attain high information measure and economical storage utilization, it is important to investigate how data are placed in fog network since data locality for computation is very important. There are similar works in the context of cloud (Agarwal et al., 2010) and sensor network (Sheng, Li & Mao, 2006). However, this downside faces new challenges in fog computing. For example, a fog node may need to compute on data that is distributed in several nearby nodes. The computation cannot begin before the end of information aggregation, which definitely adds delay to services. To solve this, we may leverage user mobility pattern and service request pattern to place data on suitable fog nodes to either minimize the cost of operation, the latency or to maximize the throughput.

FOG COMPUTING WORK SCENARIO AND ITS COMPARISON WITH CLOUD COMPUTING

Fog applications are as diverse as the Internet of Things itself. What they have in common is monitoring or analyzing real-time data from network-connected things and then initiating an action. The action can involve machine-to-machine (M2M) communications or human-machine interaction (HMI). Examples include locking a door, changing equipment settings, applying the brakes on a train, zooming a video camera, opening a valve in response to a pressure reading, creating a bar chart, or sending an alert to a technician to make a preventive repair. The possibilities are unlimited.

Production of fog applications area unit quickly proliferating in producing, oil and gas, utilities, transportation, mining, and the public sector. When to Consider Fog Computing:

1. Information is collected at the acute edge: vehicles, ships, factory floors, roadways, railways, etc.
2. Thousands or scores of things across an outsized are generating information.
3. It's necessary to research and act on the information in but a second.

The fog nodes closest to the network edge consume the information from IoT devices. Then—and this is often essential—the fog IoT application directs differing types of information to the optimum place for analysis, as shown in Table 1:

1. The foremost time-sensitive information is analyzed on the fog node closest to the items generating the information. In a Cisco good Grid distribution network, for instance, the most time-sensitive requirement is to verify that protection and control loops are operating properly. Therefore, the fog nodes closest to the grid sensors will rummage around for signs of issues so forestall them by causation management commands to actuators.
2. Information (data)that may wait seconds or minutes for action is passed on to associate degree aggregation node for analysis and action. In the good Grid example, every station may need its own aggregation node that reports the operational standing of every downstream feeder and lateral.
3. Information(data) that's less time sensitive is distributed to the cloud for historical analysis, huge information analytics, and long-term storage (see sidebar). For example, each of thousands or hundreds of thousands of fog nodes might send periodic summaries of grid data to the cloud for historical analysis and storage.

Table 1. Fog nodes extend the cloud to network edge for analysis

	Fog Nodes Closest to IoT Devices	Fog Aggregation Nodes	Cloud
Response time	Milliseconds to subsecond	Seconds to minutes	Minutes, days, weeks
Application examples	M2M communication, including telemedicine and training	Visualization Simple analytics	Big data analytics Graphical dashboards
How long IoT data is stored	Transient	Short duration: perhaps hours, days, or weeks	Months or years
Geographic coverage	Very local: for example, one city block	Wider	Global
	Fog nodes are geographically distributed, scattered all over the edges of Internet, and logically decentralized in that they are maintained by different organizations		Cloud servers are usually rack-mounted, high-end servers located in large, warehouse-like data centers. Centralized cloud servers allow for replication, load balancing, failure recovery, power management, and easy access to failed hardware for repairing and replacement
Cost Analysis	fog nodes aren't as reliable as cloud servers, and physically locating a failed fog node and repairing it is more difficult and costly.		Many financial and time costs, such as those related to power and system configuration, can't be amortized as they would be with cloud computing

There are several key differences between fog and cloud computing. .Various difference can find between Fog and Cloud Computing that was discussed in Table 2 and Pros and Cons for Edge and Fog Ccomputing was explained in Table 3

Advantages of both Technologies:

1. Real-time data analysis: Since, the data is processed at the source of data generation, it can be analyzed in real-time or near real-time.
2. Reduced costs: These technologies lower the costs as companies need less data bandwidth management solutions for local devices, as compared to the cloud or data center.
3. Lower bandwidth consumption: Companies wouldn't need high bandwidth to handle data, because processing will happen at the edge itself.

Table 2. Comparison between fog and cloud computing

Cloud Computing	Fog Computing
Cloud servers are usually rack-mounted, high-end servers located in large, warehouse-like data centers. Centralized cloud servers allow for replication, load balancing, failure recovery, power management, and easy access to failed hardware for repairing and replacement. For this reason, the reliability of cloud services can be held at a high standard. But not at all time.	Fog nodes are geographically distributed, scattered all over the edges of Internet, and logically decentralized in that they are maintained by different organizations.
Cloud Servers and its nodes aren't reliable .	Consequently, fog nodes are reliable and physically locating a failed fog node and repairing it is not more difficult. Many financial and time costs, such as those related to power and system configuration, can't be amortized as they would be with cloud computing.
The network connectivity cant be guaranteed.	The network connectivity to fog nodes can be guaranteed.
An unreachable path or network can fulfill any request even if its computational hardware is fully functional. But may or might not be guarantee.	An unreachable fog node can't fulfill any request even if its computational hardware is fully functional.
In this Cloud Computing, schedule for computational task cant be predictable but not much more complex .because it is maintained by centralized service.	A fog computing application is typically spread over the client's mobile device, one of potentially many fog nodes, and occasionally a back-end cloud server. Therefore, deciding where to schedule computational tasks in fog computing is more difficult.
Deciding the scheduling task is not possible	In short, in fog computing, more factors must be considered in deciding where and when to schedule tasks to provide the best user experience.
This is not maintained by different organizations. Because of centralized server will distribute overall services.	Fog nodes, owned and maintained by different organizations, usually have vastly different RAM capacity, CPU performance, storage space, and network bandwidth.
In this cloud computing, applications are deployed in only one cloud at a time, unless the need for scaling is beyond the capacity of a single cloud provider.	Mobility is a key feature of the fog computing paradigm, and applications deployed on fog infrastructure need to always take this into account.

4.   Lower latency levels: This is the main benefit of edge computing and fog computing. They lower the latency compared to a faraway cloud or data center by eliminating the time involved in sending data back and forth.

BUSINESS BENEFITS AS FaaS AND ITS APPLICATIONS

Platform as a service (PaaS) could be a class of cloud computing services that gives a platform permitting customers to develop, run, and manage net applications while

Table 3. Pros and Cons of Edge and Fog Computing

Pros of Edge Computing	Cons of Edge Computing	Pros Fog Computing	Cons of Fog Computing
one major benefit to edge computing is that data isn't transferred, and is more secure.	It can become a complex issue for brands to handle, as data sets that require more sophisticated algorithms are better handled in the cloud, whereas simpler analytical processes are best kept at the edge.	This is also providing better security (Rayani, Bhushan & Thakare, 2018)	Handling methods does not issue major problem .
Edge computing maintains all data and processing on the device that initially created it. This keeps the data discrete and contained within the source of truth, the originating device	This is striking the balance between keeping data at the edge and bringing it into a central cloud when necessary.	In a fog computing architecture, it enables organizations to, aggregate data from multi-devices into regional stores. That's in contrast to collecting data from a single touch point or device, or a single set of devices that are connected to the cloud.	More infrastructure [and thus more investment] is needed [for fog computing] and must rely on data consistency across a large network.
In edge computing, the data is processed right on the devices, or gateway devices closest to the sensors. So, the compute and storage systems are located at the edge, close to device, application, or component producing the data.		In fog computing, the edge computing happenings are moved to processors linked to a local area network or into the hardware of LAN. Therefore, the data in fog computing is processed within an IoT gateway or fog node in LAN.	
Applications		**Applications**	
1.Oil and Gas industry 2.Intelligent transportation and Traffic management 3.self –Driving vehicles and etc.,		1.Smart Cities 2.Smrt Building 3.Visual Security and etc.,	

not the complexness of building and maintaining the infrastructure generally related to developing and launching an application. Some consortium defines the required infrastructure to enable building Fog as a Service (FaaS) to address certain classes of business challenges. FaaS includes Infrastructure as a Service (IaaS), Platform as a Service (PaaS), Software as a Service (SaaS), and many service constructs specific to fog. The infrastructure and design building blocks below show however FaaS is also enabled and can be enlarged upon within the reference design that shown in

Figure.3 and QoS-aware service composition is building of new-valued services by combining it with the set of current existing services. Due to rapid increase in the number of services in the cloud it becomes very difficult to select an appropriate service that satisfies the user requirements. As the number of services offered by the service providers increases exponentially, the users may find difficulty in choosing the right service provider that fulfills his/her requirements. There are various techniques or methods to find the services with respect to the users expectations. One of research classifies and gives the taxonomy of approaches in QoS-aware service compositions (Bhushan & Reddy, 2016, 2018)

Business Benefits of Fog Computing (Ahmed & Ahmed, 2016)

Extending the cloud nearer to the items that generate and act on knowledge edges the business within the following ways:

1. **Larger Business Agility**: With the proper tools, developers will quickly develop fog applications and deploy them wherever needed. Machine manufacturers can offer MaaS to their customers. Fog applications program the machine to operate in the way each customer needs.

Figure 3. Applications benefitting from fog computing

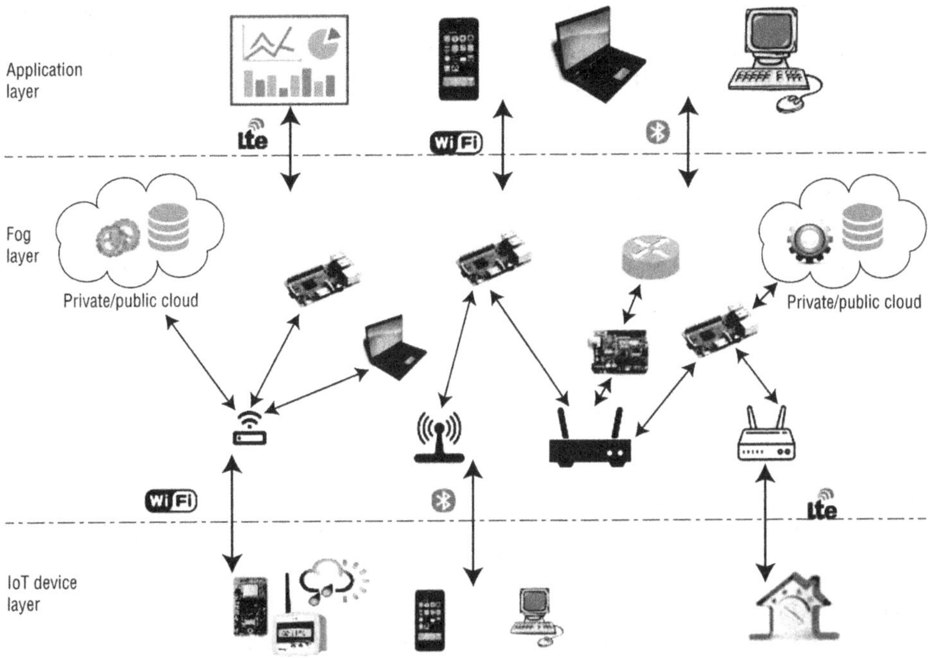

2. **Higher Security:** Defend your fog nodes exploitation a similar policy, controls, and procedures you utilize in alternative components of your IT environment. Use the same physical security and cyber security solutions.
3. **Deeper Insights, With Privacy Control:** Analyze sensitive knowledge domestically rather than causing it to the cloud for analysis. Your IT team will monitor and management the devices that collect, analyze, and store knowledge.
4. **Lower Operative Expense:** Conserve network information measure by process chosen knowledge domestically rather than causing it to the cloud for analysis.

Fog computing targets cross-cutting considerations just like the management of performance, latency and efficiency are also key to the success of fog networks. Cloud and fog computing are on a mutually beneficial, interdependent continuum. The traditional backend cloud can still stay a crucial a part of computing systems as fog computing emerges. The segmentation of what tasks move to fog and what goes to the backend cloud area unit application specific. This segmentation could be planned, but also change dynamically if the network state changes in areas like processor loads, link bandwidths, storage capacities, fault events, security threats, cost targets, etc.

The vicinity unit many issues with this scenario: The information measure to move the sensing element and mechanism information to and from the cloud might price several thousands of bucks per month; those connections could be susceptible to hackers; Now, consider placing a hierarchy of local fog nodes near the pipeline. They can connect with sensors and actuators with cheap native networking facilities. Fog nodes may be extremely secure, alteration the hacker threat. Fog nodes can react to abnormal conditions in milliseconds, quickly closing valves to greatly reduce the severity.

The Transportation in Fog

The Transportation Fog Network is comprised of a three-level hierarchy of fog nodes. The first level of the hierarchy is that the infrastructure fog nodes, or roadside fog nodes. At this level, the margin fog sensors collect knowledge from different devices like edge cameras. The fog nodes perform some native analysis for native action, like alerting the vehicle concerning poor road conditions, triggering autonomous response to slow down, and perform some autonomous functions, although connections to higher layers are inaccessible.

Data from the first level of interactions is aggregated and sent up the fog hierarchy to the second and third levels of the hierarchy— neighborhood and regional fog nodes—for further analysis and distribution. Some of the info may additionally be distributed east-west to different infrastructure nodes for his or her use. Typically, every fog layer within the hierarchy can give extra process, storage, and network capabilities in service of the vertical application at their level of the hierarchy. For example, higher level layers provide additional processing to provide data analytics or large storage capacities.

Traffic Control System

Traffic control fog nodes could receive input from different sources, like sensible light systems, municipal managers, and cloud-based systems. Data flows between the traffic control system and sensors (Bowman, Debray & Peterson, 1993), infrastructure fog nodes and vehicles in all directions, insuring all levels of the hierarchy have the data and control capabilities they need that are shown in Figure.4.

Visual Security and Surveilance Scenario

Smart cities, smart homes, retail stores, public transportation, manufacturing and enterprises increasingly rely on camera sensors to secure people, identify unauthorized access, and increase safety, reliability and efficiency. The sheer information measure of visual (and different sensor) knowledge being collected over a large-scale network makes it impractical to move all the info to the cloud to get period insights. City-

Figure 4. Smart car and traffic control system

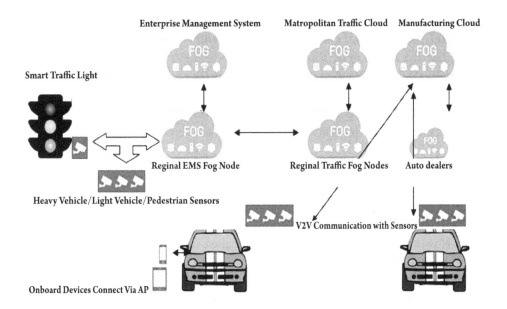

scale deployments that embrace putting cameras on traffic lights and different camera deployments in remote areas haven't got high-bandwidth property to the cloud to transfer the collected video, even if the video may work over the network infrastructure.

Additionally, privacy concerns must be addressed when using a camera as a sensor that collects image data so that the images do not reveal a person's identity or reveal confidential contextual information (e.g. intellectual property in a manufacturing plant) to any unauthorized parties. Fog Computing issuing deployments that provide the opportunity to build real-time, latency-sensitive distributed surveillance systems that maintain privacy. It leverages fog nodes to intelligently partition video processing between fog nodes colocated with cameras and the cloud so as to enable real-time tracking, anomaly detection, and insights from data collected over long time intervals. Video analytics algorithms are often settled on fog nodes near to the cameras, and take advantage of the heterogeneous processor capability of fog, running parts of the video analytics algorithm on conventional processors or accelerators.

Connected Cars Towards Fully Automated Driving

Connected cars, or Vehicle-to-Everything (V2X) communication, involves communication between vehicles and between vehicles and roadside infrastructure (Frohlich & Plate, 2000). Real-time communication allows vehicles to manage things that neither the driving force nor the vehicle's sensors may otherwise determine, enabling additional prognostic driving. In-vehicle information-based services increase road safety, improve driver comfort and enable fully automated driving in the future. When augmented with Multi-access Edge Computing (MEC), LTE advanced, NB IoT and LTE V2X, LTE can provide a viable and cost-effective solution that can accelerate the adoption of V2X communications by transport authorities and the automotive industry (Sannella, 2007). The hybrid use of the LTE portfolio will meet automotive industry needs on the way to 5G (Peng, Aved & Hua, 2012). It provides support for automated driving, increased comfort and improved infotainment and increases road safety and traffic efficiency that are shown in Figure 5.

Automative Fleet Management

In 2015, more than 51 million vehicles were recalled in the US.

1. However, some 30 percent of these recalled cars are not repaired because the owners are not aware of a recall
2. These issues can be resolved by over-the-air software management that can remotely update in-car electronic control units (ECU)(Figure 6).

122

Figure 5. High level architecture of the connected cars ecosystem

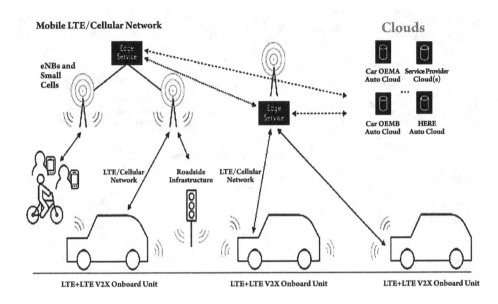

Providing advanced remote monitoring and diagnostics via over-the-air fleet management is becoming an urgent priority for the automotive industry. While Low Power Wide Area (LPWA) connectivity can support some basic fleet management monitoring apps, the need to deliver software updates will call for higher bandwidth that is best provided (Tavel, 2007) by technologies such as Wi-Fi and/or mobile broadband in shape of LTE.

Connectivity for IoT

- Mobile radio for the IoT unleashes the IoT potential of 4G networks by optimizing LTE and TD-LTE cell capacity and the smart phone user experience. The portfolio supports normal cellular protocols (EC-GSM, NB-IOT, eMTC) as well as Wi-Fi, LoRa and MuLTEfire. Plus, our LTE technologies support mission-critical public safety and initial respondent services.
- Support for all three 3GPP IoT radio technologies addresses the connection requirements of different applications with low-cost connectivity and improved indoor and rural coverage. It extends device battery life beyond 10 years for remote sensors and meters.

Virtualized MEC

Figure 6. Secure and control IoT devices for the Automotive Fleet Management

- MEC platform evolution to commercial off-the-shelf (COTS) servers Virtualized Multi-access Edge Computing (vMEC) could be a software-only resolution that may be deployed on industrial ready-to-wear (COTS) servers, creating it simple to integrate with existing IT infrastructure.
- MEC processes information about to wherever it's generated and consumed. This enables the network to deliver the ultra-low latency needed by business-critical applications and to support interactive user experiences in busy venues. By processing data locally, MEC applications can also significantly reduce data transfer costs[7]. vMEC software package parts are often purchased by subscription to greatly scale back your direct investment and business risk.

MEC Multi-Radio Connectivity

- MEC implements computing at the network edge. Nokia MEC multi-radio connectivity takes computing to the enterprise site, for example by making the current enterprise Wi-Fi and operator LTE work together for the benefit of both.
- MEC multi-radio connectivity enhances the capabilities of the Nokia MEC platform by providing an overlay approach for multi-operator and multi-access network integration that is truly independent of the radio access and core networks. This flexible framework mixes and matches different technologies

Figure 7. Block diagram of smart ID card implementation

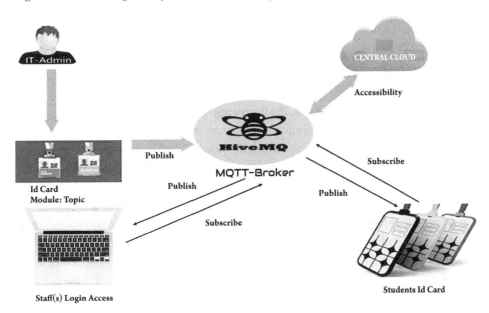

to improve capacity and is not coupled to the capacity of underlying networks. Any access for uplink/downlink can be chosen by the framework according to application need.

Bitcoin in Cloud Computing

- There are lot of method uses a block chain-based electronic wallet in the cloud computing environment. The block chain method is used to remove the information of the user who uses cloud computing. This technique installs and uses an electronic case and removes it ordinarily.
- The electronic notecase is firmly removed by causing the finished message. Leak of user info are often prevented only if the electronic notecase is totally removed. Even though many existing studies have been performed on the block chain protocol, a method for removing the electronic wallet completely is presented to ensure user anonymity and privacy protection .

Smart ID Card for Management

Smart ID card using IoT is very essential application for college, school and all types of industry management. here we are using MDTT protocol for publish and subscribe the topic. Here topic is generating the message which will transmit to corresponding staffs and students through MQTTBroker protocol. These information are stored in central cloud for accessibility purpose that are shown in Figure 7

EVALUATIONS AND RESULT DISCUSSIONS

According to smart card using IoT, the following result revealed that between various total number of students and timing. How many numbers of student received the topic which is generated message within the range. That is shown in Figure 8.

Where A,B,C,D,E,F and G are various total number of students such that 65, 80,110,120,130,50 and 45 respectively.

While connecting to total number of students, need to analyze and finalize the speed and capability of RAM usage and storage also. The Above shown in Figure 9 that storage and RAM usage while connect to the 120 students simultaneously.

Here response time is referred to as smart card activation time calculation .Where X1,X2 and X3 are various place such that play ground, Library and entrance respectively. The above Figure 10 shows that .Note: 700mt between each place.

Figure 8. Timing vs number of students connected

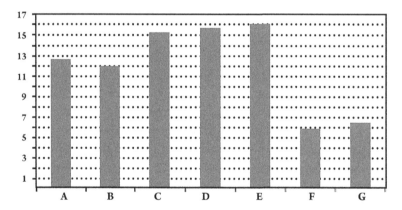

Figure 9. Memory usage while connecting number of students within range

	Storage (KB)	RAM (KB)
Free	3200	512
Used	83	4
% used	2.59%	0.78%

Figure 10. Responding time vs distance place

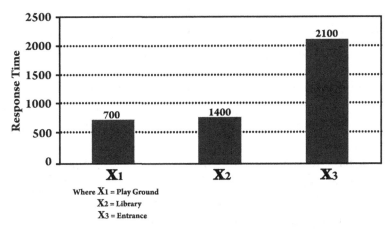

RESULT ANALYSIS

While Fog nodes provide localization, therefore enabling low latency and context awareness, the Cloud provides global centralization. Many applications need each Fog localization, and Cloud globalization, particularly for analytics and Big Data. With all the elements connected and the network deployed, several time measurements were obtained: startup time of the network elements, service response time, and Memory usage while connecting number of students within range. Also, the quantity of memory employed in the nodes to run the applications was measured.

As a results of this the Fog should support many sorts of storage, from passing at very cheap tier to semi-permanent at the best tier. Comparative analysis employs different parameters such as such as system performance, network performance, overhead of deployment and system migration overhead to measure the degree of effectiveness of different approaches (Cortes et al., 2015). Based on our thorough investigation, it can be asserted that MEC is a way forward for achieving 1 ms latency dream.

CONCLUSION

Fog computing accelerates awareness and response to events by eliminating a trip to the cloud for analysis. It avoids the requirement for pricey information measure additions by offloading gigabytes of network traffic from the core network.

It conjointly protects sensitive IoT knowledge by analyzing it within company walls. Ultimately, organizations that adopt fog computing gain deeper and quicker insights, leading to increased business agility, higher service levels, and improved safety.

We also note that the higher the tier, the wider the geographical coverage, and the longer the time scale. The final, global coverage is provided by the Cloud, which is used as repository for data that that has a permanence of months and years.

Edge-centric Computing could be a novel paradigm that moves the locus of management of Cloud Computing applications and services to the sides of the network. An edge could also be a mobile device, a wearable device but also a nano-data center or a user-controlled device.

While the basic reason is privacy, since Edge-centric Computing permits users to retake management of their data, leverage user's resources and even reducing response times build edge-centric computing appealing to novel personal and social online services (Starzyk & Quereshi, 2011; Poluru et al., 2019).

MQTT is proposed and experimented as a communication proposal between these layers .Some platform used to deliver different service by means an API .In this context, experts and professional in each subsystem are required to design and develop the effective services to offer the solution in real time .This will lead in AI services in future and then specific optimization and improvement will be developed. In addition, some of new control rules, model and analysis approach using Machine Learning platforms and AI paradigms will ensure that new smart services can be formed.

Edge and fog are transforming the digitally connected world. Without these technologies, the IoT couldn't be that effective. By breaking the silos of centralized cloud servers, these are making IoT a more flexible and distributed technology.

If the meaning of fog computing and edge computing is understood well, these technologies can bring limitless value to any domain.

REFERENCES

Agarwal, S., Dunagan, J., Jain, N., Saroiu, S., Wolman, A., & Bhogan, H. (2010). Volley: Automated data placement for geo-distributed cloud services. NSDI.

Ahmed, A., & Ahmed, E. (2016). A survey on mobile edge computing. Intelligent systems and control (ISCO), 2016 10th. doi:10.1109/ISCO.2016.7727082

Bhushan, S. B., & Reddy, P. (2016). A four-level linear discriminant analysis based service selection in the cloud environment. *International Journal of Technology*, *5*, 859–870. doi:10.14716/ijtech.v7i5.3546

Bhushan, S. B., & Reddy, P. C. (2018). A hybrid meta-heuristic approach for QoS-aware cloud service composition. *International Journal of Web Services Research*, *15*(2), 1–20. doi:10.4018/IJWSR.2018040101

Bonomi, F., Milito, R., & Natarajan, P. (2014). *Fog computing – A platform For Internet Of Things And Analytics*. San Jose, CA: Enterprise Networking Labs, Cisco Systems Inc. doi:10.1007/978-3-319-05029-4_7

BowmanDebray, & Peterson. (1993). Reasoning about naming systems. *ACM Trans. Program. Lang. Syst., 15*(5), 795-825.

Cortés, R., Bonnaire, X., Marin, O., & Sens, P. (2015). Stream Processing of Healthcare Sensor Data: Studying User Traces to Identify Challenges from a Big Data Perspective. *Procedia Computer Science*, *52*, 1004–1009. doi:10.1016/j.procs.2015.05.093

Das, A. (2014). Consistent reidentification in a camera network. In *Computer Vision–ECCV 2014* (pp. 330–345). Springer.

Forman, G. (2003, March). An extensive empirical study of feature selection metrics for text classification. *Journal of Machine Learning Research*, *3*, 1289–1305.

Frohlich, B., & Plate, J. (2000). The cubic mouse: a new device for three-dimensional input. In *Proceedings of the SIGCHI conference on Human factors in computing systems, CHI '00*, (pp. 526-531). New York, NY: ACM. 10.1145/332040.332491

Luan, Gao, & Xiang. (n.d.). *Fog Computing: Focusing on Mobile Users at the Edge*. School of Information Technology Deakin University.

Peng, R., & Alex, J. (2012). *Real-time query processing on live videos in networks of distributed cameras*. Research, Practice, and Educational Advancements in Telecommunications and Networking.

Poluru, R. K., Bhushan, B., Muzamil, B. S., Rayani, P. K., & Reddy, P. K. (2019). Applications of Domain-Specific Predictive Analytics Applied to Big Data. In *Sentiment Analysis and Knowledge Discovery in Contemporary Business* (pp. 289–306). IGI Global. doi:10.4018/978-1-5225-4999-4.ch016

Rayani, P. K., Bhushan, B., & Thakare, V. R. (2018). Multi-Layer Token Based Authentication Through Honey Password in Fog Computing. *International Journal of Fog Computing*, *1*(1), 50–62. doi:10.4018/IJFC.2018010104

Sannella. (2003). *Constraint satisfaction and debugging for interactive user interfa ces*. Academic Press.

Sheng, B., Li, Q., & Mao, W. (2006). Data storage placement in sensor networks. In *Mobihoc*. ACM. doi:10.1145/1132905.1132943

Starzyk & Qureshi. (2011). Learning proactive control strategies for ptz cameras. In *Distributed Smart Cameras (ICDSC), 2011 Fifth ACM/IEEE International Conference on*, (pp. 1–6). IEEE.

Stojmenovic, I. (2014). Fog computing: A cloud to the ground support for smart things and machine-to-machine networks. In *ATNAC*. IEEE. doi:10.1109/ATNAC.2014.7020884

Tavel. (2007). *Modeling and simulation design*. Academic Press.

Willis, D. F., Dasgupta, A., & Banerjee, S. (2014). Paradrop: a multi-tenant platform for dynamically installed third partyservices on home gateways. In *SIGCOMM workshop on Distributed cloud computing*. ACM. 10.1145/2627566.2627583

Zhang, S., Zhu, Y., & Roy-Chowdhury, A. (2015). Trackingmultiple interacting targets in a camera network. *Computer Vision and Image Understanding*, *134*(C), 64–73. doi:10.1016/j.cviu.2015.01.002

Chapter 8

Internet of Things and Fog Computing Applications in Intelligent Transportation Systems

Korupalli V. Rajesh Kumar
Vellore Institute of Technology, India

K. Dinesh Kumar
ⓘ https://orcid.org/0000-0003-0843-1561
Vellore Institute of Technology, India

Ravi Kumar Poluru
Vellore Institute of Technology, India

Syed Muzamil Basha
Vellore Institute of Technology, India

M Praveen Kumar Reddy
Vellore Institute of Technology, India

ABSTRACT

Self-driving vehicles such as autonomous cars are manufactured mostly with smart sensors and IoT devices with artificial intelligence (AI) techniques. In most of the cases, smart sensors are networked with IoT devices to transmit the data in real-time. IoT devices transmit the sensor data to the processing unit to do necessary actions based on sensor output data. The processing unit executes the tasks based on pre-defined instructions given to the processor with embedded and AI coding techniques. Continuous streaming of sensors raw data to the processing unit and for cloud storage are creating a huge load on cloud devices or on servers. In order to reduce the amount of stream data load on the cloud, fog computing, or fogging technology, helps a lot. Fogging is nothing but the pre-processing of the data before deploying it into the cloud. In fog environment, data optimization and analytical techniques take place as a part of data processing in a data hub on IoT devices or in a gateway.

DOI: 10.4018/978-1-7998-0194-8.ch008

INTRODUCTION

Intelligent Transportation Systems (ITS) developed in various paths. Since the middle of 1980's the study and development of Autonomous cars (Popularly known as Self-driving cars or Driverless cars) has started. Many Research centers, Vehicle Manufacturers and Universities took part in the design and development of Autonomous cars around the world. Since the last two decades, recent advancements in the technologies changing the path of autonomous cars to the top-notch position. In last decade advancement in automation technologies creating a huge impact on Autonomous cars development. Technologies related to ITS namely embedded systems, Internet of Things, Artificial intelligence, Cloud computing and Fog computing. Some autonomous cars were popular within their development era like UniBw Munich (E. D. Dickmanns et al., 1987), Navlab's Mobile platform (C. Thorpe et al., 1991) and Daimler-Benz's cars "Vamp" and "VITA-2" (J. Becker et al., 2014) etc.

The Defense Advanced Research Projects Agency (DARPA) organized three competitions to analyze the autonomous car's development in the last decade (M. Buehler et al., 2007), (M. Buehler et al., 2009). The key phase of autonomous cars development described in SAE International (Society of Automotive Engineers) publications. That is about the classification system based on the intervention rate of the human driver and the amount of attentiveness required by them. Here six levels of driving automation described. Later all research surveys and publications mainly focused on DAPRA competitions and respective modifications with SAE level references (Elrob et al., 2018), (SAE International, 2016).

Let's come to present and future scenarios of the Automobile industry development phase. "Self-driving cars will hit roads by 2025 with the complete integrated Autonomous System". Google was the first initiative to introduce driverless cars in 2018 (Driveless-Future.com). In every automobile industry manufacturers are trying to release self-driving cars with fully integrated autonomous structure in the future. In a recent survey by IEEE, upcoming 20 years, most of the vehicles will be autonomous (Approx. 75%). Advancements for the technologies like embedded systems, Internet of Things (IoT), Sensors, Artificial Intelligence (AI), Cloud Computing and Fog computing concepts were the key elements in the development of Autonomous Cars.

The authors (Tian, J et al., 2018) described about the evolution of intelligent vehicles from grid to autonomous level. They explained about advancements in autonomous vehicles design functional aspects like Internet connected vehicles, Vehicular Fog computing and Cloud networking methods etc. They explained in detail computing systems functional properties. The authors (Botta, A et.al., 2019) proposed alternative architectures for pure cloud systems especially in the robotic

132

applications, Fog and Dew computing architectures proposed where we can use this kind of concepts in intelligent transportation systems. The authors (Raza, S et al., 2019) described about the Vehicular Edge Computing (VEC) architecture, and coupled with the concept of the smart vehicle, its services, communication, and applications. Advancements in technology driving the things in the smart way and in efficient manner. Using technology automotive field became intelligent and autonomous domain. These concepts motivated us to go for in depth analysis about the intelligent transportation systems and its functional architecture.

The chapter organization flow starts with Introduction, here we described about the some key evaluation in the field of autonomous vehicles. After that the Literature survey and Motivation follows there we discussed about the some researchers findings and motivation. Next Autonomous cars- overview of integrated technologies, here we discussed about what all the technologies are associated in the development of self-driving cars. Next we described about Autonomous Vehicles functional architecture. Next we described about how the Hardware components associated within the self-driving cars and next about the Software structure and implementation. After that Fog computing and Internet of things applications described. After that we described about Fog computing applications in autonomous cars and finally application scenarios based on Fog computing and conclusion at the end.

AUTONOMOUS CARS: OVERVIEW OF INTEGRATED TECHNOLOGIES

An Autonomous car also called as Self-driving car or Driverless car. The Design of the vehicle consists various blocks. Important feature of the autonomous car is sensing block, which is capable of sensing the surrounding environment, and to transmit the information to the Decision making system unit. Various types of sensors integrated within autonomous cars, such are Radar, Lidar, GPS, Sonar, Inertial Measurement sensors (Accelerometer, Gyroscope, Magnetometer and Pressure sensor etc.), odometer, temperature and lightning sensors.

The main unit is Control System or Core unit, which executes the necessary actions based on input signals. Control system interprets the sensors information and processes the further actions. Actions relatively Navigation, Mapping, Moving, Obstacle avoidance, Speed controlling, Reading information of nearest vehicles and sending data to the storage units etc. Advanced Image processing, Machine Learning and Deep learning techniques are the advancements in Artificial Intelligence domain which is capable of predicting all kinds of devices performance, failure issues and all kinds of service related issues etc. In real time scenarios huge amount of data will be generates from the sensors and from the devices, in order to store the entire data is not an good choice, because it creates a huge load on servers and cloud systems. To filter the data, need a middleware mechanism. Fog computing is the technology which introduced to reduce the load on cloud. In fogging data pre-processing is the main parameter. Let's discuss about the functional architecture of the Autonomous vehicles (cars).

AUTONOMOUS VEHICLES FUNCTIONAL ARCHITECTURE (AVFA)

According to previous researchers proposed literature and methodologies for autonomous vehicles limited to a specific zone of applications (competitions, exhibitions etc.) Based on applications, semi or fully autonomous vehicles design and development takes place in many scenarios. For real-time and world scenarios, autonomous vehicles designed and developed with advanced technologies for advanced features. Autonomous vehicles functional Architecture (AVFA) describes the working functionality of the vehicle. This indicates the system functions and its interactions with associated components and how they work together to achieve the system functional goal. Functional architecture of an autonomous car is like an anatomy map of the human body, which illustrates the different interconnection between various functional organs and how they interacting to keep our body alive. Similarly, AVFA describes the functional architecture of an autonomous car, with major sections working together to meet the autonomous vehicle working goals (J. D. Wegner et al., 2015).

Mainly architecture shows the functional blocks of the Autonomous vehicle design. The AVFA had shown in Figure 1. Like other general autonomous machines, autonomous vehicles also have hardware and software blocks and also firmware sections.

HARDWARE

The hardware components and devices are the major parts of the system. Main Hardware components and devices are sensors, actuators, cameras, GPS devices, Radar, Lidar and vehicle communication devices. Here all the hardware devices should work in real time scenarios in critical embedded systems i.e. hard real time embedded systems (A. E. Gomez et al., 2014).

Figure 1. Autonomous vehicle functional architecture

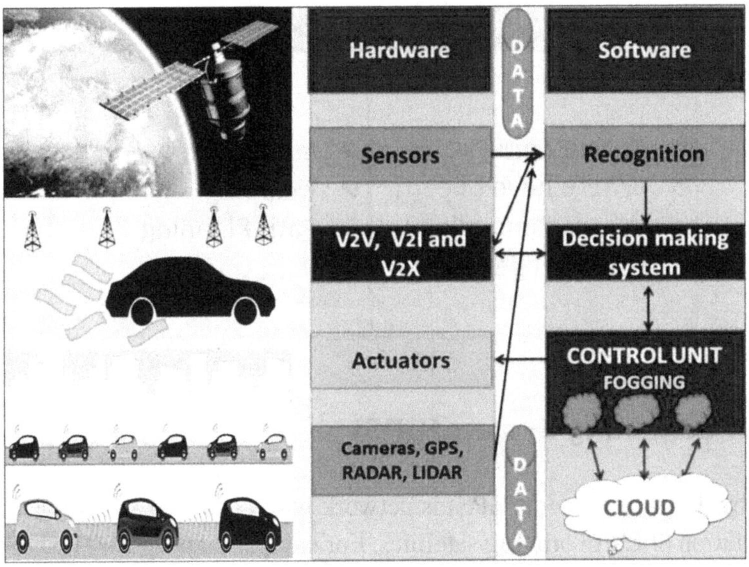

Sensors

Sensors are the input components to the system, which senses the external and internal environment of the autonomous vehicle. Sensors are able to stream the raw information about the surrounding things like the human eye. The main sensors in the autonomous vehicle are Proximity sensors, Inertial Movement Sensors, Gas sensors, ultrasonic and Range sensors etc. In addition to these sensors Cameras, Radar, Lidar and GPS units are also inbuilt in the hardware unit. Each sensor will give an individual response to the control unit for necessary actions. In some conditions, sensor data may contain noise signals or error signals. In advanced systems sensor fusion technology also included to compensate the week sensor signals. Figure 2 and 3 shows the functional aspects of sensors, how sensors are placing a vital role in autonomous cars.

Sensors for various applications in autonomous cars have shown in Figure 2 and 3. Position tracking or localization is for identifying the exact position of the cars pose in advanced terminology these all called as Yaw, Pitch and Roll angles. Generally accelerometer, gyroscope, magnetometer and pressure sensors are used to find out the car orientation sensing parameters like position, velocity, moving angle etc.

Figure 2. Sensors functional aspects

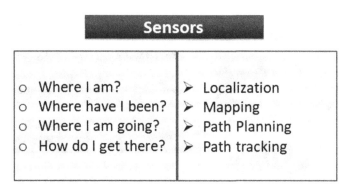

Global Positioning System (GPS)

The Global Positing system (GPS) is network based tracking system, actually it is a constellation of Earth orbiting satellites. For navigation purpose The U.S military unit developed GPS systems. Due to advancements in technologies GPS came into mobiles as tracking device. Based on the coordinate systems it tracks the object Latitude, Longitude and Altitude etc. In autonomous cars GPS is used to track the path and to find the path location (V. Mnih et al., 2010).

Obstacle Detection Sensors

For Obstacle detection most of the cases Ultrasonic sensors will be useful, in order to calculate the distance of obstacle need to perform mathematical analysis with the sensor data. Based on obstacle distance –obstacle avoidance function will be

Figure 3. Sensors functional aspects: Possibilities

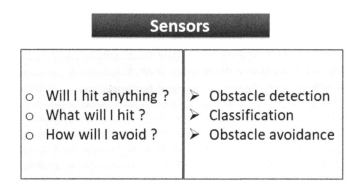

executed by the control unit. Ultrasonic and Range sensors are limited to applications in most of the cases (J. Levinson et al., 2010).

Radar

The RADAR stands for Radio Detection and Ranging; it uses radio waves for the working functionality. In the RADAR instrument, antenna is the key parameter; here antenna doubles up the radar receiver signal and as well transmitting signal. The functionality of RADAR – The RADAR emits a radio signal, which is scattered in all the directions, when these scattered signals hit any obstacle and then the time of back flight "t" from the signal consider for the distance calculation. If the object is in moving state, the frequency of the scattered wave also changes (S. Thrun et al., 2005). Model images shown in Figure 4.

However, radio signal waves have less absorption rate when compared to the light waves when contacting with objects. For long distance data calculation applications RADAR is much suitable. Sequential Lobing RADAR is mostly used in autonomous cars. It tracks min 10 obstacles closer than distance of min 30 meters. Range calculations processed with time of flight. Model devices shown in Figure 5.

LiDAR

LiDAR stands for Light Detection and Ranging, this device generates huge amount of laser signals in less time (fraction of seconds). The emission rate of the laser signals sometimes goes in the range of 150,000 to 200,000 pulses per second. These signals hit the object and then bounce back from the obstacles. The sensor placed on the device measures the amount of time it takes for each pulse to bounce back, from this measurement, obstacle distance can be calculated. Advantage of the LiDAR over RADAR, it can detect the exact size of the object. High-end LiDAR sensors

Figure 4. RADAR working model and RADAR placed in autonomous car

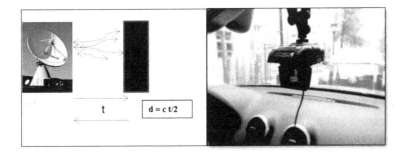

Figure 5. RADAR device and ranging graph

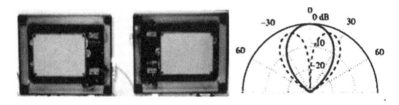

have ability to detect the object from a few centimeters to more than 100 meters (A. Segal et al., 2009).

Cameras

Mainly Cameras used to capture the images around the moving car. These images can be in 3 dimensional or 2 dimensional. Stereo cameras are used for 3-dimensional image capturing. Input images send to processing unit, where image processing techniques are performed in real time using Machine learning (K.D. Kumar et.al, 2018) and Deep learning techniques (AutoX 2018). Figure 6 shown was from Leddertech Canada.

Vehicle Communication Networks

Vehicle communication systems are designed as computer networks. In this scenario vehicles and roadside installed communication poles become communicating nodes. Both the things will share their information. Mainly about Safety precautions, warning and traffic related information. This concept can be efficient and effective in avoiding road accidents and helps in prevention of traffic congestion. Here in different types of technologies developed and implemented successfully. Development of Internet protocol-based systems or internet of things are backbone of this kind of development. This kind of networking systems named as VANET (Waymo, et al., 2018).

Vanet (VANET)

Vehicular ad-hoc Network (VANET) is developed by using the principles of Mobile ad-hoc Networks (MANET). In advancement of wireless networking systems Vehicle to Vehicle (V2V) communication developed for the exchange of information between 2 vehicles. VANETs developed in 2001 under "car to car" ad-hoc mobile communication and networking applications.

Major Applications of VANET in autonomous cars

Figure 6. Autonomous cars - Leddertech Canada, a Leader in AI

1. Electronic Breaking Lighting system (EBL),
2. Platooning,
3. Traffic Information Systems,
4. Road Transportation Emergency services and
5. On- The Road services.

These are the functional services and functioning systems using VANETs. These applications deal with vehicle to vehicle communication protocols. Interestingly V2V expanded and advanced with many features like

*   **V2I**: Vehicle to infrastructure
*   **V2X**: Vehicle to everything

V2V and V2I are the basic communication components which enable the autonomous vehicle to communicate with the environment and other systems and allow transmitting and receive the data. V2X is the vehicle to everything communication component which is communicating with every aspect in the environment affecting the vehicle. V2X component mainly classified as WLAN based and Cellular Network based. The goal of these components to avoid the risk factors like collisions (Aurora et al., 2018).

Actuators

An Actuator is another kind of transducer. Normally, an actuator functions in the reverse direction of a sensor. Here actuator is a mechanism, which turns energy into motion.

Actuators further categorized with their require energy source Vs rate of generation of motion.

- ○ **Pneumatic** actuators use compressed air to generate motion.
- ○ **Hydraulic** actuators use liquid to generate motion.
- ○ **Electric** actuators use an external power source, such as a battery, to generate motion.
- ○ **Thermal** actuators use a heat source to generate motion.

The data generated by the sensors and actuators plays an important role in the Internet of things related to autonomous cars functionality. These actuators are the main reason for car moving.

SOFTWARE

Autonomous vehicle hardware components are performing the functions like sensing, communicating and moving, on the other side software perfection also needed to maintain the autonomous vehicle efficiency. Here software unit is like the human brain, used to control the entire workflow of the system based on input data. Based on pre-defined software instructions, the control unit will execute the tasks to run the autonomous system accurately. Software unit mainly classified as Recognition unit, Decision making system and control unit, here control unit comes under firmware, which is like an embedded system.

Recognition Unit

Autonomous vehicle Recognition unit is an intelligent system which is responsible to identify the entire environment and objects with the preloaded intelligence techniques. Based on sensor signals and Hardware components response recognition unit supposed to understand the consequences going around the vehicle and sends the necessary signals to the decision-making system for vehicle control.

Decision Making System

The Decision-making system is an intelligent unit which is having the ability to take autonomous decisions based on the surrounding environment. The decisions are must be in accurate and dynamic with respect to time, even a millisecond delay in the decision making may cause serious damage. Decisions are related to the working of the vehicle (Navya et al., 2018). Examples Decisions: Start the vehicle, check the signals, follow the traffic rules, Observe the traffic lighting system, check the turning, slow down, speed up, breaks and stop the system etc. In addition to these decisions, the decision system has to follow the route maps autonomously. In order to maintain all the functions properly, the Decision-making system needs to work with V2X, V2V, and V2I hardware components. The combination of Communication components and Decision-making system results in efficient and accurate autonomous vehicle design.

Control Unit

It is like a central processing unit, like the human heart. This unit is responsible for the entire actions performed by the autonomous vehicle. The decision-making system passes the signals to the control unit and it controls the movement of the vehicle through actuators. With the control unit, other major components are in networked to exchange the data. Based on embedded coding the control unit performs the necessary tasks. On the other hand control unit is responsive to the send the raw information about the vehicle working conditions and operational strategies to the cloud (Morteza et al., 2015).

FOGGING OR FOG COMPUTING

Fogging is nothing but the preprocessing concept of the data, before deploying into the cloud. Fogging introduced to reduce the load of the cloud system. Generally, the edge devices and sensors generate the raw data. Before deployment of the raw data into the cloud, need to perform data processing, computing, analysis, and storage functions in order to reduce the load on the cloud system for that the alternative is Fog computing (Toh et al., 2001). In a fog environment, the processing takes place in a smart device or in data hub, or in a router or in gateway, thus reducing the amount of data sent to the cloud.

Figure 7. Fog computing structure

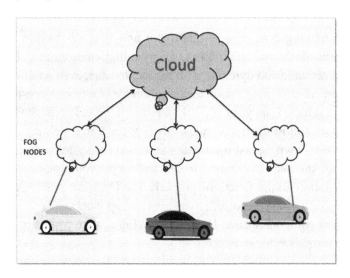

INTERNET OF THINGS (IOT) APPLICATIONS IN AUTONOMOUS CAR

The advancements in the age of internet and automation exponentially increasing; IoT – Internet of things technology is transforming the world with outstanding creativity and innovation in every aspect of our daily life. IoT technology is bringing all kinds of machines, devices, sensors and tools to one closer platform. IoT technology is rapidly occupying all the industries; from that list top place is goes to Vehicle manufacturing sector. IoT applications in Autonomous cars broadly discussed in Table 1.

Levels of Driving Automation – Autonomous Car

IoT technology empowering the devices through communication, all connected devices performs actions independently according to the situation. If it is without human interference, then it is named as Autonomous system. To develop a connected car with various features, need to use all IoT smart applications.

Autonomous Cars: IoT Devices and Its Data

Where devices with connectivity mainly IPV6 allows devices to communicate each other. In autonomous car all the digital devices are connected to the control unit and

Table 1. Levels of driving automation and its key advancements

Levels	Automation - Aspects	Key Advancements
0	No Automation	• System alerts, Alarms, Warnings • Driver has to respond and to make decisions.
1	Driver Assistance	• Automation in Acceleration, Brake control • Driver must respond accurately according to situation
2	Semi Automation	• System performs multiple tasks based on surrounding conditions or with driver's instructions. • Driver must fully control the situations.
3	Conditional Automation	• Based on parameters and conditions, system functions as autonomous vehicle in conditional mode. • Continuous monitoring not require by the driver • But driver should be ready to take over when the system request occurs.
4	High Level Automation	• System will function as Autonomous vehicle and perform all the tasks in automation mode. • At particular scenarios, when driving becomes a challenging task, then system raises request to the driver to take over.
5	Fully Automation	• The systems performs the tasks on its own knowledge • Driver intervention not needed.

share the information and responds to the commands by the control unit. Figure 8 shows the main IoT Devices associated with in the autonomous car.

The working functionalities of all the blocks discussed in above Hardware section. Coming to the Software process and algorithms for autonomous cars must be powerful and efficient to process the information from the network of sensors to make necessary actions.

Autonomous Cars: Decision Making System

In Autonomous cars Decision making system (DMS) is key unit, this unit is responsible for all the tasks execution in real time. Decision making system works with Artificial Intelligence. Based on the algorithms embedded on the control processing, DMS will act accordingly. Here Machine Learning, Deep Learning and Advanced Image Processing kind of techniques integrated within the processing unit.

Decision Making System sends the decisions to the control unit, which is responsible for all further necessary actions. DMS functional structure shown in Fig No.11 and DMS Background technology and its functionalities has shown Fig No 11. After that, data storage is the next key aspect. Data processing will happen within the connected devices at each and every time instance. In order to save the data dynamically need a huge amount of storage devices. In this context for the reduction of hardware space, virtual components came into existence as labeled as

Figure 8. Functional representation of the IoT based autonomous car

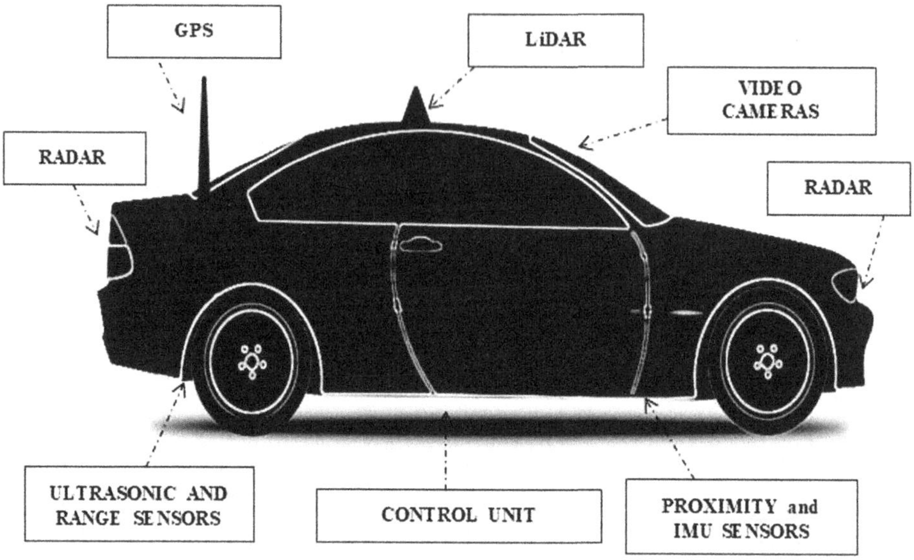

"Cloud Resources". Using these cloud resources we can save our data in the cloud based memory devices. But all the connected devices send the information in every instance, the amount of data becomes huge, this affecting the Cloud resources. In order to overcome the cloud data loading problem, Fog computing or fogging have been introduced.

FOG COMPUTING APPLICATIONS IN AUTONOMOUS CARS

Fog computing applications are a paradigm that enhances the cloud computing and applications to the edge of the network. Cloud is more centralized, where fog computing is widely distributed and deployed across the many regional points to provide services. When comparing the applications of cloud with fog, fog also providing Data, Computation, Storage and Service based applications to the end-users. For fog node point fixing- if any device having computation, storage and network connectivity can suitable for the Fog node.

In real time applications Fog computing techniques are more useful, in order to reduce the load on the cloud infrastructure. Fog computing is also known as Edge Computing. Fog computing hosts the services at the network edge or even at the end of the connected devices. The most commonly used definition comes from NIST (National institutes of standard and technology) for cloud computing is "Cloud

Figure 9. Functional structure of DMS: Associates

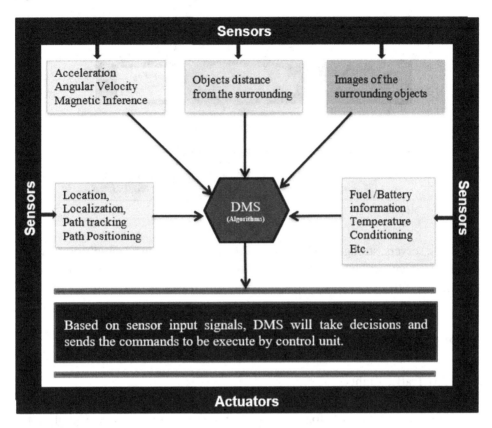

computing is a model for enabling convenient, on-demand network access to a shared pool of configurable computing resources that can be rapidly provisioned and released with minimal management effort or service providers interaction e.g.,

Figure 10. DMS background technologies: Functionalities

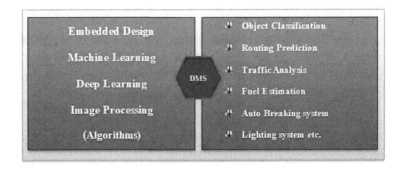

Figure 11. Fog computing distributed infrastructure for IoT based application

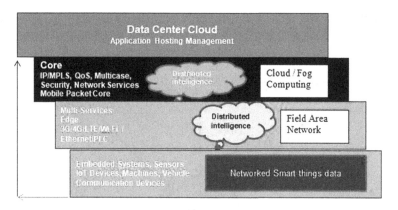

networks, servers, storage, applications, and services that can be rapidly provisioned and released with minimal management efforts or service providers interaction" (B. Paden et al., 2016).

APPLICATION SCENARIOS BASED ON FOG COMPUTING

Smart Traffic Lights

- Smart lights serves as fog devices synchronize to send warning signals to the approaching vehicles.
- The interactions between vehicle and access points are enhanced with Wi-Fi, 3G, road side units and smart traffic lights.
- A highly distributed collector of traffic data over an extended geographically data.
- Ensuring an acceptable degree of consistency between the different aggregator points is crucial for the implementation of efficient traffic policies.
- The situation of traffic lights can be changed by vehicles pass by.

For example: An ambulance flashing lights can be sensed by video camera automatically. And then, smart street lights interact with the right condition. Neighboring smart lights serving as Fog devices coordinate to create green traffic wave and send warning signals to approaching vehicles.

Parking System

- The traffic is really in a mess when the number of vehicles is increasing rapidly.
- As a consequence, finding a parking space is remarkably difficult and expensive.
- Fog computing and roadside clouds are utilized to find a vacant spot.
- By utilizing these infrastructures, any parking space at many places can be shared. Etc.

CHALLENGES

Key challenges for Autonomous vehicles are road conditions and human sudden interventions – How the artificial intelligent systems will act according to the situation is the big question. While vehicle moving in autonomous mode if any sudden change occurs then how system will give response is also key challenge to observe. According to road conditions, fully autonomous vehicles should read the conditions otherwise damage will be high.

CONCLUSION

The development of fusing and integrated technologies creating a huge impact on autonomous vehicles. Artificial intelligence solving the real-world problems effectively compare to human nature. Design and development of autonomous vehicle with these technologies are working accurately. Fog computing is not an exact replacement of cloud computing, but it reducing the workload on the cloud. The technologies all together creating sustainable and intelligent autonomous transportation systems.

REFERENCES

Aurora. (2018). *We Do Self-Driving Cars.* Available: https://aurora.tech/

Autox. (2018). *Democratizing Autonomy.* Available: https://www.autox.ai/

Becker, J., Colas, M. B. A., Nordbruch, S., & Fausten, M. (2014). *Bosch's Vision and Roadmap Toward Fully Autonomous Driving in Road Vehicle Automation.* Springer International Publishing.

Bhushan, S. B., & Pradeep, R. C. (2016). A Network QoS Aware Service Ranking Using Hybrid Ahp-Promethee Method in Multi-Cloud Domain. *International Journal of Engineering Research in Africa*, *24*, 153–164. doi:10.4028/www.scientific.net/JERA.24.153

Bhushan, S. B., & Reddy, P. (2016). A four-level linear discriminant analysis based service selection in the cloud environment. *International Journal of Technology*, *5*, 859–870. doi:10.14716/ijtech.v7i5.3546

Bhushan, S. B., & Reddy, P. C. (2018). A hybrid meta-heuristic approach for QoS-aware cloud service composition. *International Journal of Web Services Research*, *15*(2), 1–20. doi:10.4018/IJWSR.2018040101

Botta, A., Gallo, L., & Ventre, G. (2019). Cloud, Fog, and Dew Robotics: Architectures For Next Generation Applications. In *7th IEEE International Conference on Mobile Cloud Computing, Services, And Engineering (Mobilecloud)* (pp. 16-23). IEEE. 10.1109/MobileCloud.2019.00010

Buehler, M., Iagnemma, K., & Singh, S. (Eds.). (2007). *The 2005 DARPA Grand Challenge: The Great Robot Race*. Springer-Verlag Berlin Heidelberg.

Buehler, M., Iagnemma, K., Singh, S. (Eds.). (2009). *The DARPA Urban Challenge: Autonomous Vehicles In City Traffic*. Springer-Verlag Berlin Heidelberg.

Dickmanns, E. D., & Zapp, A. (1987). Autonomous High Speed Road Vehicle Guidance By Computer Vision 1. *IFAC Proceedings Volumes*, *20*(5), 221–226.

Elrob. (2018). *The European Land Robot Trial (Elrob)*. Available: Http://Www.Elrob.Org/

Gomez, A. E., Alencar, F. A. R., Prado, P. V., Osorio, F. S., & Wolf, D. F. (2014). Traffic Lights Detection and State Estimation Using Hidden Markov Models. *Intelligent Vehicles Symposium (IV)*, 750–755. 10.1109/IVS.2014.6856486

Kumar, K. D., & Umamaheswari, E. (2017). An Authenticated, Secure Virtualization Management System. In *Cloud Computing, Asian Journal Of Pharmaceutical And Clinical Research*. Advances In Smart Computing And Bioinformatics.

Kumar, K. D., & Umamaheswari, E. (2018). Prediction methods for effective resource provisioning in cloud computing: A Survey. *Multiagent and Grid Systems*, *14*(3), 283–305. doi:10.3233/MGS-180292

Kumar, K. D., & Umamaheswari, E. (2018). Efficient Cloud Resource Scaling Based On Prediction Approaches. *International Journal of Engineering & Technology*, *7*(4.10).

Levinson, J., & Thrun, S. (2010). Robust Vehicle Localization In Urban Environments Using Probabilistic Maps. *Robotics and Automation (Icra), 2010 IEEE International Conference on,* 4372-4378.

Mnih, V., & Hinton, G. E. (2010). Learning to Detect Roads in High resolution Aerial Images. *European Conference on Computer Vision,* 210–223.

Navya. (2018). *Sensors.* Available: http://navya.tech/en/autonom en/ utonomshuttle/ #storeLocator__bottomHalf

Paden, B., Cap, M., Yong, S. Z., Yershov, D., & Frazzoli, E. (2016). A Survey Of Motion Planning And Control Techniques For Self-driving Urban Vehicles. *IEEE Transactions on Intelligent Vehicles, Vol, 1*(1), 33–55. doi:10.1109/TIV.2016.2578706

Poluru, R. K., Bhushan, B., Muzamil, B. S., Rayani, P. K., & Reddy, P. K. (2019). Applications Of Domain-Specific Predictive Analytics Applied to Big Data. In *Sentiment Analysis and Knowledge Discovery in Contemporary Business* (pp. 289–306). IGI Global. doi:10.4018/978-1-5225-4999-4.ch016

Rayani, P. K., Bhushan, B., & Thakare, V. R. (2018). Multi-Layer Token Based Authentication Through Honey Password in Fog Computing. *International Journal of Fog Computing, 1*(1), 50–62. doi:10.4018/IJFC.2018010104

Raza, S., Wang, S., Ahmed, M., & Anwar, M. R. (2019). A Survey on Vehicular Edge Computing: Architecture, Applications, Technical Issues, and Future Directions. *Wireless Communications and Mobile Computing, 2019,* 1–19. doi:10.1155/2019/3159762

Segal, A., Haehnel, D., & Thrun, S. (2009). Generalized-ICP. *Robotics: Science and Systems V, 5,* 168–176.

Thorpe, C., Herbert, M., Kanade, T., & Shafter, S. (1991). Toward Autonomous Driving: The Cmu Navlab. Ii. Architecture and Systems. *IEEE Expert, 6*(4), 44–52. doi:10.1109/64.85920

Thrun, S., Burgard, W., & Fox, D. (2005). *Probabilistic Robotics.* Cambridge, MA: MIT Press.

Tian, J., Chin, A., & Yanikomeroglu, H. (2018). Connected and Autonomous Driving. *IT Professional, 20*(6), 31–34. doi:10.1109/MITP.2018.2876928

Toh & Chai. (2001). Ad Hoc Mobile Wireless Networks: Protocols and Systems. Prentice Hall.

Waymo. (2018). *Waymo 360° Experience: A Fully Self-Driving Journey*. Available: Https://Www.Youtube.Com/Watch?V=B8r148hfxpw

Wegner, J. D., Montoya-Zegarra, J. A., & Schindler, K. (2015). Road Networks As Collections Of Minimum Cost Paths. *ISPRS Journal of Photogrammetry and Remote Sensing*, *108*, 128–137. doi:10.1016/j.isprsjprs.2015.07.002

Zanjireh & Larijani. (2015). A Survey on Centralized and Distributed Clustering Routing Algorithms for Wsns. *IEEE 81st Vehicular Technology Conference.*

Chapter 9
Agribot

Ravi Kumar Poluru
iD https://orcid.org/0000-0001-8591-5266
Vellore Institute of Technology, India

M. Praveen Kumar Reddy
Vellore Institute of Technology, India

Rajesh Kaluri
Vellore Institute of Technology, India

Kuruva Lakshmanna
Vellore Institute of Technology, India

G. Thippa Reddy
Vellore Institute of Technology, India

ABSTRACT

This robotic vehicle is a farming machine of significant power and incredible soil clearing limit. This multipurpose system gives a propel technique to sow, furrow, water, and cut the harvests with the least labor and work. The machine will develop the ranch by considering specific line and a section settled at a fixed distance depending on the crop. Moreover, the vehicle can be controlled through voice commands connected via Bluetooth medium using an Android smartphone. The entire procedure computation, handling, checking is planned with engines and sensor interfaced with the microcontroller. The major modules of the vehicle are cultivating, sowing seeds, watering, harvesting the crop. The vehicle will cover the field with the help of the motors fixed which is being controlled with the help of the voice commands given by the user. The main motto of this project is to make the vehicle available and should be operated by everyone even without any technical knowledge.

DOI: 10.4018/978-1-7998-0194-8.ch009

INTRODUCTION

In the field of agribusiness, diverse tasks for dealing with overpowering material are performed. For instance, in vegetable trimming, specialists should deal with overwhelming vegetables in the gathering season. Also, in natural cultivating, which is quickly picking up notoriety, specialists should deal with substantial fertilizer packs in the preparing season. These activities are dull, tedious, or require quality and aptitude for the laborers. In the 1980s numerous horticultural robots were begun for innovative work. Kawamura and collaborators built up the organic product reaping in the plantation. Grand and collaborators built up the apple reaping robot. In any case, a large number of robots are not in the phases of diffusion but rather still in the phases of innovative work. It is imperative to discover rooms to accomplish higher execution and lower cost of the robots. Over history, horticulture has advanced from a manual occupation to a profoundly industrialized business, using a wide assortment of devices and machines. Scientists are presently looking towards the acknowledgment of independent farming vehicles. The main phase of advancement, programmed vehicle direction, has been examined for a long time, with numerous developments investigated as right on time as the 1920s. The potential advantages of computerized rural vehicles incorporate expanded profitability, expanded application exactness, and upgraded activity wellbeing.

Moreover, the fast progressions in hardware, PCs, and registering innovations have roused recharged enthusiasm for the improvement of vehicle direction frameworks. Different direction innovations, including mechanical direction, optical direction, radio route, and ultrasonic direction, have been explored. Horticulture includes the methodical creation of sustenance, bolster, and different merchandise. Notwithstanding creating nourishment for people and creatures, horticulture additionally delivers cut blossoms, timber, composts, creature shrouds, cowhide, and mechanical chemicals.

- **A robot** is a machine that can be programmed and reprogrammed to do certain tasks and usually consists of a manipulator such as a claw, hand, or tool attached to a mobile body or a stationary platform.
- **Autonomous** robots: They work completely under the control of a computer program. They often use sensors to gather data about their surroundings to navigate.
- **Tele-controlled** robots work under the control of humans and computer programs.
- **Remote-controlled** robots are controlled by humans with a controller such as a joystick or other hand-held device. Today agricultural robots can be classified into several groups: harvesting or picking, planting, weeding, pest control, or maintenance. Scientists have the goal of creating robot farms.

Where all the work will be done by machines. The main problem with this kind of robot farm is that the farms are the part of nature and nature is not uniform. It is not like the robots that work in factories building cars. Factories are built around the job at hand, whereas, farms are not. Robots in factories don't have to deal with uneven terrain or changing conditions. Scientists are working on overcoming these problems.

RELATED SYSTEM

The application of management techniques such as precision agriculture (PA) aims at better utilization of the cultivated area and opens opportunities for technological development applied to the agricultural sector. The flexibility offered by the steering is utilized fully in the trajectory planning. A two-part trajectory planning algorithm consists of the steering planning and velocity planning. The limits of vehicle mechanics and drive torque are taken into account. A technology that has been widely used as an embedded network is the CAN protocol. The implementation of the ISO11783 standard represents the standardization of the CANfor application in agricultural machinery.

PROPOSED SYSTEM

AGRIBOT is a robot for agricultural purposes. The main area of application of robots in agriculture is at the harvesting stage. Fruits picking robots, driverless tractor/sprayers, and sheep shearing robots are designed to replace human labor. In most cases, a lot of factors must be considered (e.g., the size and color of the fruit to be picked) before the commencement of a task. Robots can be used for other horticultural tasks such as pruning, weeding, spraying, and monitoring. Robots like these have many benefits for the agricultural industry, including a higher quality of the fresh procedure, lower production costs, and a smaller need for manual labor.

SOFTWARE REQUIREMENTS

The software requirements of the system are-

1. Android OS that includes Android SDK
2. Eclipse SDK
3. Arduino

HARDWARE REQUIREMENTS:

1.   Arduino
2.   DC Motors
3.   Jump Wires
4.   Bluetooth Module
5.   Water Pipe
6.   Plough
7.   Seed Sower
8.   Harvester

RESULTS

The signals are processed from the application which is given by the user using voice and moving the AGRIBOT to its left-side path.

Apart from these, there are multiple features which will be operated with the voice commands like "0" – To Stop

"5" - To water the field
"6" – To Harvest
"7" – To Sow Seeds

CONCLUSION

This multipurpose system gives an advance method to sow, plow and harvest the crops with minimum manpower and labor, making it an efficient vehicle. The machine will cultivate the farm by considering particular rows and specific column at a fixed distance depending on the crop. This project may provide a great scope in agricultural vehicles over the past 20 years. Although the research developments are abundant, there are some shortcomings (e.g., low robustness of versatility and dependability of technologies) that are delaying the improvements required for commercialization of the guidance systems. The application of new popular robotic technologies for agricultural guidance systems will augment the realization of agricultural vehicle automation in the future. In agriculture, the opportunities for robot-enhanced productivity are immense –, and the robots are appearing on farms in various guises and increasing numbers. The other problems associated with autonomous farm equipment can probably be overcome with technology. This equipment may

Figure 1.

be in our future, but there are important reasons for thinking that it may not be just replacing the human driver with a computer. It may mean a rethinking of how crop production is done. Crop production may be done better and cheaper with a swarm of small machines than with a few large ones. One of the advantages of the smaller machines is that they may be more acceptable to the non-farm community. The jobs in agriculture are a drag, dangerous, require intelligence and quick, though highly repetitive decisions hence robots can be rightly substituted with a human operator. Robots can improve the quality of our lives, but there are downsides.

ADDITIONAL READING

Bakker, T., Bontsema, J., & Müller, J. (2010). Systematic design of an autonomous platform for robotic weeding. *Journal of Terramechanics, 47*(2), 63–73. doi:10.1016/j.jterra.2009.06.002

Cariou, C., Lenain, R., Thuilot, B., & Berducat, M. (2009). Automatic guidance of a four-wheel-steering mobile robot for accurate field operations. *Journal of Field Robotics, 26*(6-7), 504–518. doi:10.1002/rob.20282

Chen, Y., Peng, X., & Zhang, T. (2011). Application of wireless sensor networks in the field of agriculture. In *2011 Louisville, Kentucky, August 7-10, 2011* (p. 1). American Society of Agricultural and Biological Engineers.

Gondchawar, N., & Kawitkar, R. S. (2016). IoT based smart Agriculture. *International Journal of Advanced Research in Computer and Communication Engineering, 5*(6).

Hamner, B., Bergerman, M., & Singh, S. (2011). Autonomous orchard vehicles for specialty crops production. In *2011 Louisville, Kentucky, August 7-10, 2011* (p. 1). American Society of Agricultural and Biological engineers.

Heraud, J. A., & Lange, A. F. (2009). *Agricultural automatic vehicle guidance from horses to GPS: How we got here, and where we are going.* American Society of Agricultural and Biological Engineers.

Ryerson, A. F., & Zhang, Q. (2007). Vehicle path planning for complete field coverage using genetic algorithms. *Agricultural Engineering International: CIGR Journal.*

Xue, J., & Xu, L. (2010, March). Autonomous agricultural robot and its row guidance. In *Measuring Technology and Mechatronics Automation (ICMTMA), 2010 International Conference on* (Vol. 1, pp. 725-729). iEEE. 10.1109/ICMTMA.2010.251

Xue, J., Zhang, L., & Grift, T. E. (2012). Variable field-of-view machine vision based row guidance of an agricultural robot. *Computers and Electronics in Agriculture, 84*, 85–91. doi:10.1016/j.compag.2012.02.009

Yaghoubi, S., Akbarzadeh, N. A., Bazargani, S. S., Bazargani, S. S., Bamizan, M., & Asl, M. I. (2013). Autonomous robots for agricultural tasks and farm assignment and future trends in agro robots. *International Journal of Mechanical and Mechatronics Engineering, 13*(3), 1–6.

Yaghoubi, S., Akbarzadeh, N. A., Bazargani, S. S., Bazargani, S. S., Bamizan, M., & Asl, M. I. (2013). Autonomous robots for agricultural tasks and farm assignment and future trends in agro robots. *International Journal of Mechanical and Mechatronics Engineering*, *13*(3), 1–6.

Chapter 10

Towards Efficient Resource Management in Fog Computing:
A Survey and Future Directions

M. Sudhakara
Vellore Institute of Technology, India

Ravi Kumar Poluru
Vellore Institute of Technology, India

K Dinesh Kumar
Vellore Institute of Technology, India

R Lokesh Kumar
Vellore Institute of Technology, India

S Bharath Bhushan
Sree Vidyanikethan Engineering College (SVEC), India

ABSTRACT

Cloud computing is an emerging field. With its three key features and its natural favorable circumstances, it has had a few difficulties in the recent years. The gap between the cloud and the end devices must be reduced in latency specific applications (i.e., disaster management). Right now, fog computing is an advanced mechanism to reduce the latency and congestion in IoT networks. It emphasizes processing the data as close as possible to the edge of the networks, instead of sending/receiving the data from the data centre by using large quantity of fog nodes. The virtualization of these fog nodes (i.e., nodes are invisible to the users) in numerous locations across the data centres enabled the fog computing to become more popular. The end users need to purchase the computing resources from the cloud authorities to process their excessive workload. Since computing resources are heterogeneous and resource are constrained and dynamic in nature, allocating these resources to the users becomes an open research issue and must be addressed as the first priority.

DOI: 10.4018/978-1-7998-0194-8.ch010

INTRODUCTION

Internet of Things, abbreviated as IoT, is now a burning trend in technology and by 2025, the count of connected components will increase and almost 26 billion gadgets are estimated for installation at typical speed. IoT implementation result in creating huge repository of data which is to be processed and also do analyse in real time. So that it enhance the quantity of workloads related to data centres, requiring wide range of computing resources and make the providers to face new challenges. To engage with challenges and satisfy the services of computing, several wide ranging data centres or clouds are implemented. Cloud data centres belonging to cloud computing, are able to categorize some portion of computing resources (like servers, storage, applications, services and networks) which are shareable. These can be accessed with ease by the users based on their requirements. Although the clouds are commonly be created in remote locations which are far away from users. It leads to have more transmission cost and also congestion in transmission. Additionally it is not endurable with applications which need real-time collaboration in IoT aspects (IDC, Worldwide Internet of Things Forecast 2015 -2019).

Fog computing in IoT, was introduced by Cisco and they recommended a challenging solution. In this computing, the relevant information is given to data centres and performs computing, decision making and so on occurs through various computing gadgets which consumes less power. Those gadgets are known as Fog Nodes (FNs) and these are implemented at the network edges so that to offload the services of data computing from cloud. Hence Fog computing yields minimum latency and speed response. Network virtualization is deployed in fog computing in which Fog nodes are not visible to users and they could only buy the computing resources from the cloud data centres in order to process their more workloads. The requests from the users to data centres and each of those data centres are able to gather the computing resources from total FNs. The noticeable thing here is that every cloud data centre allocates different computing resources from multiple FNs to multiple users. Therefore the computing resources are used by users properly (B. P. Rimal et.al, 2014).

In conventional cloud computing, to minimize the workloads related to data centres Fog computing provides an alternate way in supporting locally distributed, less latency and QoS related IoT applications. As mentioned earlier Fog computing was proposed by Cisco to elaborate the cloud computing to the edges of a network. In simple terms 'Fog' is 'a cloud somewhat closer to ground' which is from Core to edge computing allowing better services otherwise applications. Fog computing is highly essential platform which gives computing, storage and services related to networking between EU and DC belonging conventional cloud computing (L. M. Vaquero et.al, 2014)

In general data created by the user gadgets like smart mobiles and some other wearable's in smart city are transferred to clouds and is to be processed and stored as well. But in real time applications it is ineffective in future because it is essential to improve the communication latencies when huge collection of devices connected to Internet (M. Aazam et.al, 2016). The applications will have adverse effects when there is increase in the communication latencies, so that it leads to degrade the total Quality of Service and Quality of Experience. Similarly another computing type which minimize the above issue is getting the computing resources near to user gadgets and sensors and can utilize them to perform processing of data. It will reduce the data size which was sent to cloud and consequently minimizes the communication latencies. To comprehend this kind of computing the present research notion is to divide few of computing resources which are in available at many data centres by getting them closer to network edges to users and to sensors. A type of computing which utilizes the resources which are closer to network edges is known as "Edge computing". Adversely to the cloud resources, those resources at edge are:

1. **Resource Constrained**: Restricted resources for computing as the edge devices contain small processors and a controlled power cost.
2. **Heterogeneous**: The processors with varied systems.

Hence handling resources is said to be one of the major challenges in both the Fog and also in edge computing.

RELATED WORK

Though, resource management is still a challenging task and the novel techniques to be addressed. Up to now, several authors proposed techniques to address this issue and each method has its own advantages and limitations. Few of these techniques are introduced in this section. One of the critical research concepts is RAP because it raised in many research fields and also found in many recent studies specifically in modern information system. The best way for resource allocation in the computer systems is being discussed since from decades because it highly influences the total system's performance. The motive of resource allocation problem is when a group of tasks and resources are given then it is need to allocate those resources to finish that tasks by considering some predefined constraints.

In earlier studies, Jain et al, 1994 proposed fairness index to evaluate the solution preciseness for algorithm of resource allocation which can be used to increase the information system's performance wholly like network management. Among various RAP related problems one of the well-known problems is how to allocated minimum resources on cloud system to accomplish the tasks, in earlier years (A. Balasubramanian et.al.,2007) on best power transmission resource allocation problem in integral network to reduce the power transmission for Time Division (TD) and Frequency Division (FD) Multiple Access strategies. Dahrouj et al., 2015 later analysed the challenges related to resource allocation problem in diverse cloud radio accessible network and also presented coordinated scheduling model to overcome this problem. These RAPs also prevails in IoT environment like assignment of tasks to minimize the total energy consumption by IoT gadgets. B. Manate et al, 2016, utilized a multi-user system to manage three kinds of Virtual Machines (VM) for an IoT system over cloud. Those are compute Virtual machine, DB virtual machine and also GPU instances. As IoT gadgets might have various diversified network interfaces and those are allowed to give some services.

(Angelakis et al., 2016) assumed this case as RAP and focused in providing an optimal solution to allocation of services to interfaces which is so called as SIA (Service-to Interface Assignment (SIA). Based on their evaluations, this problem is an NP-complete problem. One more research trend is that management of gateways, appliances and IoT devices is now a hot topic. So that,(Kim and Ko, 2015), provided a RAP of IoT and is transformed it in to a updated version of the Degree-Constrained Minimum-Spanning Tree (DCMST). This RAP considers how to reduce the data size while the transmission done between gateways and IoT resources by taking some conditions into sight.

KEY TECHNOLOGIES

Fog computing rely on few of the available and prevalent technologies in order to hold up its formation along with application. Figure 1 represents the inclusion of technologies belonging to computing, communication and storage technologies along with naming and resolution, resource management and security and privacy. These are the primary technologies where the fog computing properties are completely taken into sight so that to satisfy its application. On this basis, fog computing delivers many informative and robust services to the users. In this section, the authors discussed the overview of the key technologies in Fog Computing.

Computing Technologies

Fog computing is an efficient computing approach in which fog nodes instantly serves neighboring evaluation and data processing request to users. The efficient and less latency service capacity must be supported by few computing technologies. Computation offloading process can overcome resource conditions over the edge

Figure 1. Key technologies of fog computing

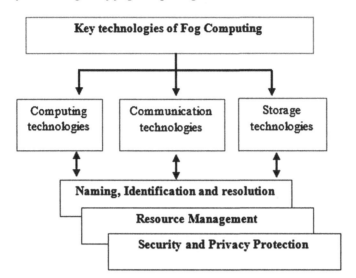

devices, particularly for computation-intensive activities. It helps with increasing the performance and saving the life time of a battery (Zheng et al., 2017). (Chen et al., 2015) researched the multi-user computation offloading issue in the mobile-edge cloud computing and suggested distributed computational offloading model. The aim of latency management of fog computing to bound the response time of service within considerable threshold. (Zeng et al., 2016) investigated the consumption time in reduction problem with the service requests by assuming task image placement and scheduling tasks together. Intharawijitr et al., 2016 introduced least latency for the architecture of fog computing. To overcome the delay in computation and also in communication, there defined a mathematical model to the nodes selection in the fog network to yield minimum delay.

Communication Technologies

A fog node acts as a component in intermediate networking; it maps with the end users and also connects the devices, fog nodes and cloud. The three connections included are wireless links between the fog nodes and the end components, links among the fog nodes, links between fog nodes and cloud data center. Such wireless communication technologies supports Fog application by including 3G,4G,WiFi, WLANs, ZigBee and Bluetooth. Particularly to support mobile fog computing. We have described some more communication technologies in the below:

Software Defined Networking

SDN is an emerging paradigm of computing and networking. It is also known to be a method for implementing network virtualization. This model partitions control plane and planes of information to obtain the robustness in controlling the traffic in a network. S. Truong et al, 2015 recommended a novel model of vehicular based ad hoc networks by considering SDN and FSDN (Fog Computing) to overcome the high complexities with poor connectivity, low scalability, and low flexibility and also with low awareness. Long-Reach Passive Optical Network (LRPON) is suggested to widen the network till it reaches 100km with huge optical network units. (Zhang et al., 2017) introduced the combination of Fog Computing and LRPON to minimize the model of network and obtains a related optimal solution to the gigantic Fog networks by generating an efficient heuristic paradigm.

Storage Technologies

In the Fog Computing, Pre-cache technology is preferred so that to satisfy the conditions of least-latency property. Fog nodes will forecasts the user requirements and stimulates by choosing the most essential data for caching decentralized nodes. (Hassan et al., 2015) introduced a secure and efficient storage expansion approach by using personal space for mobile gadgets. It combines the total space storage of user by fog computing to build a distributed storage service and augment storage capacity.

Naming, Identification and Resolution

There exists many components and objects in fog computing. On the basis of fog algorithm, the availability of many applications actively offering different services. As DNS (Domain Name System) of a computer network, naming, identification and resolution patterns in the Fog computing is most essential to address, authentication of identity, objects handling, data communication, services and object tracking and so on. The conventional naming approaches like DNS and URI (Uniform Resource Identifier) have been widely utilized in present networks. For satisfying the fog computing criterion few of the novel approaches are recommended; for instance NDN (Named Data Networking) (Zhang et al., 2014) and Mobility First (Raychaudhuri et al., 2012).

Resource Management

Resource Management is to be prioritized in providing the resources and also services. To enable process with less latency, few of the techniques related to resource management and also scheduling must be examined. Those technologies will highly influence the latency during processing and at the time of decision making. Resources virtualization of the fog nodes is a way of effective management where there is possibility of allocating to too many users. Context-awareness technology contributes to the efficient resources and also service provisioning in the fog computing. Based on the energy and resource management approach, the context awareness will effectively increases the utilization of resources and saves energy (Sharma et al., 2017) and further details about resource management will be discussed in the Resource management section of this chapter.

Security and Privacy Protection

Being associated with the end users, fog node gadgets are generally arranged in few of the locations at which the security and surveillance is poor. So that they can find harmful attack (Hu et al., 2017; Qiu et al., 2017). For instance, man-in-the-middle attack is considered as one of the way to intrude the information (Lee et al., 2015). During this fog node components are replaced with the illegal ones. To overcome this issue there adopted encryption and decryption schemes. (Dsouza et al., 2015) introduced policy-based resource management and control of access in the fog environment to obtain safe interaction along with the interoperability between varied resources requested by the user.

RESOURCE MANAGEMENT

The main aim of this chapter is to address the issues of managing the resources in fog computing. In this section, the authors introduced the basic definition of resource management and the system model of fog computing. Resource management is said to an organised process of scheduling the available resources to the user's workloads through internet (Sukhpal Singh and Inderveer Chana, 2015). Virtual resources are allocated by the applications in optimized way whereas workloads should run at less time with low cost. In virtual environment, the effectiveness of resource management improves the utilization of resources along with user satisfaction. The issues regarding equipped and under equipped resources in available resource allocation methods. To overcome the above two issues a new technique is introduced called QoS aware resource management. Fog gadgets contains extra computational and also storage power. But for those gadgets it is impossible to give the resource power than by cloud. Hence a process known as efficient resource management in which a user can send requests on timely basis. Besides, the techniques of resource management which are available in fog computing are also run on timely basis.

A common 3-layered network of Fog computing is described in Figure 2. This architecture includes Cloud, Fog and User layers. A Cloud layer which comprises of several Cloud Data Centres (CDCs) with best performance computational parameters belonging to remote area which is far from where users been. Fog layer contains a group of some fog nodes (FNs) that extensively establishes nearer to users. The User layer comprises the user equipment which requires less latency with greater services by QoE computing. In Figure 2, the arrow denotes a virtual connection, denotes a physical connection and denotes a local connection between the nodes.

BACKGROUND

To better understand the resource management techniques, it is better to introduce the basic terminology used in it, which includes architectures and infrastructure and algorithms used in resource management in fog computing.

Architecture

The models used to resource management in Fog/Edge computing are categorized based on three factors such as Data flow, control and tenancy. Data flow architectures relies on direction of workloads and the data in computing ecosystem. For instance, workloads need to be moved from user gadgets to edge nodes otherwise from the cloud servers to edge nodes. Control architectures depend on the resource controlling in the computing ecosystem. Consider a mono controller which might be used to control multiple edge nodes otherwise a distributed model might be engaged. Tenancy architectures rely on support given to host various users in ecosystem. Suppose either one or more applications are to be hosted at an edge node.

Figure 2. System model of fog computing network

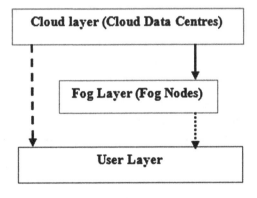

Data Flow Architectures

Data Flow Architectures concentrates mainly on the data/work load transfers with in the fog computing. Aggregation, sharing, and offloading are three types of architectures discussed in this section. In an *aggregation model*, each of the edge nodes retrieves data which is generated from various end gadgets. The objective of this model is optimizing the overheads by communication by ignoring the unwanted congestion during the data transmission out of the network's edge. The aggregation is broadly classified based on:

1. Techniques for Modelling and Implementing Aggregation: The basic techniques applied to support aggregation have created a major part of WSNs (Wireless Sensor Networks) (R. Raja gopalan et.al, 2006) and also distributed data flow processing. Denser and gigantic sensor networks are unable to route the complete information developed from the sensors to the centralized server. But instead it is necessary to utilize the intermediary nodes through the data path that aggregates the data. It is known as in-network data aggregation.
2. Techniques for Improving Aggregation: The implementation of aggregation is done so that to reduce various objectives existing in computing field. Those objectives bounds in between the efficiency of communication concerning bandwidth, key energy constraints and latency and the real aggregation quality that performs on an edge node.

In contrast to an aggregation model, another model known as a *Sharing model* is generally used only whenever the workload is distributed among peers. It aims at satisfying the computing needs of workloads over a mobile gadget with no offloading it to a cloud. It leads to provide a huge dynamic network in which the gadgets may connect or disconnect with the network without intimation. The research in this domain is usually done under the Mobile Cloud Computing (MCC) environment and also Mobile Edge Computing (MEC) and is considered as a successor for the peer-to-peer computing. The techniques of this sharing model are classified according to the basis of Control, Optimization and Cooperation (M D Assun et.al, 2018).

Offloading is considered as one of the techniques of dataflow architectures where a server, an application and relative data are moved towards the network's edge. It may augment the computing essentials of a user or cluster of user components or provide services in a cloud which processes the requests from source related gadgets. Offloading might be discriminated in dual ways are i. offloading from a User Device to an Edge: ii. Offloading from a Cloud to an Edge.

Control Architectures

Control Architectures are classified into two categories such as Centralized control architectures and Distributed Control architectures as shown in Figure 3. Centralized control architectures refer to utilization of individual controller which performs decision making over the evaluations, networks or interactions of edge resources. In contrast, during the distribution of decision making over the edge nodes then it refers to distributed architecture. Many research procedures are applied over *centralized architectures* and we identified two kinds of centralized architecture are Solver based and Graph Matching based. The former kind is said as the mathematical solvers which are usually utilized to generate the deployment and redeployment the schedules of workloads in the grids, clouds and also in clusters. Relative techniques are also adopted to the edge environments. The latter kind of architecture resembles an offloading structure which regards with device-to-device and also proposed the techniques of cloud offloading (X. Chen and J. Zhang, 2017).

There identified four distributed architecture such as (i) block chain-based, (ii) game theoretic-based, (iii) genetic algorithm-based, and (iv) sensor function virtualization-based. Block chain approach is considered as an underlying approach to implement the distributed control on edge computing systems (A. Stanciu, 2017). This technique is being built based on a generic standard IEC 61499 specifically for the distributed control systems. Game theoretic based approach is applied in order to obtain the offloading activities of distributed control in multi-channel wireless interference environment of mobile-edge cloud computing (X. Chen et.al, 2016).

In Genetic Algorithm-based the end components are the sensors that send the data to computing node through a network and makes decisions regarding total

Figure 3. Classification of control architectures

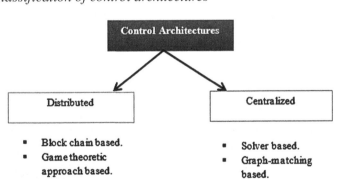

concerns of networking, computation and also on communication. The aim of Edge Mesh technique is to distribute the decision making on various edge nodes. Sensor Function Virtualization (SFV) is said as visionary concept where the decision making is modularized and also be deployed at any point in IoT network (Y. Sahni et.al, 2017).

Tenancy Architectures

The third classified architecture for the resource management in a fog/edge computing environment is Tenancy. In distributed systems tenancy refers whether the basis resources are distributed or not among various entities so that to reduce the utilization of resources and also energy efficiency. A multitenant is an ideal distributed system which has open access. The Open Fog reference architecture brings out multitenancy as a key feature for fog/edge computing. Figure 4 shows the four possibilities in the taxonomy.

Infrastructure

The framework to Fog/Edge computing allows equipment which includes with both the hardware and software to handle computation, network and resources for store. A framework to resource management belonging fog or edge computing is divided into three categories are Hardware, software and middleware. Recommended gadgets in hardware include, network gateways, Wi-Fi Access Points etc. for better resource efficiency. Currently these devices are equipped with SBCs (Single Board Computers) which gives better computational capabilities. System software runs directly over fog/edge computing resources. It controls the resources and administers those to applications of fog or edge computing. On the other hand, middleware runs

Figure 4. Taxonomy of tenancy based architectures

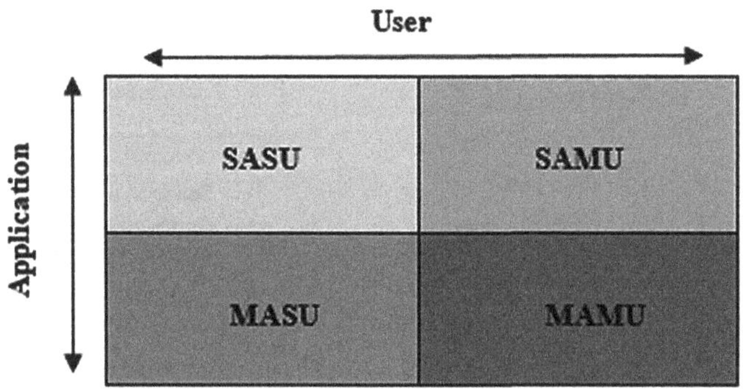

on operating system and contributes supportive services which are not supported by system software.

Hardware

Fog/edge computing develops computing environment which allows us to use less power mobile gadgets, home gateways and also routers. Hardware which is used in fog/edge computing is divided into two kinds namely Computation devices and network devices as shown in Figure 5. Computation devices to fog/edge computing comprises of SBCs and also commodity products specifically modelled to process fog/edge information. On the other side, Network devices used for in fog/edge computing includes with gateways, edge racks, Wi-Fi and routers which locates at the edge and primarily process the network traffics.

System Software

System software is said as a platform to the fog/edge and is specially modelled to run directly over the fog/edge nodes and controls computation, network along with the device's storage resources. Virtual Machines (VMs) and the containers are the instances. The system software that is used in fog/edge computing is divided into two types i.e. system virtualization and network virtualization as shown in Figure 6.

System Virtualization enables many Operating systems to work over an individual physical machine. It also enables the defects and isolation of the performance among many tenants in fog/edge. System virtualization bounds to usage of every tenant's resources so that they cannot monopolize total system resources which are available. In order to support system virtualization there included virtual machines, recent containers, and VM/container migration software. A collection of *virtualized resources* which are utilized for emulating a physical system constitutes a virtual

Figure 5. Classification of hardware

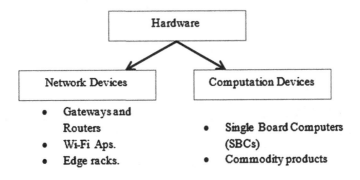

Figure 6. Classification of system software

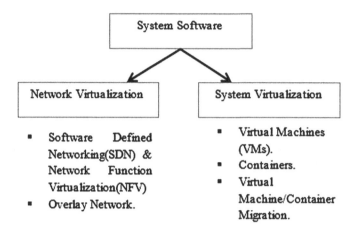

machine. A Virtualization software which is called as a hypervisor will virtualizes physical resources and yields the virtualized resources as a VM. (C.-H. Hong et.al, 2017). One of the emerging technologies in Cloud computing is Containers. These gives process-level a lightweight virtualization (N. Haydel et.al, 2015) As containers are multiplexed with one Linux kernel there is no need an extra layer of virtualization when compared to VMs. Even though they shares similar OS kernel, but still allows OS virtualization principles where every user is provided a separate environment to run the applications.

Network Virtualization includes the resources of hardware and software network to a virtual network which is a software-based administrative entity to a tenant. To support network virtualization; SDN and NFV and Overlays are included. A fog/edge cloud have a choice for adopting a *software-defined networking (SDN) and network functions virtualization (NFV)* to manage the network by software. NFV is complementary concept for SDN and is independent of it, even though they are usually integrated together in present clouds (D. Kreutz et.al, 2015). This is a virtual network which relies on a basic physical network and offers extra network services (for instance, peer-to- peer networks). An *overlay network* for the edge computing which is decentralized. No controller will be there in the decentralized edge computing as in cloud computing, hence every node is bound to network view.

Middleware

Middleware provides some complementary services for the system software. The middleware that is used in fog/edge computing is divided into four forms and is represented in Figure 7.

Figure 7. Classification of middleware

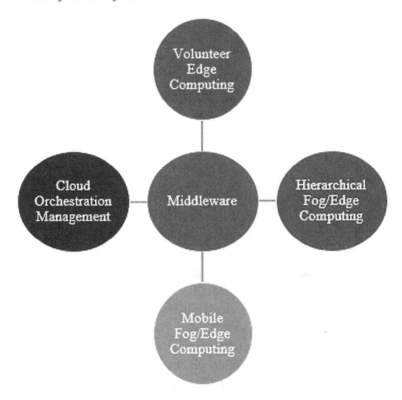

Algorithms

There exists numerous algorithms which can be used to implement Fog/Edge computing in an easy way (K.D. Kumar et.al, 2018). Under this phase, four algorithms such as discovery, benchmarking, load balancing and placement are to be discussed, and the broad classification of these algorithm is shown in in Figure 8. Discovery algorithm identifies the edge resources in a network which can be utilized for the distributed computation. Benchmarking apprehend the resource's performance so that to do decision making in improving the performance while implementation. Load balancing assigns workloads over resources on the basis of different criteria like priorities, fairness and so on. Placement identifies the related resources to organize workloads.

Figure 8. Classification of RM algorithms

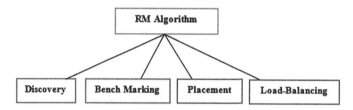

Discovery

Discovery is the process of finding the edge resources in order to deploy the workloads from cloud or from the user gadgets/sensors. Typically the research on edge computing considers that the edge resources are identified. Anyways it is hard to perform. During discovery process there employed three techniques which use programming requirements, handshaking protocols and sending messages. The first approach employs with programming essentials like Foglets and introduced a method to edge resources to connect with a cloud edge environment. The second technique utilizes handshaking protocols. The Edge-as-a-Service (EaaS) platform suggests a lightweight discovery protocol to gather similar edge resources (B. Varghese et.al, 2017). The platform needs a major node which might evaluate the existing network device that interacting with every node. The third technique employs by sending messages. The research suggests that the messages are delivered in network in which the services provided by nodes (referred to as processing nodes) that are Internet connected (G. Tato et.al, 2017).

Benchmarking

Benchmarking is said as de facto approach to evaluate performance (of entities like memory, CPU, storage etc.) of computing system. Prevailing benchmarks are typically the scientific applications which are not exactly suited for an edge (B. Varghese et.al, 2017). Instead, the voice-driven benchmarks and Internet-of-Things (IoT) applications are used (S. Sridhar et.al, 2017). It is necessary to use lightweight benchmarking tools for an edge.

Load-Balancing

As the edge data centers are arranged over a network edge, the issue in sharing tasks while using an efficient load balancing paradigm attains greater attention. (He et al., 2016) introduced SDCFN architecture (Software Defined Cloud/Fog Networking) for IoV (Internet of Vehicles). CooLoad (R. Beraldi et.al, 2017) introduced a supportive model of load-balancing between fog/edge data centers to reduce the suspension time of service. CooLoad allocates buffer to every data center in order to get clients requests. (Song et al., 2016) stated that prevailing algorithms of load balancing are unable to apply directly on the architectures of dynamic and peer-to-peer fog computing. (Puthal et al., 2018) concentrated on generating an efficient dynamic load-balancing algorithm by an authentication process for the edge data centers (R.A. Cherrueau et.al, 2017).

Placement

The available techniques are classified into dynamic condition-aware techniques and iterative techniques. Iterative techniques are again classified into two spaces: iterative over resources, and iterative over the problem spaces. Wang et al. find out that present work clears the placement related issues in the fog/edge computing based on some standard network conditions and already defined demands of resources (S. Wang et.al, 2017). (Taneja et al., 2017) introduced a placement paradigm for the hierarchical fog computing which exploits both the conventional cloud and present fog computing. The algorithm repeats from a fog towards a cloud for keeping the computation modules initially on existing fog nodes.

REINFORCEMENT LEARNING BASED RESOURCE MANAGEMENT

For the past decades, 5G and the IoT related concepts remained as an interesting for various researchers in the field of wireless communications. Currently some of the best studies in literature concentrate on attaining less latency to IoT applications. Reinforcement learning is an efficient framework for allocating the resources in F-RAN for 5G for guaranteeing the effective utilization of limited fog-nodes resources while preserving the latency. According to (J. Oueis et.al, 2015), determined load balancing problem in the fog computing and have used the fog clustering to enhance the user's experiences quality. (T. Gao et.al, 2017), cloud forecasts the user's mobility structures and mentions the essential resources to users requested contents and can be stored over clouds and in small cells. (Y. Sahni et.al, 2017) was studied about Cooperative computing and allocation of resources to attain ultra-low latency in FRAN in their paper. Along with the authors proposed and algorithm for edge mesh computing is suggested as a substitute than using centralized server in which the distribution of decision making tasks is done between the edge devices. (A. Pang et.al., 2017), considered different F-RAN models, small cells and macro base stations and proposed a paradigm to select F-RAN nodes for serving resource allocation in a proper way. (G.M Shafiqur Rahman, et.al, 2018) proposed a method content fetching is to improve the delivery rates when there is availability of requested content in cache about fog access edges. The issue with congestion raises while doing resource allocation with best signals obtained by an end user and it is spotlighted in (D. Vu, et.al, 2018).

In the recent years many research works are done to allocate the resources using reinforcement learning. One of such work is with the help of Fog Radio Access Network (FRAN) proposed by (Almuthanna T et.al, 2017). The general architecture of F-RAN is shown in Figure 9, in which the Fog Nodes (FNs) are associated to the Cloud Controller (CC) which contains Storage Pool (SP), Base Band Units (BBU). To overcome the expanding number of IoT devices and less-latency applications, fog networks are enabled at the network edge. Consequently, they are furnished with caching and computation and other signal processing abilities, in addition these resources are constrained and need to be used proficiently. The end user sends a request for the neighbouring FN to have network access. The FN evaluates the levels of priority and makes decision whether to give local service near edge by utilizing its own computing and processing resources otherwise to enable for cloud reference. We assume FNs capacity in terms of computational and processing is bound to n slots. In depth, we divided the timings into minimum steps as T=1,2 and so on and considering the high rate serial attending of users, single user at one time-step. Reinforcement Learning is considered as a third algorithm in Machine Learning (ML) whereas the first and second are supervised and unsupervised ML respectively. The notable thing in RL is, FN studies IoT environment through communication and later adapts in IoT environment. FN obtains betterment from environment for each and every task it performs and when the optimum based tasks learned, FN will increases its rewards at an average and meets its goal. Consider u_T as a request access from user with the utility at 'T' time. If FN confirms in taking action then a_T = serve and reward $r_{T+1} = u_T$ and a slot of FNs resources is occupied.

Load Balancing

In context of Fog networks, Load balancing refers to efficient sharing of workloads over a network of enabled fog nodes. It leads to increase the ability of the concurrent users and requested tasks reliability. It is classified into two kinds of methods namely static and dynamic methods of load balancing [20]. Static method of load balancing shares workload by forecasting the requested tasks, which are determined during the start of execution. The major drawback with such static methods is tasks allocation cannot be altered during execution to show the changes in the traffic load. Contrary

Figure 9. Fog-RAN based model

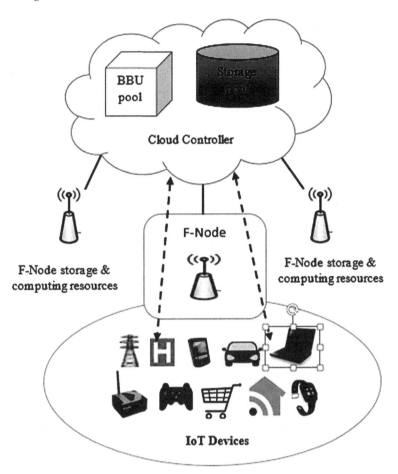

to a static method, dynamic load balancing assigns tasks at runtime when a node is under loaded. On the other side; it can alter the tasks allocation serially on the basis of recent knowledge on traffic loads. In the previous section, the authors has given the brief introduction about Software Defined Networking. In continuation Figure 10 shows the SDN based fog network. Here it considers dynamic method of load balancing by using mechanism of distributed fog computing where the nodes have ability to offload its computation tasks to relative node with existing queue spaces concerning computational abilities and sharing of demanded tasks. Classical DP algorithms have limited characteristics in the context of Reinforcement learning because of its assumption of precise model and computational cost. Q-learning is one of the classic-model free algorithms using reinforcement. It is usually used to identify the optimal state action policy to any MDP with no basic policy. Assume

Figure 10. SDN based fog architecture

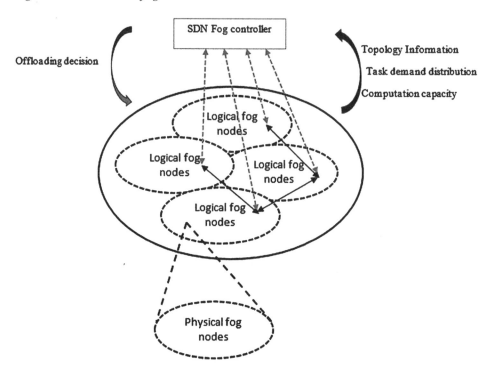

a control system, a learning controller iteratively tracks the present state's' and 'r' as reward. From those observations, it can alter its Q-function estimation for the state's' and action 'a' as shown in equation (1).

$$Q\big(s,a\big) \leftarrow (1-\alpha)Q\big(s,a\big) + \alpha\left[R\big(s,a\big) + \gamma' \overset{\max}{\in} A_{s'} Q\big(s',a'\big) \right] \tag{1}$$

Where 'α' is rate of learning (0<α<1), balancing the weight of what was already learned with weight of recent observation

CONCLUSION

Cloud computing is an emerging field with its three key features and its natural favourable circumstances, has few difficulties in the recent years. The key technologies of fog computing such as computing, communication and storage technologies along with naming conventions, resource management, security and privacy protection are addressed. The technical challenges to deal with the limited resources in fog computing have been routed. In any case, a couple of difficulties still exists to be made to improve the resource management in terms of capacity and execution time in fog computing. The key contributions in the three fields of architectures, infrastructures and algorithms are presented briefly. In the context of fog/edge computing, the architectures which are used for the resource management are classified based on the flow of data, control and tenancy. Infrastructure provides services to handle the evaluation, network and resources related to storage. The basic paradigms particularly for facilitating the fog/edge computing such as discovery, benchmarking, load balancing, and placement are presented. Resource management is said to an organised process of scheduling the available resources to the user's workloads through internet. This framework for allocating the resources in F-RAN for 5G for guaranteeing the effective utilization of limited fog-nodes is efficient compared with the state-of-the art techniques. Although, reinforcement learning is giving the better results, still many challenges require the progress in research towards the efficient allocation of the nodes in the fog environment.

REFERENCES

Aazam, M., & Huh, E. N. (2016). Fog computing: The cloud-iot/ioe middleware paradigm. *IEEE Potentials*, *35*(3), 40–44. doi:10.1109/MPOT.2015.2456213

Ahmad, R. W., Gani, A., Hamid, S. H. A., Shiraz, M., Yousafzai, A., & Xia, F. (2015). A survey on virtual machine migration and server consolidation frameworks for cloud data centers. *Journal of Network and Computer Applications*, *52*, 11–25. doi:10.1016/j.jnca.2015.02.002

Angelakis, V., Avgouleas, I., Pappas, N., Fitzgerald, E., & Yuan, D. (2016). Allocation of heterogeneous resources of an IoT device to flexible services. *IEEE Internet of Things Journal*, *3*(5), 691–700. doi:10.1109/JIOT.2016.2535163

Balasubramanian, A., Levine, B., & Venkataramani, A. (2007, August). DTN routing as a resource allocation problem. *Computer Communication Review*, *37*(4), 373–384. doi:10.1145/1282427.1282422

Beraldi, R., Mtibaa, A., & Alnuweiri, H. (2017, May). Cooperative load balancing scheme for edge computing resources. In *2017 Second International Conference on Fog and Mobile Edge Computing (FMEC)* (pp. 94-100). IEEE. 10.1109/FMEC.2017.7946414

Bhushan, S. B., & Pradeep, R. C. (2016). A Network QoS Aware Service Ranking Using Hybrid AHP-PROMETHEE Method in Multi-Cloud Domain. *International Journal of Engineering Research in Africa*, *24*, 153–164. doi:10.4028/www.scientific. net/JERA.24.153

Bhushan, S. B., & Reddy, P. (2016). A four-level linear discriminant analysis based service selection in the cloud environment. *International Journal of Technology*, *5*, 859–870. doi:10.14716/ijtech.v7i5.3546

Bhushan, S. B., & Reddy, P. C. (2018). A hybrid meta-heuristic approach for QoS-aware cloud service composition. *International Journal of Web Services Research*, *15*(2), 1–20. doi:10.4018/IJWSR.2018040101

Chen, X., Jiao, L., Li, W., & Fu, X. (2015). Efficient multi-user computation offloading for mobile-edge cloud computing. *IEEE/ACM Transactions on Networking*, *24*(5), 2795–2808. doi:10.1109/TNET.2015.2487344

Chen, X., Jiao, L., Li, W., & Fu, X. (2015). Efficient multi-user computation offloading for mobile-edge cloud computing. *IEEE/ACM Transactions on Networking*, *24*(5), 2795–2808. doi:10.1109/TNET.2015.2487344

Chen, X., & Zhang, J. (2017, May). When D2D meets cloud: Hybrid mobile task offloadings in fog computing. In 2017 IEEE international conference on communications (ICC) (pp. 1-6). IEEE.

Cherrueau, R. A., Pertin, D., Simonet, A., Lebre, A., & Simonin, M. (2017, May). Toward a holistic framework for conducting scientific evaluations of openstack. In *Proceedings of the 17th IEEE/ACM International Symposium on Cluster, Cloud and Grid Computing* (pp. 544-548). IEEE Press. 10.1109/CCGRID.2017.87

Dahrouj, H., Douik, A., Dhifallah, O., Al-Naffouri, T. Y., & Alouini, M. S. (2015). Resource allocation in heterogeneous cloud radio access networks: Advances and challenges. *IEEE Wireless Communications*, *22*(3), 66–73. doi:10.1109/ MWC.2015.7143328

de Assuncao, M. D., da Silva Veith, A., & Buyya, R. (2018). Distributed data stream processing and edge computing: A survey on resource elasticity and future directions. *Journal of Network and Computer Applications*, *103*, 1–17. doi:10.1016/j. jnca.2017.12.001

Gao, T., Chen, M., Gu, H., & Yin, C. (2017, October). Reinforcement learning based resource allocation in cache-enabled small cell networks with mobile users. In *2017 IEEE/CIC International Conference on Communications in China (ICCC)* (pp. 1-6). IEEE. 10.1109/ICCChina.2017.8330448

Haydel, N., Madey, G., Gesing, S., Dakkak, A., de Gonzalo, S. G., Taylor, I., & Hwu, W. M. W. (2015, December). Enhancing the usability and utilization of accelerated architectures via docker. In *Proceedings of the 8th International Conference on Utility and Cloud Computing* (pp. 361-367). IEEE Press.

He, X., Ren, Z., Shi, C., & Fang, J. (2016). A novel load balancing strategy of software-defined cloud/fog networking in the Internet of Vehicles. *China Communications*, *13*(Supplement2), 140–149. doi:10.1109/CC.2016.7833468

IDC. (2019). *Forecasts Worldwide Shipments of Wearables to Surpass 200 Million in 2019, Driven by Strong Smartwatch Growth and the Emergence of Smarter Watches, document #prUS41100116*. Framingham, MA: IDC.

IDC. (2015-2019), *Worldwide Internet of Things Forecast Update*. document #US40983216. IDC.

Intharawijitr, K., Iida, K., & Koga, H. (2016, March). Analysis of fog model considering computing and communication latency in 5G cellular networks. In *2016 IEEE International Conference on Pervasive Computing and Communication Workshops (PerCom Workshops)* (pp. 1-4). IEEE. 10.1109/PERCOMW.2016.7457059

Jain, R. K., Chiu, D. M. W., & Hawe, W. R. (1984). *A quantitative measure of fairness and discrimination*. Hudson, MA: Eastern Research Laboratory, Digital Equipment Corporation.

Kim, M., & Ko, I. Y. (2015, June). An efficient resource allocation approach based on a genetic algorithm for composite services in IoT environments. In *2015 IEEE International Conference on Web Services* (pp. 543-550). IEEE. 10.1109/ICWS.2015.78

Kreutz, D., Ramos, F. M., Verissimo, P., Rothenberg, C. E., Azodolmolky, S., & Uhlig, S. (2015). Software-defined networking: A comprehensive survey. *Proceedings of the IEEE*, *103*(1), 14–76. doi:10.1109/JPROC.2014.2371999

Kumar, K. D., & Umamaheswari, E. (2017). *An Authenticated, Secure Virtualization Management System in Cloud Computing*. Advances in Smart Computing and Bioinformatics.

Kumar, K.D., & Umamaheswari, E. (2018). Efficient Cloud Resource Scaling based on Prediction Approaches. *International Journal of Engineering & Technology*, *7*(4.10).

Kumar, K. D., & Umamaheswari, E. (2018). Prediction methods for effective resource provisioning in cloud computing: A Survey. *Multiagent and Grid Systems*, *14*(3), 283–305. doi:10.3233/MGS-180292

Manate, B., Fortis, T. F., & Negru, V. (2014). Optimizing cloud resources allocation for an Internet of Things architecture. *Scalable Computing: Practice and Experience*, *15*(4), 345–355.

Ningning, S., Chao, G., Xingshuo, A., & Qiang, Z. (2016). Fog computing dynamic load balancing mechanism based on graph repartitioning. *China Communications*, *13*(3), 156–164. doi:10.1109/CC.2016.7445510

Oueis, J., Strinati, E. C., & Barbarossa, S. (2015, May). The fog balancing: Load distribution for small cell cloud computing. In *2015 IEEE 81st Vehicular Technology Conference (VTC Spring)* (pp. 1-6). IEEE.

Pang, A. C., Chung, W. H., Chiu, T. C., & Zhang, J. (2017, June). Latency-driven cooperative task computing in multi-user fog-radio access networks. In *2017 IEEE 37th International Conference on Distributed Computing Systems (ICDCS)* (pp. 615-624). IEEE. 10.1109/ICDCS.2017.83

Poluru, R. K., Bhushan, B., Muzamil, B. S., Rayani, P. K., & Reddy, P. K. (2019). Applications of Domain-Specific Predictive Analytics Applied to Big Data. In *Sentiment Analysis and Knowledge Discovery in Contemporary Business* (pp. 289–306). IGI Global. doi:10.4018/978-1-5225-4999-4.ch016

Puthal, D., Obaidat, M. S., Nanda, P., Prasad, M., Mohanty, S. P., & Zomaya, A. Y. (2018). Secure and sustainable load balancing of edge data centers in fog computing. *IEEE Communications Magazine*, *56*(5), 60–65. doi:10.1109/MCOM.2018.1700795

Rahman, G. S., Peng, M., Zhang, K., & Chen, S. (2018). Radio resource allocation for achieving ultra-low latency in fog radio access networks. *IEEE Access: Practical Innovations, Open Solutions*, *6*, 17442–17454. doi:10.1109/ACCESS.2018.2805303

Rajagopalan, R., & Varshney, P. K. (2006). Data aggregation techniques in sensor networks. *Survey (London, England)*.

Rayani, P. K., Bhushan, B., & Thakare, V. R. (2018). Multi-Layer Token Based Authentication Through Honey Password in Fog Computing. *International Journal of Fog Computing*, *1*(1), 50–62. doi:10.4018/IJFC.2018010104

Raychaudhuri, D., Nagaraja, K., & Venkataramani, A. (2012). Mobilityfirst: A robust and trustworthy mobility-centric architecture for the future internet. *Mobile Computing and Communications Review*, *16*(3), 2–13. doi:10.1145/2412096.2412098

Rimal, B. P., Choi, E., & Lumb, I. (2009, August). A taxonomy and survey of cloud computing systems. In *2009 Fifth International Joint Conference on INC, IMS and IDC* (pp. 44-51). IEEE. 10.1109/NCM.2009.218

Sahni, Y., Cao, J., Zhang, S., & Yang, L. (2017). Edge Mesh: A new paradigm to enable distributed intelligence in Internet of Things. *IEEE Access: Practical Innovations, Open Solutions, 5*, 16441–16458. doi:10.1109/ACCESS.2017.2739804

Singh, S., & Chana, I. (2016). QoS-aware autonomic resource management in cloud computing: A systematic review. *ACM Computing Surveys, 48*(3), 42.

Sridhar, S., & Tolentino, M. E. (2017, June). Evaluating Voice Interaction Pipelines at the Edge. In *2017 IEEE International Conference on Edge Computing (EDGE)* (pp. 248-251). IEEE. 10.1109/IEEE.EDGE.2017.46

Stanciu, A. (2017, May). Blockchain based distributed control system for edge computing. In *2017 21st International Conference on Control Systems and Computer Science (CSCS)* (pp. 667-671). IEEE. 10.1109/CSCS.2017.102

Taneja, M., & Davy, A. (2017, May). Resource aware placement of IoT application modules in Fog-Cloud Computing Paradigm. In *2017 IFIP/IEEE Symposium on Integrated Network and Service Management (IM)* (pp. 1222-1228). IEEE. 10.23919/INM.2017.7987464

Tato, G., Bertier, M., & Tedeschi, C. (2017, December). Designing Overlay Networks for Decentralized Clouds. In *2017 IEEE International Conference on Cloud Computing Technology and Science (CloudCom)* (pp. 391-396). IEEE. 10.1109/CloudCom.2017.64

Truong, N. B., Lee, G. M., & Ghamri-Doudane, Y. (2015, May). Software defined networking-based vehicular adhoc network with fog computing. In *2015 IFIP/IEEE International Symposium on Integrated Network Management (IM)* (pp. 1202-1207). IEEE. 10.1109/INM.2015.7140467

Vaquero, L. M., & Rodero-Merino, L. (2014). Finding your way in the fog: Towards a comprehensive definition of fog computing. *Computer Communication Review, 44*(5), 27–32. doi:10.1145/2677046.2677052

Varghese, B., Akgun, O., Miguel, I., Thai, L., & Barker, A. (2016). *Cloud benchmarking for maximising performance of scientific applications. IEEE Transactions on Cloud Computing.*

Varghese, B., Wang, N., Li, J., & Nikolopoulos, D. S. (2017). *Edge-as-a-Service: Towards distributed Cloud architectures.* arXiv preprint arXiv:1710.10090

Vu, D. N., Dao, N. N., & Cho, S. (2018, January). Downlink sum-rate optimization leveraging Hungarian method in fog radio access networks. In *2018 International Conference on Information Networking (ICOIN)* (pp. 56-60). IEEE. 10.1109/ICOIN.2018.8343083

Wang, S., Urgaonkar, R., He, T., Chan, K., Zafer, M., & Leung, K. K. (2016). Dynamic service placement for mobile micro-clouds with predicted future costs. *IEEE Transactions on Parallel and Distributed Systems*, *28*(4), 1002–1016. doi:10.1109/TPDS.2016.2604814

Zeng, D., Gu, L., Guo, S., Cheng, Z., & Yu, S. (2016). Joint optimization of task scheduling and image placement in fog computing supported software-defined embedded system. *IEEE Transactions on Computers*, *65*(12), 3702–3712. doi:10.1109/TC.2016.2536019

Zhang, W., Lin, B., Yin, Q., & Zhao, T. (2017). Infrastructure deployment and optimization of fog network based on microdc and lrpon integration. *Peer-to-Peer Networking and Applications*, *10*(3), 579–591. doi:10.100712083-016-0476-x

Zheng, X., Cai, Z., Li, J., & Gao, H. (2016). A study on application-aware scheduling in wireless networks. *IEEE Transactions on Mobile Computing*, *16*(7), 1787–1801. doi:10.1109/TMC.2016.2613529

Compilation of References

2015 . Hack my laundry card? (n.d.). Available: https://www.reddit. com/r/hacking/\ comments/2pjy5x/hack my laundry card

Aazam, M., & Huh, E.-N. (2014). Fog computing and smart gateway based communication for cloud of things. *Proc. Future Internet of Things and Cloud (Fi Cloud).International Conference on*, 464–70.

Aazam, M., & Huh. (2015). Dynamic resource provisioning through Fog micro datacenter. *2015 IEEE International Conference on Pervasive Computing and Communication Workshops.* 10.1109/PERCOMW.2015.7134002

Aazam, M., & Huh, E. N. (2016). Fog computing: The cloud-iot/ioe middleware paradigm. *IEEE Potentials*, *35*(3), 40–44. doi:10.1109/MPOT.2015.2456213

Agarwal, S., Dunagan, J., Jain, N., Saroiu, S., Wolman, A., & Bhogan, H. (2010). Volley: Automated data placement for geo-distributed cloud services. NSDI.

Agarwal, S., Yadav, S., & Yadav, A. K. (2017). An Efficient Architecture for Resource Provisioning in Fog Computing. *International Journal of Science and Research*, *6*(1), 2065–2069.

Ahmad, R. W., Gani, A., Hamid, S. H. A., Shiraz, M., Yousafzai, A., & Xia, F. (2015). A survey on virtual machine migration and server consolidation frameworks for cloud data centers. *Journal of Network and Computer Applications*, *52*, 11–25. doi:10.1016/j.jnca.2015.02.002

Ahmed, A., & Ahmed, E. (2016). A survey on mobile edge computing. Intelligent systems and control (ISCO), 2016 10th. doi:10.1109/ISCO.2016.7727082

Alrawais, A., Alhothaily, A., Hu, C., & Cheng, X. (2017). Fog Computing for the Internet of Things: Security and Privacy Issues. *IEEE Internet Computing*, *21*(2), 34–42. doi:10.1109/MIC.2017.37

Anbarasi, S. R., & Gunasekaran, S. (2014, October). The Feasibility of SETOIBS and SRT-IBOOS protocols in Cluster-based wireless sensor networks. *International Journal of Innovative Research in Computer and Communication Engineering*, *2*(10).

Angelakis, V., Avgouleas, I., Pappas, N., Fitzgerald, E., & Yuan, D. (2016). Allocation of heterogeneous resources of an IoT device to flexible services. *IEEE Internet of Things Journal*, *3*(5), 691–700. doi:10.1109/JIOT.2016.2535163

Angra, S., & Ahuja, S. (2017). Machine learning and its applications: A review. *2017 International Conference on Big Data Analytics and Computational Intelligence (ICBDAC)*, 57-60. 10.1109/ICBDACI.2017.8070809

Atlam, H. F., Alenezi, A., Hussein, R. K., & Wills, G. B. (2018). Validation of an Adaptive Risk-Based Access Control Model for the Internet of Things. *Int. J. Comput. Netw. Inf. Secur.*, *10*, 26–35.

Atlam, H. F., Alenezi, A., Walters, R. J., & Wills, G. B. (2017). An Overview of Risk Estimation Techniques in Risk-based Access Control for the Internet of Things. *Proceedings of the 2nd International Conference on Internet of Things, Big Data and Security (IoTBDS 2017)*, 254–260. 10.5220/0006292602540260

Atlam, H., Walters, R., & Wills, G. (2018). Fog Computing and the Internet of Things: A Review. *Big Data and Cognitive Computing*, *2*(2), 10. doi:10.3390/bdcc2020010

Aurora. (2018). *We Do Self-Driving Cars.* Available: https://aurora.tech/

Autox. (2018). *Democratizing Autonomy.* Available: https://www.autox.ai/

Bahrpeyma, F., Haghighi, H., & Zakerolhosseini, A. (2015). An adaptive RL based approach for dynamic resource provisioning in Cloud virtualized data centers. *Computing*, *97*(12), 1209–1234. doi:10.100700607-015-0455-8

Bakker, T., Bontsema, J., & Müller, J. (2010). Systematic design of an autonomous platform for robotic weeding. *Journal of Terramechanics*, *47*(2), 63–73. doi:10.1016/j.jterra.2009.06.002

Balasubramanian, A., Levine, B., & Venkataramani, A. (2007, August). DTN routing as a resource allocation problem. *Computer Communication Review*, *37*(4), 373–384. doi:10.1145/1282427.1282422

Balevi & Gitlin. (2018). Optimizing the Number of Fog Nodes for Cloud-Fog-Thing Networks. *IEEE Access, 6*, 11173-11183.

Baresi, L., Guinea, S., Quattrocchi, G., & Tamburri, D. A. (2016). MicroCloud: A Container-Based Solution for Efficient Resource Management in the Cloud. In *2016 IEEE International Conference on Smart Cloud (SmartCloud)* (pp. 218–223). New York: IEEE. 10.1109/SmartCloud.2016.42

Bechkit, W., Challal, Y., Bouabdallah, A., & Tarokh, V. (2013, February). A Highly Scalable Key Pre-distribution Scheme for wireless sensor networks. *IEEE Transactions on Wireless Communications*, *12*(2), 948–959. doi:10.1109/TWC.2012.010413.120732

Becker, J., Colas, M. B. A., Nordbruch, S., & Fausten, M. (2014). *Bosch's Vision and Roadmap Toward Fully Autonomous Driving in Road Vehicle Automation.* Springer International Publishing.

Ben Zhang, Kolb, Chan, Lutz, Allman, Wawrzynek, … Kubiatowicz. (2015). The cloud is not enough: Saving iot from the cloud. HotStorage.

Beraldi, R., Mtibaa, A., & Alnuweiri, H. (2017, May). Cooperative load balancing scheme for edge computing resources. In *2017 Second International Conference on Fog and Mobile Edge Computing (FMEC)* (pp. 94-100). IEEE. 10.1109/FMEC.2017.7946414

Bhushan, S. B., & Pradeep, R. C. (2016). A Network QoS Aware Service Ranking Using Hybrid AHP-PROMETHEE Method in Multi-Cloud Domain. *International Journal of Engineering Research in Africa*, *24*, 153–164. doi:10.4028/www.scientific.net/JERA.24.153

Bhushan, S. B., & Reddy, P. (2016). A four-level linear discriminant analysis based service selection in the cloud environment. *International Journal of Technology*, *5*, 859–870. doi:10.14716/ijtech.v7i5.3546

Bhushan, S. B., & Reddy, P. C. H. (2018). A Hybrid Meta-Heuristic Approach for QoS-Aware Cloud Service Composition. *International Journal of Web Services Research*, *15*(2), 1–20. doi:10.4018/IJWSR.2018040101

Bkassiny, M., Li, Y., & Jayaweera, S. K. (2013). A Survey on Machine-Learning Techniques in Cognitive Radios. *IEEE Communications Surveys and Tutorials*, *15*(3), 1136–1158. doi:10.1109/SURV.2012.100412.00017

Boneh & Franklin. (2003). Identity-Based Encryption from the weil pairing. *Society for Industrial and Applied Mathematics (SIAM). Journal of Computers*, *32*(3), 586–615.

Bonomi, F., Milito, R., Zhu, J., & Addepalli, S. (2012). Fog computing and its role in the internet of things. In *Proceedings of the First Edition of the MCC Workshop on Mobile Cloud Computing*. ACM. Available: http://doi.acm.org/10.1145/2342509.2342513

Bonomi, F., Milito, R., Natarajan, P., & Zhu, J. (2014). *Fog computing: A platform for internet of things and analytics, Big Data and Internet of Things: A Roadmap for Smart Environments*. Springer.

Bonomi, F., Milito, R., Natarajan, P., & Zhu, J. (2014). Fog Computing: A Platform for Internet of Things and Analytics. In N. Bessis & C. Dobre (Eds.), *Big Data and Internet of Things: A Roadmap for Smart Environments* (Vol. 546, pp. 169–186). Cham: Springer International Publishing. doi:10.1007/978-3-319-05029-4_7

Bonomi, F., Milito, R., Zhu, J., & Addepalli, S. (2012). Fog computing and its role in the internet of things. *Proceedings of the first edition of the MCC workshop on Mobile cloud computing*, 13–16. 10.1145/2342509.2342513

Bonomi, F., Milito, R., Zhu, J., & Addepalli, S. (2017). Fog computing and its role in the internet of things. *Proc. Proceedings of the first edition of the MCC workshop on Mobile cloud computing*.

Botta, A., Gallo, L., & Ventre, G. (2019). Cloud, Fog, and Dew Robotics: Architectures For Next Generation Applications. In *7th IEEE International Conference on Mobile Cloud Computing, Services, And Engineering (Mobilecloud)* (pp. 16-23). IEEE. 10.1109/MobileCloud.2019.00010

Boujelben, M., Youssef, H., Mzid, R., & Abid, M. (2011, April). IKM – An identity-based key management scheme for heterogeneous sensor networks. *Journal of Communication*, *6*(2).

BowmanDebray, & Peterson. (1993). Reasoning about naming systems. *ACM Trans. Program. Lang. Syst., 15*(5), 795-825.

Brogi, A., Forti, S., Ibrahim, A., & Rinaldi, L. (2018). Bonsai in the Fog: An active learning lab with Fog computing. In *2018 Third International Conference on Fog and Mobile Edge Computing (FMEC)* (pp. 79–86). Barcelona: IEEE. 10.1109/FMEC.2018.8364048

Buehler, M., Iagnemma, K., & Singh, S. (Eds.). (2007). *The 2005 DARPA Grand Challenge: The Great Robot Race.* Springer-Verlag Berlin Heidelberg.

Buehler, M., Iagnemma, K., Singh, S. (Eds.). (2009). *The DARPA Urban Challenge: Autonomous Vehicles In City Traffic.* Springer-Verlag Berlin Heidelberg.

Butun, I., Kantarci, B., & Erol-Kantarci, M. (2015). Anomaly detection and privacy preservation in cloud-centric internet of things. In *Communication Workshop (ICCW), 2015 IEEE International Conference on.* IEEE. 10.1109/ICCW.2015.7247572

Cariou, C., Lenain, R., Thuilot, B., & Berducat, M. (2009). Automatic guidance of a four-wheel-steering mobile robot for accurate field operations. *Journal of Field Robotics, 26*(6-7), 504–518. doi:10.1002/rob.20282

Casalicchio, E., Menascé, D. A., & Aldhalaan, A. (2013). Autonomic resource provisioning in cloud systems with availability goals. In *Proceedings of the 2013 ACM Cloud and Autonomic Computing Conference on - CAC '13* (p. 1). Miami, FL: ACM Press. 10.1145/2494621.2494623

Chang. (2004). Cryptanalysis of the Tseng-Jan anonymous conference key distribution system without using a one-way hash function. *Information and Security. International Journal (Toronto, Ont.), 15*(1), 110–114.

Chatterjee, K. (2012). *An Improved ID-Based Key Management Scheme in Wireless Sensor Network* (Vol. 7332). Springer.

Chen & Kudla. (2003). *Identity-based Authenticated Key agreement protocols from pairings.* Academic Press.

Chen, Cheng, Malone-Lee, & Smart. (2006). Efficient ID-KEM based on the Sakai-Kasahara key construction. *IEEE Proceedings Information Security, 153*(1).

Chen, N., Chen, Y., Blasch, E., Ling, H., You, Y., & Ye, X. (2017). Enabling smart urban surveillance at the edge. *2017 IEEE International Conference on Smart Cloud (Smart Cloud),* 109–119. 10.1109/SmartCloud.2017.24

Chen, N., Chen, Y., Song, S., Huang, C.-T., & Ye, X. (2016). Smart urban surveillance using fog computing. *Edge Computing (SEC), IEEE/ACM Symposium on,* 95–96.

Chen, X., & Zhang, J. (2017, May). When D2D meets cloud: Hybrid mobile task offloadings in fog computing. In *2017 IEEE international conference on communications (ICC)* (pp. 1-6). IEEE.

Chen, Y., Peng, X., & Zhang, T. (2011). Application of wireless sensor networks in the field of agriculture. In *2011 Louisville, Kentucky, August 7-10, 2011* (p. 1). American Society of Agricultural and Biological Engineers.

Chen, X., Jiao, L., Li, W., & Fu, X. (2015). Efficient multi-user computation offloading for mobile-edge cloud computing. *IEEE/ACM Transactions on Networking*, 24(5), 2795–2808. doi:10.1109/TNET.2015.2487344

Cherrueau, R. A., Pertin, D., Simonet, A., Lebre, A., & Simonin, M. (2017, May). Toward a holistic framework for conducting scientific evaluations of openstack. In *Proceedings of the 17th IEEE/ACM International Symposium on Cluster, Cloud and Grid Computing* (pp. 544-548). IEEE Press. 10.1109/CCGRID.2017.87

Choie. (2005). Efficient identity-based authenticated key agreement protocol from pairings. In Applied Mathematics and Computation (vol. 162, pp. 179–188). Elsevier.

Christopher, M. (1995). *Bishop, Neural networks for pattern recognition.* Oxford University Press.

Cisco. (2015). *Fog computing and the internet of things: Extend the cloud to where the things are.* Cisco White Paper.

Coin base laundromat hack. (n.d.). Available: https://www.youtube. com/watch?v=YS7rguwrauo

Cortes, C., & Vapnik, V. (1995). Support-vector Networks. *Machine Learning*, 20(3), 273–297. doi:10.1007/BF00994018

Cortés, R., Bonnaire, X., Marin, O., & Sens, P. (2015). Stream Processing of Healthcare Sensor Data: Studying User Traces to Identify Challenges from a Big Data Perspective. *Procedia Computer Science*, 52, 1004–1009. doi:10.1016/j.procs.2015.05.093

Coutinho, E. F., Gomes, D. G., & de Souza, J. N. (2015). An Autonomic Computing-based architecture for cloud computing elasticity. In *2015 Latin American Network Operations and Management Symposium (LANOMS)* (pp. 111–112). Joao Pessoa, Brazil: IEEE. 10.1109/LANOMS.2015.7332681

da Silva, R. A. C., & da Fonseca, N. L. S. (2018) Resource Allocation Mechanism for a Fog-Cloud Infrastructure. In *2018 IEEE International Conference on Communications (ICC)*, Kansas City, MO. 10.1109/ICC.2018.8422237

Dahrouj, H., Douik, A., Dhifallah, O., Al-Naffouri, T. Y., & Alouini, M. S. (2015). Resource allocation in heterogeneous cloud radio access networks: Advances and challenges. *IEEE Wireless Communications*, 22(3), 66–73. doi:10.1109/MWC.2015.7143328

Dai, Y., Du Xu, S. M., & Zhang, Y. (2018). Joint Computation Offloading and User Association in Multi-Task Mobile Edge Computing. *IEEE Transactions on Vehicular Technology*, 67(12), 12313–12325. doi:10.1109/TVT.2018.2876804

Das, A. (2014). Consistent reidentification in a camera network. In *Computer Vision–ECCV 2014* (pp. 330–345). Springer.

Dastjerdi, A. V., & Buyya, R. (2016). Fog Computing: Helping the Internet of Things Realize Its Potential. *Computer*, *49*(8), 112–116. doi:10.1109/MC.2016.245

de Assuncao, M. D., da Silva Veith, A., & Buyya, R. (2018). Distributed data stream processing and edge computing: A survey on resource elasticity and future directions. *Journal of Network and Computer Applications*, *103*, 1–17. doi:10.1016/j.jnca.2017.12.001

Delicato, F. C., Pires, P. F., & Batistal, T. (2017). *Resource Management for the Internet of Things*. SpringerBriefs in Computer Science. doi:10.1007/978-3-319-54247-8

Deng, R., Lu, R., Lai, C., & Luan, H. (2016). *Optimal Workload Allocation in Fog-Cloud Computing Towards Balanced Delay and Power Consumption. IEEE Internet of Things Journal.*

Dickmanns, E. D., & Zapp, A. (1987). Autonomous High Speed Road Vehicle Guidance By Computer Vision 1. *IFAC Proceedings Volumes*, *20*(5), 221–226.

Dutreilh, X., Kirgizov, S., Melekhova, O., Malenfant, J., & Rivierre, N. (2011). *Using Reinforcement Learning for Autonomic Resource Allocation in Clouds: Towards a Fully Automated Workflow*. Academic Press.

Elrob. (2018). *The European Land Robot Trial (Elrob)*. Available: Http://Www.Elrob.Org/

Ferrández-Pastor, F.-J., Mora, H., Jimeno-Morenilla, A., & Volckaert, B. (2018). Deployment of IoT Edge and Fog Computing Technologies to Develop Smart Building Services. *Sustainability, MDPI, Open Access Journal*, *10*(11), 1–23.

Forman, G. (2003, March). An extensive empirical study of feature selection metrics for text classification. *Journal of Machine Learning Research*, *3*, 1289–1305.

Friedman, V. (2018). *On the edge: Solving the challenges of edge computing in the era of iot*. Available: https://data-economy.com/ on-the-edge-solving-the-challenges-of-edge-computing-in-the-era-of-iot/

Frohlich, B., & Plate, J. (2000). The cubic mouse: a new device for three-dimensional input. In *Proceedings of the SIGCHI conference on Human factors in computing systems, CHI '00*, (pp. 526-531). New York, NY: ACM. 10.1145/332040.332491

Gao, T., Chen, M., Gu, H., & Yin, C. (2017, October). Reinforcement learning based resource allocation in cache-enabled small cell networks with mobile users. In *2017 IEEE/CIC International Conference on Communications in China (ICCC)* (pp. 1-6). IEEE. 10.1109/ICCChina.2017.8330448

Gentry, C., & Halevi, S. (2010). *Implementing Gentry's fully-homomorphic encryption scheme*. Preliminary version. Retrieved from https://researcher.ibm

Giang, N., Kim, S., Kim, D., Jung, M., & Kastner, W. (2014). Extending the EPCIS with Building Automation Systems: A New Information System for the Internet of Things. *Proceedings of the 2014 Eighth International Conference on Innovative Mobile and Internet Services in Ubiquitous Computing*, 364–369. 10.1109/IMIS.2014.50

Gomez, A. E., Alencar, F. A. R., Prado, P. V., Osorio, F. S., & Wolf, D. F. (2014). Traffic Lights Detection and State Estimation Using Hidden Markov Models. *Intelligent Vehicles Symposium (IV)*, 750–755. 10.1109/IVS.2014.6856486

Gondchawar, N., &Kawitkar, R. S. (2016). IoT based smart Agriculture. *International Journal of Advanced Research in Computer and Communication Engineering, 5*(6).

Hafizul Islam, S. K., & Biswas, G. P. (2012). An improved pairing-free identity-based authenticated key agreement protocol based on ECC. *Procedia Engineering, 30*, 499–507. doi:10.1016/j. proeng.2012.01.890

Hamner, B., Bergerman, M., & Singh, S. (2011). Autonomous orchard vehicles for specialty crops production. In *2011 Louisville, Kentucky, August 7-10, 2011* (p. 1). American Society of Agricultural and Biological engineers.

Haydel, N., Madey, G., Gesing, S., Dakkak, A., de Gonzalo, S. G., Taylor, I., & Hwu, W. M. W. (2015, December). Enhancing the usability and utilization of accelerated architectures via docker. In *Proceedings of the 8th International Conference on Utility and Cloud Computing* (pp. 361-367). IEEE Press.

Hengartner, U., & Steenkiste, P. (2005). Exploiting hierarchical identity-based encryption for access control to pervasive computing information. *First International Conference on Security and Privacy for Emerging Areas in Communications Networks (SECURECOMM'05)*, 384–396. 10.1109/SECURECOMM.2005.18

Heraud, J. A., & Lange, A. F. (2009). *Agricultural automatic vehicle guidance from horses to GPS: How we got here, and where we are going*. American Society of Agricultural and Biological Engineers.

He, X., Ren, Z., Shi, C., & Fang, J. (2016). A novel load balancing strategy of software-defined cloud/fog networking in the Internet of Vehicles. *China Communications, 13*(Supplement2), 140–149. doi:10.1109/CC.2016.7833468

Holbl, Welzer, & Brumen. (2012). An improved two-party identity-based authenticated key agreement protocol using pairings. *Journal of Computer and System Sciences, 78*, 142-150.

Holbl, M. (2010). *Two proposed identity-based three-party authenticated key agreement protocols from pairings. Computer and Security, 29*, 244–252.

Hou, M., Xu, Q., Shanqimg, G., & Jiang, H. (2010, July). Cryptanalysis on Identity-based Authenticated Key agreement protocols from Pairings. *Journal of Networks, 5*(7). doi:10.4304/jnw.5.7.855-862

Hu, Dhelim, Ning, & Qiu. (2017). Survey on fog computing: architecture, key technologies, applications and open issues. *Journal of Network and Computer Applications*.

Huang, Wang, & Guan, Chen, & Jian. (2013). Applications of Machine Learning to Resource Management in Cloud Computing. *International Journal of Modeling and Optimization, 3*(2).

Hyytia, Spyropoulos, & Ott. (2015). Offload (only) the right jobs: Robust offloading using the Markov decision processes. *World of Wireless, Mobile and Multimedia Networks (WoWMoM), 2015 IEEE 16th International Symposium*, 1–9.

IDC. (2015-2019), *Worldwide Internet of Things Forecast Update*. document #US40983216. IDC.

IDC. (2019). *Forecasts Worldwide Shipments of Wearables to Surpass 200 Million in 2019, Driven by Strong Smartwatch Growth and the Emergence of Smarter Watches, document #prUS41100116*. Framingham, MA: IDC.

Intharawijitr, K., Iida, K., & Koga, H. (2016, March). Analysis of fog model considering computing and communication latency in 5G cellular networks. In *2016 IEEE International Conference on Pervasive Computing and Communication Workshops (PerCom Workshops)* (pp. 1-4). IEEE. 10.1109/PERCOMW.2016.7457059

Iorga, M., Feldman, L., Barton, R., Martin, M. J., Goren, N., & Mahmoudi, C. (2018). *Fog computing conceptual model (No. NIST SP 500-325)*. Gaithersburg, MD: National Institute of Standards and Technology. doi:10.6028/NIST.SP.500-325

Jain, R. K., Chiu, D. M. W., & Hawe, W. R. (1984). *A quantitative measure of fairness and discrimination*. Hudson, MA: Eastern Research Laboratory, Digital Equipment Corporation.

James, G. (2013). *An Introduction to Statistical Learning with Applications in R. In Springer Texts in Statistics*. Springer.

Jung, B. E. (2004, February). On the forward secrecy of Chikazawa-Yamagishi ID based key Sharing Scheme. *IEEE Communications Letters, 8*(2), 114–115. doi:10.1109/LCOMM.2004.823407

Khalid & Shahbaz. (2017). Service Architecture Models For Fog Computing: A Remedy for Latency Issues in Data Access from Clouds. *KSII Transactions on Internet and Information Systems, 11*(5).

Kim, M., & Ko, I. Y. (2015, June). An efficient resource allocation approach based on a genetic algorithm for composite services in IoT environments. In *2015 IEEE International Conference on Web Services* (pp. 543-550). IEEE. 10.1109/ICWS.2015.78

Kingma, D., & Ba, J. (2014). *Adam: A method for stochastic optimization*. Ar Xiv preprint ar Xiv: 1412.6980

Kishore. (2012). Improved ID Based Key Agreement Protocol Using Timestamp. *International Journal of Computer Science and Information Technology, 3*(5), 5200–5205.

Kreutz, D., Ramos, F. M., Verissimo, P., Rothenberg, C. E., Azodolmolky, S., & Uhlig, S. (2015). Software-defined networking: A comprehensive survey. *Proceedings of the IEEE, 103*(1), 14–76. doi:10.1109/JPROC.2014.2371999

Kuhn, M. (2013). *Predictive Modeling with R and the caret Package useR!* Retrieved from https://www.r-project.org/nosvn/conferences/useR- 2013/Tutorials/kuhn/user_caret_2up.pdf

Kumar, K.D., & Umamaheswari, E. (2018). Efficient Cloud Resource Scaling based on Prediction Approaches. *International Journal of Engineering & Technology, 7*(4.10).

Kumar, K.D., & Umamaheswari, E. (2018). Efficient Cloud Resource Scaling Based On Prediction Approaches. *International Journal of Engineering & Technology, 7*(4.10).

Kumar, K. D., & Umamaheswari, E. (2017). *An Authenticated, Secure Virtualization Management System in Cloud Computing.* Advances in Smart Computing and Bioinformatics.

Kumar, K. D., & Umamaheswari, E. (2017). An Authenticated, Secure Virtualization Management System. In *Cloud Computing, Asian Journal Of Pharmaceutical And Clinical Research.* Advances In Smart Computing And Bioinformatics.

Kumar, K. D., & Umamaheswari, E. (2018). Prediction methods for effective resource provisioning in cloud computing: A Survey. *Multiagent and Grid Systems, 14*(3), 283–305. doi:10.3233/MGS-180292

La, Q. D., Ngo, M. V., Dinh, T. Q., Quek, T. Q. S., & Shin, H. (2018). *Enabling intelligence in fog computing to achieve energy and latency reduction.* Digital Communications and Networks.

Laundromat hack with lock pick. (n.d.). Available: https://www. youtube.com/watch?v=YsuLzCfNqYo

Lee, K., Kim, D., Ha, D., Rajput, U., & Oh, H. (2015). On security and privacy issues of fog computing supported Internet of Things environment. *2015 6th International Conference on the Network of the Future (NOF)*, 1–3.

Leopold & Mack. (2017). *Buzzfeed: A bunch of cia contractors got fired for stealing snacks from vending machines.* Available: https://www.buzzfeed.com/jasonleopold/cia-vending-thefts

Levinson, J., & Thrun, S. (2010). Robust Vehicle Localization In Urban Environments Using Probabilistic Maps. *Robotics and Automation (Icra), 2010 IEEE International Conference on*, 4372-4378.

Li, J., Song, D., Chen, S., & Lu, X. (2012). A simple fully homomorphic encryption scheme available in cloud computing. *IEEE 2nd International Conference*, 214-217. 10.1109/CCIS.2012.6664399

Li, F., Zhong, D., & Takagi, T. (2012, December). Di Zhong and Tsuyoshi Takagi, "Practical Identity-based Signature for wireless sensor networks. *IEEE Wireless Communications Letters, 1*(6), 637–640. doi:10.1109/WCL.2012.091312.120488

Luan, Gao, & Xiang. (n.d.). *Fog Computing: Focusing on Mobile Users at the Edge.* School of Information Technology Deakin University.

Luan, T. H., Gao, L., Li, Z., Xiang, Y., & Sun, L. (2015). *Fog computing: Focusing on mobile users at the edge.* Available: http://arxiv.org/abs/1502.01815

Lu, H., Li, J., & Guizani, M. (2014, March). Secure and efficient data transmission for Cluster based wireless sensor networks. *IEEE Transactions on Parallel and Distributed Systems, 25*(3), 750–761. doi:10.1109/TPDS.2013.43

Mahmud, R., & Buyya, R. (2017). Fog computing: A taxonomy, survey and future directions. In *Internet of Everything*. Springer.

Mahmud, R., Kotagiri, R., & Buyya, R. (2018). Fog Computing: A Taxonomy, Survey and Future Directions. In B. Di Martino, K. C. Li, L. Yang, & A. Esposito (Eds.), *Internet of Everything. Internet of Things (Technology, Communications and Computing)* (pp. 103–130). Singapore: Springer. doi:10.1007/978-981-10-5861-5_5

Malan, D. J., Welsh, M., & Smith, M. D. (2004). A public-key infrastructure for key distribution in tinyos based on elliptic curve cryptography. *Sensor and Ad Hoc Communications and Networks, 2004. IEEE SECON 2004. 2004 First Annual IEEE Communications Society Conference on,* 71–80. 10.1109/SAHCN.2004.1381904

Manate, B., Fortis, T. F., & Negru, V. (2014). Optimizing cloud resources allocation for an Internet of Things architecture. *Scalable Computing: Practice and Experience, 15*(4), 345–355.

Markmann, T., Schmidt, T. C., & Wahlisch, M. (2015). Federated end-to-end ̈ authentication for the constrained internet of things using ibc and ecc. *Proceedings of the 2015 ACM Conference on Special Interest Group on Data Communication,* 603–604. 10.1145/2785956.2790021

Microsoft IoT. (2017). *Five ways edge computing will transform business.* Available: https://blogs. microsoft.com/iot/2017/09/ 19/five-ways-edge-computing-will-transform-business/

Mitchell. (1997). *Machine Learning.* McGraw-Hill Science/Engineering/Math.

Mnih, V., & Hinton, G. E. (2010). Learning to Detect Roads in High resolution Aerial Images. *European Conference on Computer Vision,* 210–223.

Mukherjee, M., Matam, R., Shu, L., Maglaras, L., Ferrag, M. A., Choudhury, N., & Kumar, V. (2017). Security and Privacy in Fog Computing: Challenges. *IEEE Access: Practical Innovations, Open Solutions, 5,* 19293–19304. doi:10.1109/ACCESS.2017.2749422

Muthukrishnan & Radha. (2011). Edge Detection Techniques for Image Segmentation. *International Journal of Computer Science & Information Technology, 3*(6).

Nadeem. (2016). *Fog Computing: An Emerging Paradigm.* IEEE Xplorer.

Navya. (2018). *Sensors.* Available: http://navya.tech/en/autonom en/ utonomshuttle/ #storeLocator__bottomHalf

Ningning, S., Chao, G., Xingshuo, A., & Qiang, Z. (2016). Fog computing dynamic load balancing mechanism based on graph repartitioning. *China Communications, 13*(3), 156–164. doi:10.1109/CC.2016.7445510

Oliveira, L. B., Scott, M., Lopez, J., & Dahab, R. (2008). Tinypbc: Pairings for authenticated identity-based non-interactive key distribution in sensor networks. *Networked Sensing Systems, 2008. INSS 2008. 5*th *International Conference on*, 173–180. 10.1109/INSS.2008.4610921

Oueis, J., Strinati, E. C., & Barbarossa, S. (2015, May). The fog balancing: Load distribution for small cell cloud computing. In *2015 IEEE 81st Vehicular Technology Conference (VTC Spring)* (pp. 1-6). IEEE.

Paden, B., Cap, M., Yong, S. Z., Yershov, D., & Frazzoli, E. (2016). A Survey Of Motion Planning And Control Techniques For Self-driving Urban Vehicles. *IEEE Transactions on Intelligent Vehicles, Vol, 1*(1), 33–55. doi:10.1109/TIV.2016.2578706

Pang, A. C., Chung, W. H., Chiu, T. C., & Zhang, J. (2017, June). Latency-driven cooperative task computing in multi-user fog-radio access networks. In *2017 IEEE 37th International Conference on Distributed Computing Systems (ICDCS)* (pp. 615-624). IEEE. 10.1109/ICDCS.2017.83

Park, Wan, Yi, & Lee. (2010). Simple ID-based Key Distribution Scheme. *IEEE, fifth International Conference on Internet and Web applications and Service.* 10.1109/ICIW.2010.61

Parsian. (2015). *Data Algorithms.* O'Reilly Media, Inc.

Peng, R., & Alex, J. (2012). *Real-time query processing on live videos in networks of distributed cameras.* Research, Practice, and Educational Advancements in Telecommunications and Networking.

Poluru, R. K., Bhushan, B., Muzamil, B. S., Rayani, P. K., & Reddy, P. K. (2019). Applications of Domain-Specific Predictive Analytics Applied to Big Data. In *Sentiment Analysis and Knowledge Discovery in Contemporary Business* (pp. 289–306). IGI Global. doi:10.4018/978-1-5225-4999-4.ch016

Puthal, D., Obaidat, M. S., Nanda, P., Prasad, M., Mohanty, S. P., & Zomaya, A. Y. (2018). Secure and sustainable load balancing of edge data centers in fog computing. *IEEE Communications Magazine, 56*(5), 60–65. doi:10.1109/MCOM.2018.1700795

Qin, Z., Zhang, X., Feng, K., Zhang, Q., & Huang, J. (2014). An Efficient Identity-based Key Management scheme for wireless sensor networks using the Bloom Filter. *Sensors (Basel), 14*(10), 17937–17951. doi:10.3390141017937 PMID:25264955

Rahman, G. S., Peng, M., Zhang, K., & Chen, S. (2018). Radio resource allocation for achieving ultra-low latency in fog radio access networks. *IEEE Access: Practical Innovations, Open Solutions, 6*, 17442–17454. doi:10.1109/ACCESS.2018.2805303

Rajagopalan, R., & Varshney, P. K. (2006). Data aggregation techniques in sensor networks. *Survey (London, England).*

Rasmussen, C. E., & Williams, C. K. (2006). Gaussian processes for machine learning. MIT Press.

Ray, P. P. (2018). A survey on the Internet of Things architectures. *Journal of King Saud University - Computer and Information Sciences, 30*(3), 291–319.

Rayani, P. K., Bhushan, B., & Thakare, V. R. (2018). Multi-Layer Token Based Authentication Through Honey Password in Fog Computing. *International Journal of Fog Computing*, *1*(1), 50–62. doi:10.4018/IJFC.2018010104

Raychaudhuri, D., Nagaraja, K., & Venkataramani, A. (2012). Mobilityfirst: A robust and trustworthy mobility-centric architecture for the future internet. *Mobile Computing and Communications Review*, *16*(3), 2–13. doi:10.1145/2412096.2412098

Raza, S., Wang, S., Ahmed, M., & Anwar, M. R. (2019). A Survey on Vehicular Edge Computing: Architecture, Applications, Technical Issues, and Future Directions. *Wireless Communications and Mobile Computing*, *2019*, 1–19. doi:10.1155/2019/3159762

Ribeiro, M., Lazzaretti, A. E., & Lopes, H. S. (2017). A study of deep convolutional auto-encoders for anomaly detection in videos. *Pattern Recognition Letters*.

Rimal, B. P., Choi, E., & Lumb, I. (2009, August). A taxonomy and survey of cloud computing systems. In *2009 Fifth International Joint Conference on INC, IMS and IDC* (pp. 44-51). IEEE. 10.1109/NCM.2009.218

Rivest, R., Adleman, L., & Dertouzos, M. (1978). *On data banks and privacy homomorphisms*. *Academic Press*.

Ryerson, A. F., & Zhang, Q. (2007). Vehicle path planning for complete field coverage using genetic algorithms. *Agricultural Engineering International: CIGR Journal*.

Sahni, Y., Cao, J., Zhang, S., & Yang, L. (2017). Edge Mesh: A new paradigm to enable distributed intelligence in Internet of Things. *IEEE Access: Practical Innovations, Open Solutions*, *5*, 16441–16458. doi:10.1109/ACCESS.2017.2739804

Sankaran, S. (2016). Lightweight security framework for IoTs using identity-based cryptography. *2016 International Conference on Advances in Computing, Communications and Informatics (ICACCI)*, 880-886. 10.1109/ICACCI.2016.7732156

Sannella. (2003). *Constraint satisfaction and debugging for interactive user interfaces*. Academic Press.

Sayed, S. (n.d.). K nearest neighbors – classification. *Saed Sayed*. Retrieved from: https://www.saedsayad.com/k_nearest_neighbors.htm

Segal, A., Haehnel, D., & Thrun, S. (2009). Generalized-ICP. *Robotics: Science and Systems V*, *5*, 168–176.

Segal, M. R. (2004). *Machine learning benchmarks and random forest regression*. Center for Bioinformatics & Molecular Biostatistics.

Shamir. (1984). Identity-based cryptosystems and signature schemes. *Advances in Cryptology*, *196*, 47-53.

Sheng, B., Li, Q., & Mao, W. (2006). Data storage placement in sensor networks. In *Mobihoc*. ACM. doi:10.1145/1132905.1132943

Sifre, L. (2014). *Rigid-motion scattering for image classification* (Ph.D. dissertation). PSU.

Singh, A., Thakur, N., & Sharma, A. (2016). A review of supervised machine learning algorithms. *2016 3rd International Conference on Computing for Sustainable Global Development (INDIACom)*, 1310-1315.

Singh, S., & Singh, N. (2016). Containers & Docker: Emerging roles & future of Cloud technology. In *2016 2nd International Conference on Applied and Theoretical Computing and Communication Technology (iCATccT)* (pp. 804–807). Bangalore, India: IEEE.

Singh, A., & Viniotis, Y. (2017). Resource allocation for IoT applications in cloud environments. In *2017 International Conference on Computing, Networking and Communications (ICNC)* (pp. 719–723). Silicon Valley, CA: IEEE. 10.1109/ICCNC.2017.7876218

Singh, S., & Chana, I. (2016). QoS-aware autonomic resource management in cloud computing: A systematic review. *ACM Computing Surveys, 48*(3), 42.

Skarlat, O., Nardelli, M., Schulte, S., & Dustdar, S. (2017). Towards QoS-Aware Fog Service Placement. In *2017 IEEE 1st International Conference on Fog and Edge Computing (ICFEC)* (pp. 89–96). Madrid, Spain: IEEE. 10.1109/ICFEC.2017.12

Sridhar, S., & Tolentino, M. E. (2017, June). Evaluating Voice Interaction Pipelines at the Edge. In *2017 IEEE International Conference on Edge Computing (EDGE)* (pp. 248-251). IEEE. 10.1109/IEEE.EDGE.2017.46

Stallings, W., & Brown, L. (2018). *Computer security: principles and practice*. Pearson Education.

Stanciu, A. (2017, May). Blockchain based distributed control system for edge computing. In *2017 21st International Conference on Control Systems and Computer Science (CSCS)* (pp. 667-671). IEEE. 10.1109/CSCS.2017.102

Starzyk & Qureshi. (2011). Learning proactive control strategies for ptz cameras. In *Distributed Smart Cameras (ICDSC), 2011 Fifth ACM/IEEE International Conference on*, (pp. 1–6). IEEE.

Stojmenovic, I., & Wen, S. (2014, September 29). *The Fog Computing Paradigm: Scenarios and Security Issues*. Academic Press.

Stojmenovic, I. (2014). Fog computing: A cloud to the ground support for smart things and machine-to-machine networks. In *ATNAC*. IEEE. doi:10.1109/ATNAC.2014.7020884

Stojmenovic, I., Wen, S., Huang, X., & Luan, H. (2016). An overview of Fog computing and its security issues: An overview of fog computing and its security issues. *Concurrency and Computation, 28*(10), 2991–3005. doi:10.1002/cpe.3485

Taneja, M., & Davy, A. (2017, May). Resource aware placement of IoT application modules in Fog-Cloud Computing Paradigm. In *2017 IFIP/IEEE Symposium on Integrated Network and Service Management (IM)* (pp. 1222-1228). IEEE. 10.23919/INM.2017.7987464

Tato, G., Bertier, M., & Tedeschi, C. (2017, December). Designing Overlay Networks for Decentralized Clouds. In *2017 IEEE International Conference on Cloud Computing Technology and Science (CloudCom)* (pp. 391-396). IEEE. 10.1109/CloudCom.2017.64

Tavel. (2007). *Modeling and simulation design*. Academic Press.

Teetor, P. (2011). R Cookbook. O'Reilly Media, Inc.

Tesauro, G., Jong, N. K., Das, R., & Bennani, M. N. (2006). A Hybrid Reinforcement Learning Approach to Autonomic Resource Allocation. In *2006 IEEE International Conference on Autonomic Computing* (pp. 65–73). Dublin, Ireland: IEEE. 10.1109/ICAC.2006.1662383

Thorpe, C., Herbert, M., Kanade, T., & Shafter, S. (1991). Toward Autonomous Driving: The Cmu Navlab. Ii. Architecture and Systems. *IEEE Expert*, *6*(4), 44–52. doi:10.1109/64.85920

Thrun, S., Burgard, W., & Fox, D. (2005). *Probabilistic Robotics*. Cambridge, MA: MIT Press.

Tian, J., Chin, A., & Yanikomeroglu, H. (2018). Connected and Autonomous Driving. *IT Professional*, *20*(6), 31–34. doi:10.1109/MITP.2018.2876928

Toh & Chai. (2001). Ad Hoc Mobile Wireless Networks: Protocols and Systems. Prentice Hall.

Truong, N. B., Lee, G. M., & Ghamri-Doudane, Y. (2015, May). Software defined networking-based vehicular adhoc network with fog computing. In *2015 IFIP/IEEE International Symposium on Integrated Network Management (IM)* (pp. 1202-1207). IEEE. 10.1109/INM.2015.7140467

van Dijk, M., Gentry, C., Halevi, S., & Vaikuntanathan, V. (2010). Fully homomorphic encryption over the integers. In H. Gilbert (Ed.), EUROCRYPT. LNCS (Vol. 6110, pp. 24–43). Springer. http://epubs.siam.org/doi/abs/10.1137/120868669

Vaquero, L. M., & Rodero-Merino, L. (2014). Finding your way in the fog: Towards a comprehensive definition of fog computing. *Computer Communication Review*, *44*(5), 27–32. doi:10.1145/2677046.2677052

Varghese, B., Wang, N., Li, J., & Nikolopoulos, D. S. (2017). *Edge-as-a-Service: Towards distributed Cloud architectures*. arXiv preprint arXiv:1710.10090

Varghese, B., Akgun, O., Miguel, I., Thai, L., & Barker, A. (2016). *Cloud benchmarking for maximising performance of scientific applications. IEEE Transactions on Cloud Computing*.

Vu, D. N., Dao, N. N., & Cho, S. (2018, January). Downlink sum-rate optimization leveraging Hungarian method in fog radio access networks. In *2018 International Conference on Information Networking (ICOIN)* (pp. 56-60). IEEE. 10.1109/ICOIN.2018.8343083

Waheetha & Fernandez. (2016). Fog Computing And Its Applications. *International Journal of Advanced Research in Basic Engineering Sciences and Technology, 2*(19), 56-62. Retrieved from https://www.networkworld.com/article/3243111/what-is-fog-computing-connecting-the-cloud-to-things.html

Wakefield, K. (n.d.). Predictive analytics and machine learning. *Sas.* Retrieved from: https://www.sas.com/en_gb/insights/articles/analytics/a-guide-to-predictive-analytics-and-machine-learning.html

Wang, S., Urgaonkar, R., He, T., Chan, K., Zafer, M., & Leung, K. K. (2016). Dynamic service placement for mobile micro-clouds with predicted future costs. *IEEE Transactions on Parallel and Distributed Systems, 28*(4), 1002–1016. doi:10.1109/TPDS.2016.2604814

Waymo. (2018). *Waymo 360° Experience: A Fully Self-Driving Journey.* Available: Https://Www.Youtube.Com/Watch?V=B8r148hfxpw

Wegner, J. D., Montoya-Zegarra, J. A., & Schindler, K. (2015). Road Networks As Collections Of Minimum Cost Paths. *ISPRS Journal of Photogrammetry and Remote Sensing, 108*, 128–137. doi:10.1016/j.isprsjprs.2015.07.002

Wikipedia. (n.d.). *Cloud computing* [EB/OL]. Retrieved from http://en.wikipedia.org/wiki/Cloud_Computing

Wikipedia. (n.d.). K nearest neighbors algorithm. *Wikipedia.* Retrieved from: https://en.wikipedia.org/wiki/K-nearest_neighbors_algorithm

Willis, D. F., Dasgupta, A., & Banerjee, S. (2014). Paradrop: a multi-tenant platform for dynamically installed third partyservices on home gateways. In *SIGCOMM workshop on Distributed cloud computing.* ACM. 10.1145/2627566.2627583

Xue, J., & Xu, L. (2010, March). Autonomous agricultural robot and its row guidance. In *Measuring Technology and Mechatronics Automation (ICMTMA), 2010 International Conference on* (Vol. 1, pp. 725-729). iEEE. 10.1109/ICMTMA.2010.251

Xue, J., Zhang, L., & Grift, T. E. (2012). Variable field-of-view machine vision based row guidance of an agricultural robot. *Computers and Electronics in Agriculture, 84*, 85–91. doi:10.1016/j.compag.2012.02.009

Xu, K., & Zhu, H. (Eds.). (2015). *Wireless Algorithms.* Systems, and Applications. doi:10.1007/978-3-319-21837-3

Yagan, O. (2012, June). Performance of the Eschenauer-Gligor key distribution scheme under an ON/OFF Channel. *IEEE Transactions on Information Theory, 58*(6), 3821–3835. doi:10.1109/TIT.2012.2189353

Yaghoubi, S., Akbarzadeh, N. A., Bazargani, S. S., Bazargani, S. S., Bamizan, M., & Asl, M. I. (2013). Autonomous robots for agricultural tasks and farm assignment and future trends in agro robots. *International Journal of Mechanical and Mechatronics Engineering, 13*(3), 1–6.

Yang, Rong, Veigner, Wang, & Cheng. (2006). Identity Based Key Agreement and Encryption for Wireless Sensor Networks. *International Journal of Computer Science and Network Security, 6*(5B).

Yi, S., Li, C., & Li, Q. (2015). A Survey of Fog Computing: Concepts, Applications, and Issues. In *Proceedings of the 2015 Workshop on Mobile Big Data - Mobidata '15* (pp. 37–42). Hangzhou, China: ACM Press. 10.1145/2757384.2757397

Yi, S., Li, C., & Li, Q. (2017). A survey of fog computing: concepts, applications and issues. *Proc. Proceedings of the 2015 Workshop on Mobile Big Data*, 37–42.

You, C., Zeng, Y., Zhang, R., & Huang, K. (2018). Asynchronous Mobile-Edge Computation Offloading: Energy-Efficient Resource Management. *IEEE Transactions on Wireless Communications, 17*(11), 7590–7605. doi:10.1109/TWC.2018.2868710

Yousefpour, Fung, Nguyen, Kadiyala, Jalali, Niakanlahiji, … Jue. (2018). *All one needs to know about fog computing and related edge computing paradigms: A complete survey.* CoRR, abs/1808.05283

Yuan & Li. (2005). *A new efficient ID based Authenticated Key Agreement protocol.* Academic Press.

Zahoor, S., & Mir, R. N. (2018). Resource management in the pervasive Internet of Things: A survey. *Journal of King Saud University - Computer and Information Sciences.*

Zanjireh & Larijani. (2015). A Survey on Centralized and Distributed Clustering Routing Algorithms for Wsns. *IEEE 81st Vehicular Technology Conference.*

Zeng, D., Gu, L., Guo, S., Cheng, Z., & Yu, S. (2016). Joint optimization of task scheduling and image placement in fog computing supported software-defined embedded system. *IEEE Transactions on Computers, 65*(12), 3702–3712. doi:10.1109/TC.2016.2536019

Zhang, B., Mor, N., Kolb, J., Chan, D. S., Lutz, K., Allman, E., … Kubiatowicz, J. (2015). *The cloud is not enough: Saving iot from the cloud.* HotStorage.

Zhang, S., Zhu, Y., & Roy-Chowdhury, A. (2015). Tracking multiple interacting targets in a camera network. *Computer Vision and Image Understanding, 134*(C), 64–73. doi:10.1016/j.cviu.2015.01.002

Zhang, W., Lin, B., Yin, Q., & Zhao, T. (2017). Infrastructure deployment and optimization of fog network based on microdc and lrpon integration. *Peer-to-Peer Networking and Applications, 10*(3), 579–591. doi:10.100712083-016-0476-x

Zhao, F., Li, C., & Chun, F. L. (2014). A cloud computing security solution based on fully homomorphic encryption. *IEEE 16th International Conference*, 485-488.

Zheng, X., Cai, Z., Li, J., & Gao, H. (2016). A study on application-aware scheduling in wireless networks. *IEEE Transactions on Mobile Computing, 16*(7), 1787–1801. doi:10.1109/TMC.2016.2613529

About the Contributors

Sam Goundar is an Editor-in-Chief of the International Journal of Blockchains and Cryptocurrencies (IJFC) - Inderscience Publishers, Editor-in-Chief of the International Journal of Fog Computing (IJFC) - IGI Publishers, Section Editor of the Journal of Education and Information Technologies (EAIT) - Springer and Editor-in-Chief (Emeritus) of the International Journal of Cloud Applications and Computing (IJCAC) - IGI Publishers. He is also on the Editorial Review Board of more than 20 high impact factor journals. He is currently working (writing/editing) on six book projects expected to be published between July to December 2019: As a researcher, apart from Blockchains, Cryptocurrencies, Fog Computing, Mobile Cloud Computing, Cloud Computing, Educational Technologies, Dr. Sam Goundar also researches on Management Information Systems, Technology Acceptance Model (TAM), Massive Open Online Courses (MOOC), Gamification in Learning, Cyber Security, Artificial Intelligence, ICT in Climate Change, ICT Devices in the Classroom, Using Mobile Devices in Education, e-Government, and Disaster Management. He has published on all these topics. He was a Research Fellow with the United Nations University. As an academic, Dr. Sam Goundar has been teaching Information Systems (IS), Information Technology (IT), Management Information Systems (MIS) and Computer Science (CS) over the last 25 years at several universities in a number of countries at all levels. Currently, he is a Senior Lecturer in Information Systems at the University of the South Pacific, Adjunct Lecturer in Information Systems at Victoria University of Wellington (Malaysian Partner Campus) and an Affiliate Professor of Information Technology at Pontificia Universidad Catolica Del Peru (Peru). Dr. Sam Goundar is a Senior Member of IEEE, a member of ACS, a member of the IITP, New Zealand, Certification Administrator of ETA-I, USA and Past President of the South Pacific Computer Society. He also serves on the IEEE Technical Committee for Internet of Things, Cloud Communication and Networking, Big Data, Green ICT, Cyber security, Business Informatics and Systems, Learning Technology and Smart Cities. He is a member of the IEEE Technical Society and a panellist with the IEEE Spectrum for Emerging Technologies.

S. Bharath Bhushan received his PhD in Computer Science and Engineering (from VIT University Vellore in 2018. He did his Masters in Computer Networks and Information Security from JNTUA in 2013. He is an Associate Professor in the Department of Computer Science and Systems Engineering, Sree Vidyanikethan Engineering College, Tirupathi. His area of interest includes Cloud Computing, networks, Data Analytics, Internet of Things (IoT). He published more than 20 journal articles in highly reputed journals and conferences. He is an Editorial board member of International journal of web service research and International journal of fog computing. He is serving as reviewer for more than 10 reputed journals.

* * *

P. Shanthi Bala received her Ph.D from Pondicherry University, India. She is presently working as a Assistant Professor in Department of Computer Science, Pondicherry University, Puducherry. She has around 10 years of teaching and 6 years of research experience. Her research interests include Knowledge Engineering, Artificial intelligence, Ontology and Networks. She has published more than 30 papers in International Journal and conferences.

P. Bhargavi is working as Assistant Professor in the Department of Computer Science, Sri Padmavati Mahila Visvavidyalayam, Tirupati. She Received her Ph.D. from Sri Padmavati Mahila Visvavidyalayam, Tirupati in Data Mining. She has 20 years of teaching experience and 12 years of research experience. Now she is guiding 8 Ph. D. students. She is member in IEEE, CSI, ISTE, ACM, IAENG and, MEACSE. Her areas of interest are Data mining, Soft Computing, Big Data Analytics, Bioinformatics and GIS. She published 25 research papers in reputed journals and presented 17 papers in International & National Conferences. She acted as Editorial Board Member of International Journal of IJCAR, Technical Committee Member of IndiaCOM2016 and Reviewer of IndiaCOM2016 and IGI book chapter.

Kartheek D. N. has completed Bachelor's degree from JNTU Anantapur and master's from MIT, Manipal. Currently pursuing Doctoral degree from VIT, Vellore. His areas of interest are Computer Networks, Cloud Computing and Internet of Things.

A. S. Gowri did her Masters of Computer Science and Engineering from Anna University, India. Her area of interest includes mobile computing, networking and cloud computing. She has 13 years of teaching experience. Her research area includes cloud computing and machine learning techniques.

X. Alphonse Inbaraj completed Master of Engineering in Anna University, Coimbatore, Tamil Nadu and having five years of teaching experience in computer field. His Domain is cloud computing and published research papers in national and international journals. Currently working as assistant professor under department of Computer Science and Engineering in PACE Institute of Technology and Engineering, Ongole, Andra Pradesh. He got award "Best Innovator" from university of JNTUK, Kakinda.

S. Jyothi did her M.Sc. in Applied Mathematics & Ph.D in Theoritical Computer Science from S.V.University, Tirupati and M.S. from BITS, Pilani. She got Gold Medal in Mathematics and 6th Rank in Under Graduate studies, 1st Rank in Post Graduate studies, and awarded prestegious UGC – JRF. Dr. S. Jyothi is a Professor in Computer Science. She worked as Director, University Computer Centre, Head, Dept. of Computer Science, Head (I/C), Dept of Computer Science and Engineering, BOS Chairperson, BOS member and so on. She has 25 years teaching experience and 30 years research experience. She is handling core and electives subjects of Computer Science for post graduate and graduate level. She is honored and awarded Rashtriya Gaurav Award, inclusion of her Biography in 2000 Outstanding Intellectuals of the 21st Century~10th Edition, Great Britain, nominated for Top 100 Professional by International Biographical Centre, Cambridge. She is also member of SIG-IE of CSI, India, Member of "IoT SIG" on IEEE Standards at Hyderabad Section, India and Mentor of Initiative for Research and Innovation Science(IRIS) for southern region. Prof. S. Jyothi acted as Editorial Board member of Intenational Journals, Technical Committee Member of International Conferences, Reviewer of many research papers for International Journals and International Conferences and Invited speaker. Seventeen Ph.Ds, seven M.Phil were awarded and eight Ph.D. scholars are being guided under her supervision. More than 150 papers published presented in International and National Journals and conferences. 10 books were authored and edited by her. She has conducted 2 national and 2 international conferences and acted as session chair of International and National Conferences. She has completed UGC & DBT major Projects and handling one DBT project. Her areas of interest in Image Processing, Soft Computing, Data Mining, Big Data analytics, Bioinformatics and Hyperspectra Image Analysis. She is senior member of IEEE & IACSIT, fellow of RSS, ISCA, IETE & SSARSC, member of IEEE CS, GSRS & WS, ACM, IET, IAENG & Gyancity Research Labs and life member of CSI, ISTE, ISCA, IFERP, IUPRAI and ISRS.

Aravind Karrothu is a Research Scholar in the Information Technology and Engineering Department at the Vellore Institute of Technology - Vellore, Tamilnadu, India. His main research interests are information security.

K. Dinesh Kumar is currently pursuing the Ph.D, in the School of Computing Science and Engineering, VIT University, Chennai. He received his B.Tech and M.Tech degrees under JNTU-Hyderabad. He has published national and International publications to his credit and participated in various national and international conferences. His research area is cloud computing and machine learning and also interests in IoT, grid computing, and computer networks.

Kuruva Lakshmanna has received his Ph.D. in the year 2017 from VIT Vellore, India, B-Tech in Computer Science and Engineering from Sri Venkateswara University College of Engineering -Tirupathi, India in the year 2006, M-Tech in Computer Science and Engineering(Information Security) from National Institute of Technology Calicut, Kerala, India in the Year 2009. He is working as an Assistant professor - senior in VIT University, India. His research interests are Data Mining in DNA sequences, algorithms, Knowledge Mining, etc.

Shanthi Thangam Manukumar is pursuing her Ph.D. degree in the Department of Information Science and Technology, College of Engineering, Guindy, Anna University. She received M.E. degree in Network Engineering from Anna University Coimbatore in 2011 and B.E degree in the specification of Computer Science and Engineering, Anna University in 2009. Her research interests are in the area of Mobile Cloud Computing, Fog Computing, Data Analytics, Computer Networks, and Optimization Techniques.

Vijayalakshmi Muthuswamy is currently working as Associate Professor in the Department of Information Science and Technology, College of Engineering, Guindy, Anna University, Chennai. She received her M.E and Ph. D from Anna University and B.E. degree from NIT Trichy. She has published 50 articles in journals and conferences. Her area of interest includes Mobile Database, Computer Networks, Mobile Cloud, Cloud Computing, Fog Computing, and Security.

Jasmine Norman is an Associate Professor in School of Information Technology and Engineering at the Vellore Institute of Technology, Vellore, Tamilnadu, India.

Ravi Kumar Poluru received M.Tech. from JNTU Anantapur, Anantapuram in 2014. Currently, he is a Research Scholar in the School of Computer Science & Engineering, Vellore Institute of Technology, Vellore and pursuing his Ph.D. work in the field of Internet of Things. His main areas of research include the Internet of Things, Wireless Sensor Networks and Nature Inspired Optimization Techniques.

G. Thippa Reddy has received his B-Tech in Computer Science and Engineering from Nagarjuna University, India in the year 2003, M-Tech in Computer Science and Engineering from Anna University, India in the Year 2010, his Ph.D in VIT Vellore, India in teh year 2017. He is working as an Assistant professor in VIT University, India. His research interests are Data Mining in Healthcare, Natural Language Processing, Knowledge Mining, Big Data Analytics, etc.

M. Sudhakar, currently working as Research Associate in Vellore Institute of technology, Chennai Campus. He finished his master's degree in the stream of Computer Science and Engineering in the year of 2012 from JNTU University, Anantapur. He started his teaching career in Modugula Kalavathamma Engineering College located in Rajampet and he also worked as Assistant Professor in the department of C.S.E in Sri Sai Institute of Technology and Science around 3.5 years. He started his research work in 2015 in the school of Computing Science and Engineering in VIT Chennai Campus. He published several UGC and Scopus Indexed journals. He was conducted multiple workshops for the engineering students on the topic of python programming, C Programming etc. His research interests include Image Analytics, Image Processing and Deep Learning in computer vision.

Vaishali Ravindra Thakare is a Research Scholar and pursuing PhD at VIT University (TN), India. She was Research Associate in the School of Information Technology and Engineering, VIT University and received MS (by Research) degree from VIT University (TN), India. She received Bachelor of Engineering in Information Technology from Rashtrasant Tukdoji Maharaj Nagpur University, Nagpur in 2012. She has published many research articles in peer-reviewed journals and in international conferences. Her area of interests includes cloud security and virtualization, security protocols in cloud computing, cloud computing architectures.

Index

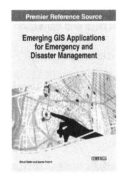
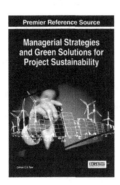

IGI Global Author Services

Providing a high-quality, affordable, and expeditious service, IGI Global's Author Services enable authors to streamline their publishing process, increase chance of acceptance, and adhere to IGI Global's publication standards.

Benefits of Author Services:

- **Professional Service:** All our editors, designers, and translators are experts in their field with years of experience and professional certifications.
- **Quality Guarantee & Certificate:** Each order is returned with a quality guarantee and certificate of professional completion.
- **Timeliness:** All editorial orders have a guaranteed return timeframe of 3-5 business days and translation orders are guaranteed in 7-10 business days.
- **Affordable Pricing:** IGI Global Author Services are competitively priced compared to other industry service providers.
- **APC Reimbursement:** IGI Global authors publishing Open Access (OA) will be able to deduct the cost of editing and other IGI Global author services from their OA APC publishing fee.

Author Services Offered:

English Language Copy Editing
Professional, native English language copy editors improve your manuscript's grammar, spelling, punctuation, terminology, semantics, consistency, flow, formatting, and more.

Scientific & Scholarly Editing
A Ph.D. level review for qualities such as originality and significance, interest to researchers, level of methodology and analysis, coverage of literature, organization, quality of writing, and strengths and weaknesses.

Figure, Table, Chart & Equation Conversions
Work with IGI Global's graphic designers before submission to enhance and design all figures and charts to IGI Global's specific standards for clarity.

Translation
Providing 70 language options, including Simplified and Traditional Chinese, Spanish, Arabic, German, French, and more.

Hear What the Experts Are Saying About IGI Global's Author Services

"Publishing with IGI Global has been *an amazing experience* for me for sharing my research. The *strong academic production* support ensures quality and timely completion." – **Prof. Margaret Niess, Oregon State University, USA**

"The service was *very fast, very thorough, and very helpful* in ensuring our chapter meets the criteria and requirements of the book's editors. I was *quite impressed and happy* with your service." – **Prof. Tom Brinthaupt, Middle Tennessee State University, USA**

Learn More or Get Started Here: For Questions, Contact IGI Global's Customer Service Team at cust@igi-global.com or 717-533-8845

Publisher of Peer-Reviewed, Timely, and
Innovative Academic Research Since 1988

www.igi-global.com

IGI Global's Transformative Open Access (OA) Model:
How to Turn Your University Library's Database Acquisitions Into a Source of OA Funding

Well in advance of Plan S, IGI Global unveiled their OA Fee Waiver (Read & Publish) Initiative. Under this initiative, librarians who invest in IGI Global's InfoSci-Books and/or InfoSci-Journals databases will be able to subsidize their patrons' OA article processing charges (APCs) when their work is submitted and accepted (after the peer review process) into an IGI Global journal.

How Does it Work?

Step 1: **Library Invests in the InfoSci-Databases:** A library perpetually purchases or subscribes to the InfoSci-Books, InfoSci-Journals, or discipline/subject databases.

Step 2: **IGI Global Matches the Library Investment with OA Subsidies Fund:** IGI Global provides a fund to go towards subsidizing the OA APCs for the library's patrons.

Step 3: **Patron of the Library is Accepted into IGI Global Journal (After Peer Review):** When a patron's paper is accepted into an IGI Global journal, they option to have their paper published under a traditional publishing model or as OA.

Step 4: **IGI Global Will Deduct APC Cost from OA Subsidies Fund:** If the author decides to publish under OA, the OA APC fee will be deducted from the OA subsidies fund.

Step 5: **Author's Work Becomes Freely Available:** The patron's work will be freely available under CC BY copyright license, enabling them to share it freely with the academic community.

Note: This fund will be offered on an annual basis and will renew as the subscription is renewed for each year thereafter. IGI Global will manage the fund and award the APC waivers unless the librarian has a preference as to how the funds should be managed.

Hear From the Experts on This Initiative:

"I'm very happy to have been able to make one of my recent research contributions *freely available* along with having access to the *valuable resources* found within IGI Global's InfoSci-Journals database."

– **Prof. Stuart Palmer**,
Deakin University, Australia

"Receiving the support from IGI Global's OA Fee Waiver Initiative *encourages me to continue my research work without any hesitation*."

– **Prof. Wenlong Liu**, College of Economics and Management at Nanjing University of Aeronautics & Astronautics, China

For More Information, Scan the QR Code or Contact:
IGI Global's Digital Resources Team at eresources@igi-global.com.

Printed in the United States
By Bookmasters